ENGLISH AND COMMUNICATIONS FOR BUSINESS STUDENTS

FIFTH EDITION

John F. Scott

Catherine Fox

D1464925

GILL & MACMILLAN

Gill & Macmillan Ltd

Hume Avenue

Park West

Dublin 12

with associated companies throughout the world

www.gillmacmillan.ie

© John F. Scott and Catherine Fox 2005

ISBN-13: 978 0 7171 4034 3

ISBN-10: 0 7171 4034 2

Print origination in Ireland by O'K Graphic Design

The paper used in this book is made from the wood pulp of managed forests. For
every tree felled, at least one tree is planted, thereby renewing natural resources.

A catalogue record is available for this book from the British Library.

For Bernadette, Enda, Conor and Iseult.

For Marty and Áine.

Support Material for

ENGLISH & COMMUNICATIONS FOR BUSINESS STUDENTS,

FIFTH EDITION

by John F. Scott & Catherine Fox

Dynamic and easy to use, online support material for this book

provides **lecturers** with:
- PowerPoint slides
- Extra examples and letters
- Solutions to quizzes

To access Lecturer support material on our secure site,
1) Go to www.gillmacmillan.ie/lecturers
2) Logon using your username and password. If you don't have a password, register online and we will email your password to you.

provides **students** with:
- Extra examples and letters
- Solutions to quizzes

To access Student support material
1) Go to www.gillmacmillan.ie/student
2) Click on the link for Student Support material

CONTENTS

Preface

Acknowledgements

PREFACE

The fifth edition of this book has been updated to take account of the new and developing trends and technology in communications and business. When the first edition of this book appeared in 1981, the internet was but a technological invention yet to be launched, the telephone a landline and mail items delivered by An Post. Now, as we approach the end of the first decade of a new century, the web, mobiles and e-mail are all essential tools in communication. This edition largely reflects the impact technology has had on communicating.

The emphasis on written communication skills continues in this edition, with a new section in Chapter 4 focusing on the correct use of tenses. Personal writing skills are addressed in Chapter 6, with emphasis placed on approaching the writing of a review and the contents of personal letters. The importance of oral communication skills continues to be emphasised in Part 3, with the key skill of listening highlighted in Chapter 13.

Part 4, 'Research Skills', has been updated to take account of the new challenges facing researchers as they confront technological developments, including the use of the internet. Advice on planning and approaching a piece of research is also contained in Chapter 15, which also focuses on the importance of referencing and acknowledging sources.

Chapter 18, 'Media Analysis', continues to offer thought-provoking ideas for use both in the classroom and for independent study. It is intended that this chapter will lead to further research on the part of students.

Chapter 20, 'Communications Technology', reinforces the emphasis on technology and examines the various technological methods of communicating that a student is likely to find in a modern working environment.

Part 7 on career skills has been revamped to reflect the changing challenges faced by students as they set out to find their first post-study job. It looks at the demands of employers and interview boards and contains advice on approaching an interview and how to conduct oneself during an interview.

Each chapter ends with sections headed 'Review', 'Pitfalls', 'Confusing

Words', 'Quiz' and 'Spellings'. It has been decided to retain this format, as it reinforces the points raised in the chapter.

Users of this book can access support material through the Gill & Macmillan website at www.gillmacmillan.ie.

ACKNOWLEDGMENTS

I would like to thank a number of people who have helped me in preparing the fifth edition of this book.

To John Scott, who graciously allowed me tamper with his excellent material.

To all at Gill & Macmillian, especially Marion O'Brien, Aoileann O'Donnell and those editors who despaired at times of ever seeing a finished book.

To Colm McEvoy, Principal of Cavan College of Further Studies, and the staff of the College for their continued friendship and support.

To Lorraine Audley, Brenda Hennesessy, Cara McDermott and Sue Donohoe, who between them provided babysitting services and endless assistance.

To my former colleagues in Carr Communications, RTÉ and other media organisations who provided me with material and many wise words.

To the School of Marketing, DIT, for their help on the subject of referencing in chapter 15.

To my family, my parents, Noel and Patricia Fox, my brothers Christopher, Oliver and Alan, my sisters Bernadette and Noelle and my nieces Aoife and Eimear, for their constant support and encouragement.

Finally, to Marty and Aine, who assisted in their own way in ensuring that no deadline was ever met without love and support.

Catherine Fox

INTRODUCTION

TO

COMMUNICATION

1

INTRODUCTION TO COMMUNICATION

INTRODUCTION

Communication is the lifeblood of any organisation. People are constantly transmitting information. An organisation's need for an effective communication system increases as the firm gets bigger.

But we, as individuals, communicate constantly every day. Most of the time we are not even aware of it. From the time you got out of bed this morning, and perhaps even before that, you have engaged in communicating several times.

Definition of communication: *communication is the passing on of feelings, ideas, opinions and information from one person or group to another person or group and the eliciting of a discriminating response.*

A few elements of this definition are important.

1. Communication is not just the passing on of information. When you transmit information, you also transmit, to some extent, your feelings about the information.

2. Communication is a two-way process. You must get a response to your message. Thus you transmit a communication to another person, but the other must respond in some way. Our definition says it must be a 'discriminating response'. That means that the response must be a reaction to the specific communication.

FIG. 1 — A MODEL OF ONE-WAY COMMUNICATION

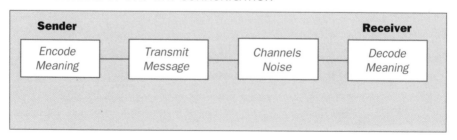

Sender			Receiver
Encode Meaning	Transmit Message	Channels Noise	Decode Meaning

FIG. 2 – A MODEL OF TWO-WAY COMMUNICATION

Sender			Receiver
Encode Meaning	Transmit Message	Channels Noise	Decode Meaning
Decode Receiver	Channels Noise	Transmit Message	Encode Sender

- The *sender* is the person or group who wishes to transmit a meaning to another person or group.

- To *encode* is to put the message in a form understood by the receiver. The usual form used is words. Other ways of transmitting meaning would be sign language, smoke signals, flags and silence.

- *Channel* is the medium by which you transmit a communication. You could send a memo, hold a meeting, use the telephone or send the message by e-mail.

- All channels contain *noise*, which is any interference that may hinder the communication. A meeting held before dinner when people are hungry would be an example of noise.

- To *transmit* a message is to send it across to the receiver. Timing can be very important here, as transmitting a message at an inappropriate time could result in it being misunderstood.

- The *receiver* is the person or group which perceives the sender's message. If there is no receiver, there is no communication.

- To *decode* a message is to translate the symbols in the message into meaning for the receiver. If you are told to do something 'as soon as you can', does that mean you are to do it immediately, or when you have your present task completed?

- *Feedback* is the reaction to a communication. There are three types of feedback:

  ■ *Informational feedback* is when the receiver simply provides the sender with non-evaluative information. For example, the sender asks how many students study at the Institute of Technology, Carlow, and the receiver provides the information.

  ■ *Corrective feedback* is when the receiver responds by challenging or correcting the original message. For instance, the receiver may point out that it is not his responsibility to monitor student numbers.

■ *Reinforcing feedback* is when the receiver acknowledges clear receipt of the intended message. An example of this would be the grade a student receives in an examination. It is important to note that reinforcing feedback can be either positive or negative.

GROUP ACTIVITY

One-way communication

Form the class into groups of five. One person is appointed as the sender of the communication, three are the receivers and the fifth person is the timekeeper. The sender of the communication can use only words to transmit the message. The receivers, who must have a pen and blank page, cannot ask questions. The timekeeper simply records the time it took to complete the exercise. The sender must transmit the following message to the receivers:

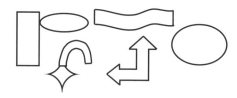

When the receivers have the message recorded on paper to their satisfaction, the exercise is complete. Do not show the message to the receivers before going on to the second part of the exercise.

Two-way communication

Again, form the class into groups of five. One person is appointed as the sender of the communication, three are the receivers and the fifth person is the timekeeper. The sender of the communication can use all the techniques available to transmit the message. However, the message must not be shown to the receivers. The receivers, who must have a pen and blank page, may ask as many questions as they wish and the sender may answer all questions. The timekeeper again simply records the time it took to complete the exercise. The sender must transmit the following message to the receivers:

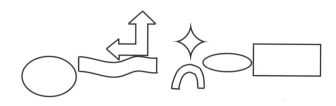

Normally, two-way communication will take longer but the message will be transmitted more accurately. Discuss the difficulties the senders and the receivers experienced during the exercise. What mistakes did the senders make? How did the receivers misinterpret the message?

ACTIVITY I

1. *List five communications you engaged in today in which you were the sender of the communication.*

2. *List five communications you engaged in today in which you were the receiver of the communication.*

3. *In what way were the five messages encoded? For example, did you write, speak or give signs?*

4. *What feedback did you get to the five messages you sent?*

5. *What was the purpose of each of the five communications you sent?*

6. *What problems did you have in decoding the five messages you received?*

7. *What feedback did you give to the five messages you received?*

8. *In what way were the five messages you received encoded?*

9. *What channels were used in each of the five messages you sent?*

10. *What channels were used in each of the five messages you received?*

11. *Give examples of any noise which occurred in the messages you sent.*

12. *Give examples of any noise which occurred in the messages you received.*

ORGANISATIONAL COMMUNICATION

Once the decision to communicate has been taken, the next step is to select the method. The style of the communication can be formal or informal. The reason for the communication, its priority and the recipients will all determine the selection of method and style of communication.

Formal communication

Formal communication follows the hierarchy as depicted in the organisation chart. It is standard acceptable procedure within an organisation and hence carries with it a degree of authority.

- *Upward*: goes from a person or group to a higher level of the organisation.
- *Downward*: goes from a person or group to a lower level in the organisation.
- *Horizontal (lateral)*: goes from a person or group on one level of the organisation to a person or group on the same level of the organisation.

Examples of formal communications include:

- traditional written forms, e.g. memo, circular, letters, reports
- notice or bulletin board
- meetings or briefings
- company publications, e.g. staff report, magazine, induction manua
- corporate video.

Advantages and disadvantages of formal communication

The advantages of formal communication are:

- Information is distributed in a predicable way, following the hierarchy of the organisation.
- The message is well prepared and less likely to be distorted in transmission.
- The authority of the sender is transmitted with the message, so the message carries a high degree of success, as it is seen as a direct order or instruction.
- Formal communication tends to involve a medium, which means a record of the message is often kept.

The disadvantages are:

- The message may have a management bias and thus may be viewed with suspicion.
- Employees may find formal channels intimidating to use.

Informal communication

All organisations have informal communication networks. Examples of informal communications may include a chat in the corridor, the office grapevine or a short, informal e-mail. Good managers are aware of the importance of informal communication and use it as part of the communication process. Informal communication flows up, down and across the organisation independently of the organisation chart and outside of management control.

Advantages and disadvantages of informal communication

The advantages are:

- It can often be the only real source of information for employees.
- It is speedy and used more often than formal channels.
- It is normally accurate, despite its dismissal by many as just gossip.
- A good manager can use the grapevine to float new ideas and gauge staff reaction prior to launching a new policy.

The disadvantages are:

- Everyone may not hear the information, as it can be selective, i.e. some groups may be bypassed or excluded.
- Information travels by word of mouth, so errors can occur as it passes along the line.
- The grapevine can include rumor and gossip, which can be damaging to individuals or the organisation as a whole.

ACTIVITY 2

1. Give three examples of formal communication you engaged in during the past week.

2. Give three examples of informal communication you engaged in during the past week.

3. Give an example of upward communication.

4. Give an example of downward communication.

5. Give an example of horizontal communication.

6. The tutor asks you a question in class. What type of communication is this?

7. You respond to the tutor's question. What type of communication is taking place?

8. You have a discussion with your friend during lunch hour. What type of communication is taking place?

9. Draw an organisation chart of your college and show how upward, downward and horizontal communication take place.

10. Give one example of a communication you are aware of that is both formal and downward.

BARRIERS TO COMMUNICATION

Barriers to communication are any elements which may hinder or prevent communication from taking place. It is possible to generate a lengthy list of such barriers. The most important ones are:

- *Language*: using too many words or words people are not familiar with can be a barrier to communication. For example, Samuel Johnson is said to have defined a window as 'an orifice in an edifice for the admission of luminary particles'.

- *Jargon*: jargon is technical language belonging to a profession, e.g. economists use such terms as 'GDP' and 'GNP'. You should be careful of using jargon with people who do not understand it.

- *Status*: people at different levels of an organisation may have difficulty in communicating with each other. What the managing director may express as merely a desire may be taken as a command by someone further down the line.

- *Education*: this can be a barrier, as educated people tend to see matters not as black and white, but as various shades of grey.

- *Timing*: if a communication is badly timed, it can be misunderstood.

- *Placing*: if a communication is placed or posted in an incorrect position, it may not be noticed by the people for whom it is intended. This can happen frequently at work when notices are placed on the wrong notice board.

- *Noise:* noise can be physical or psychological. If people cannot hear a speaker clearly, they may not understand the message. If a room is too hot, this can interfere with communication. When a person is tired, communication may be less successful.

  There are a number of different kinds of noise.

  - *Psychological noise:* a person's mind may be tired, and they will not be as successful in communication as if their mind was fresh.

  - *Emotional noise:* if a person is upset or disturbed about something, it will hinder their communication.

  - *Social noise:* if the communicator dislikes the person with whom they are communicating, this will be a barrier to successful communication.

  - *Technical noise:* some people may be uncomfortable with some of the new technology used in communication, and this can be an obstruction to communication.

- *Observation/inference confusion*: this barrier arises when you observe something and based on that evidence you infer or arrive at some conclusion. For example, when you are driving up the street and the traffic lights are green, you infer that the other lights are red. That is a reasonable inference to arrive at. However, you may sometimes make an incorrect inference. For instance, if you see a person with a tattoo, you may come to certain conclusions about the person which may not be accurate.

- *Information overload*: this occurs when so much information is available to a person that he or she cannot process or understand all of it. It is becoming more and more of a problem, as computers generate so much information.

Some examples of barriers to communication

The Black Hole of Calcutta

In 1756 the Nawab (governor) of Calcutta led a successful rising against the British East India Company. The British surrendered and the Nawab ordered the 146 captives to be put in prison for the night. He then went to bed. There was only one cell available and this was just twenty feet by twenty feet. All 146 captives were placed in the cell. Without air, panic broke out among the captives. In the morning 123 of the prisoners were dead.

'Get me coffee'

The former president of the US, Mr Richard Nixon, was working late one night in his hotel room while on a trip. He opened the door and asked his aide to 'Get me coffee.' It was late and the hotel kitchen was closed. Some hotel personnel were contacted and a fresh pot of coffee was brewed. On a number of occasions while this was being done the president kept asking for coffee. Finally, a tray arrived with the coffee. It was only then that it was discovered that the president did not want coffee to drink, but wanted to talk to his assistant whose name was Coffee.

(Recounted in D. Rather and G. Gates, *The Palace Guard*, New York: Harper & Row, 1974, p. 109.)

The Duggan case

Mr Harry Whelehan, the attorney general, was nominated president of the

High Court by the government on Friday, 11 November 1994. Before his appointment, the Labour members of the government withdrew from the Cabinet meeting because of the delay in executing an extradition warrant for Fr Brendan Smith. Within a few hours, Mr Whelehan was sworn in as High Court president at Áras an Uachtarán by President Robinson. Mr Eoghan Fitzsimons was appointed as the new attorney general. On Monday, 14 November the Fianna Fáil ministers were meeting to discuss and work on the Taoiseach, Mr Reynolds's, speech to be delivered in the Dáil on the following day. The new attorney general was called to the meeting and he told those present that he had discovered a new case similar to the Smith case. Mr Fitzsimons later said he made it clear that the Duggan case should be referred to in the Taoiseach's speech the next day. Others present said his information was not clear. Fianna Fáil ministers and advisers spent all day and late into the night drafting the speech. Some of them admitted to being very tired. For example, Mr McCreevy was just back from a trip to India and had had very little sleep. When the Taoiseach spoke in the Dáil on Tuesday, 15 November he did not mention the Duggan case. He was accused of misleading the Dáil and the future of the government was threatened. The question was asked later whether the Fianna Fáil ministers deliberately misled the Dáil, did not understand the significance of the Duggan case because of tiredness and confusion, or if the attorney general's advice was unclear.

This was the beginning of an episode that ended in the fall of a government which was very popular, as it had just helped to negotiate a ceasefire in Northern Ireland.

ACTIVITY 3

1. 'Be back as soon as you can.' How might a person misinterpret that message?

2. 'Move it over a little.' What barrier to communication might be present in this sentence?

3. Give two examples of jargon which you have experienced.

4. A manager in a company calls an important meeting for 3.00 p.m. on 23 December. Comment on this.

5. Give two examples of notices which you think were posted in the wrong place.

6. A company puts a memo about threatened redundancies in with the monthly cheques. Comment on the barriers to communication which might arise.

7. Give two examples of observation/inference confusion from your own experience.

8. *Judges in court wear wigs. Comment on this as a barrier to communication.*

9. *Give examples of other clothes which may be a barrier to communication.*

10. *'All I expect of you is that you do your best in the exam.' What different interpretations might a student put on this sentence?*

DELIVERING THE MESSAGE

In business, it is important that your message is delivered, understood and acted upon. By paying particular attention to some key factors before you communicate, you will ensure a high degree of success in your communication.

In deciding to communicate, it is important to consider all the factors.

- Ask yourself why you are communicating this information. What is your purpose and objective in sending this information?
- Consider your target audience and their expertise and knowledge.
- Select the most appropriate method (medium) and style to deliver your message. Draft the message, paying particular attention to using codes understood by the receiver.
- Attempt to see the message from the receiver's point of view.
- Select the most appropriate time (context) to deliver the message.
- Check for understanding and feedback.

As a receiver, you have an important role in the communication process.

- Pay full attention, listen actively and observe all verbal and non-verbal codes.
- Decode the message carefully. If you are unsure of the meaning, seek clarification.
- Be objective, regardless of your personal feelings or prejudices. Focus on the message, not the sender.
- Provide appropriate feedback, acknowledge receipt of the message, note important details and take the necessary action.

PERCEPTION

Definition of perception: *perception is the process by which a person selects, organises and interprets stimuli to give them meaning.* Stimulus or stimuli (the plural) are anything we see, feel, hear, etc. We get stimuli through our senses. The senses are seeing, hearing, smelling, tasting and touching. An old philosopher said that there is nothing in the mind that was not first in the senses. We learn through our senses. Perception is a very individual aspect of behaviour. We all perceive in our own way. Perception is the interpretation of a message by the receiver.

There are a multitude of objects and stimuli that vie for our attention. We select the ones that are important to us. This is called *perceptual selectivity*. In driving a car we perceive what is important, such as traffic lights, people crossing the road and road signs. We tend to perceive what we are motivated to perceive.

Many things compete for our attention. Why do we pay attention to some and not to others? The following are the factors which influence our attention:

- *Size*: we will perceive a big object before a small object.

- *Intensity*: we will pay attention to a loud sound rather than a whisper.

- *Contrast*: if three people are sitting down and one person is standing, we will pay attention to the person standing. Directors of plays make use of this technique frequently.

- *Novelty*: something we have not seen before will engage our attention.

- *Movement*: most advertisements make use of this fact and have plenty of movement. They also tend to use intensity in speech and music. Guinness had an advertisement in contrast to this which had no sound at all. A quiet voice said at the end of the ad: 'This twenty seconds of darkness was brought to you by Guinness.'

- *Repetition*: if something is repeated often enough, you will pay attention to it.

Social perception

Social perception is concerned with the processes by which we perceive people. Social perception is far more complex than the perception of inanimate objects such as chairs, tables and signs. This is true for two reasons: (i) people are more complex than things, and (ii) an accurate perception of people is far more important to us personally than perception of inanimate objects. The consequences of misperceiving people are great. Failure to perceive a desk in a room may mean that we will bump into it. Failure to accurately perceive a social situation may have serious consequences at work.

Factors which influence social perception include physical appearance, verbal and non-verbal communication and ascribed attributes.

FIG. 3 – MAJOR INFLUENCES ON SOCIAL PERCEPTION IN ORGANISATIONS

	Characteristics of the situation 1. Organisational role 2. Location of event	
Characteristics of the person perceived 1. Physical appearance 2. Verbal communication 3. Non-verbal communication 4. Ascribed attributes		
	Characteristics of the perceiver 1. Self-concept 2. Previous experience with individual	

Characteristics of the person perceived: we partly perceive people on the basis of how they look. Clothing, which is part of physical appearance, also influences our perception. Our use of words (verbal) and such elements as tone of voice and accent (non-verbal) also help to determine our perception of others.

We often ascribe or give certain attributes to a person before or at the beginning of an encounter. These attributes can influence how we perceive the person. Status, occupation and personal characteristics are three ascribed attributes. If we are told the person we are about to meet is the managing director, we will have certain perceptions of the person before she arrives. Likewise, if you are told that the medical consultant will see you now, you will begin to behave towards the person who arrives with a certain amount of deference. An example of a personal characteristic would be intelligence. If you are told by someone whose view you respect that a person is very intelligent, you will conjure up a picture of what you think an intelligent person is like.

Characteristics of the situation: a person's place in the organisation can influence her perceptions. Production workers in a firm will see production as the most important department; members of the sales force will tend to put sales and marketing at the top. Also, where an event takes place may influence perception. To walk about in your bare feet in your home may be acceptable, but a different view of it would be taken at work.

Characteristics of the perceiver: people with a positive self-concept tend to see favourable characteristics in others. Also, our previous experience with others will often influence how we view their current behaviour.

1. List the items that gain your attention when coming to college each morning.

2. What techniques does your tutor use to attract your attention?

3. Explain how the organisation of your classroom helps your tutor to gain the attention of the class.

4. Explain why social perception is more complicated than the perception of inanimate objects.

5. Why is it important to understand the process of perception?

6. Give three examples of when you and your friend had different perceptions of the same event.

7. What is meant by saying that 'perception is a very individual aspect of behaviour'?

8. What attributes would you ascribe to a person with red hair?

9. What attributes would you ascribe to a person with a tattoo on his arm?

10. What attributes would you ascribe (a) to a man who dyes his hair (b) to a woman who dyes her hair?

REVIEW

1. Explain why communication is not just 'sending information from one person to another'.

2. Look up the origin of the word 'communication'.

3. Why is an understanding of perception important in communication?

4. Find two other meanings for the word 'communication'.

5. A lecturer once went into his classroom when no students were present and locked the door. He then proceeded to deliver his lecture. He explained afterwards that his contract obliged him to teach ten hours a week but it made no mention of students having to be present. Did communication take place in this instance?

6. What is meant by self-concept?

7. What is meant by organisational role?

8. Why is it important to plan your communication in business?

PITFALLS

prostrate prostate

The two words *prostrate* and *prostate* are very similar. The word 'prostrate' means lying with face to the ground. The word 'prostate' refers to a gland near the neck of the bladder.

CONFUSING WORDS

commissar	commissariat	commonable	commonage
commonality	commoner	commutable	commutate
countervail	countervalue	covey	covin

QUIZ

The following words all have their origins in languages other than English. Can you find which languages they spring from?

apartheid, blitz, coup d'état, ersatz, slogan.

SPELLINGS

The words most commonly misspelled are highlighted.

abolition	admittance	anonymous
absence	advertisement	**anxiety**
accelerate	**aerial**	**appearance**
accessible	**agreeable**	appreciate
accidental	agriculture	architecture
accommodation	already	**argument**
accomplished	alteration	**arrangement**
ache	alternate	**ascend**
achieved	although	assassin
acknowledge	altogether	**athletic**
acquainted	amiable	atmosphere
acquiesce	**among**	auctioneer
address	**analysis**	**awful**
admirable	anniversary	awkward

PART 2

WRITTEN

COMMUNICATION

SKILLS

2

IN WORDS THERE IS POWER

VOCABULARY

It is possible to communicate messages without using words. This is called non-verbal communications. However, in business we rely on verbal and written communication.

English is a growing language. Every year new words are added to English dictionaries. Modern technology has had a more rapid impact on language than any previous developments. The speed communication can take place at results in a need to draft the message more quickly, with shorter forms or letters replacing words. Ten years ago the word 'text' would not have been used as a verb, but now 'I will text you' is a standard and acceptable sentence in the English language.

In business, however, and indeed in life, words are very important and your success as a communicator will largely depend on your ability to use words. You should always strive for conciseness and accuracy. While our spoken language has been influenced by modern technological developments, our written communications have also come under attack.

A common sentence, 'Before I see you at 5.00 pm I have to wait for Mary', is commonly texted as 'B4 I c u @ 5 I hv 2 wait 4 Mary'. While this may be acceptable in text communication, its use is not acceptable in business communication. E-mail messages often use 'SMS'-type abbreviations, such as BTW (by the way), IMHO (in my humble opinion). Such abbreviations should not be used in formal written communication.

Do not simply use the first word that enters your head. The English language may have several other words that are more appropriate. By constantly practising and by expanding your reading, your ability to communicate will improve.

Express the meaning of each of the following phrases in a single word. The first letter of each word is given to help you.

happening each year	annually
a person seventy years old	s ....
a person one hundred years old	c ....
a non-drinker	t ....
celebration of an event that happened one hundred years ago	c ....
occurring at the same time	s ....
not capable of being heard	i ....
not enough	i ....
cannot be rubbed out	i ....
not capable of being explained	i ....
a person who collects stamps	p ....
a person who writes plays	p ....
a person who carves in stone	s ....
a book that has been shortened	a ....
a person who pleads in court	b ....

In the blank spaces in the continuous passage below, insert the appropriate words from the list provided at the end.

Why is the industrial .... problem in Ireland so acute? Do Irish workers have a self-destructive ....? Is the good of the .... put before selfish .... gain any longer? All strikes are .... settled. Why can't they be solved sooner rather than later? It is well known that the .... a strike goes on, the more .... it is to settle. The great problem is that each side refuses to .... for fear of losing face. To find a .... that each side can agree to without losing dignity is the .... to many of the strikes which occur at present. One of the .... questions to be decided is whether the findings of the Labour Court should be .... But what happens if people refuse to .... by the Labour

Court findings? Should they be fined or ....? If the latter, will many people see them as ....? Despite all the talk about the problem of strikes, there seems to be general .... when it comes to solving the problem. If all .... people involved with the problem would sit down and work ...., surely a solution could be found which would not .... the .... of any party.

Words to insert:

principles	eventually	relations	longer	personal
community	difficult	formula	solution	vital
binding	conscientious	compromise	abide	jailed
apathy	impulse	diligently	martyrs	compromise

ACTIVITY 3

Always use simple words rather than complex words. Use familiar words rather than unfamiliar ones.

For the words below, insert a more commonly used word in the blanks provided.

approximately	....	promulgate	....
accomplished	....	masticate	....
ameliorate	....	employment	....
cognisant	....	diminish	....
demonstrate	....	expensive	....
modification	....	terminate	....

ACTIVITY 4

For each of the following sentences, choose the correct word in the parentheses.

1. The (coarse, course) was (formally, formerly) approved.

2. The actress missed her (cue, queue) because she was short of (breath, breathe).

3. The (current, currant) affairs programme could not be seen because the electrical (current, currant) was switched off.

4. The (site, sight) of the house was in a terrible state because of the weather.

5. The mother heard the telephone (ring, wring).

6. It is very difficult living in a (desert, dessert).

7. The car accident had a terrible (effect, affect) on him.

8. He was delighted he (passed, past) his examination.

9. What are the responsibilities of county (councils, counsels)?

10. The boy had a (flare, flair) for music.

11. I left the (stationery, stationary) in the car.

12. My lace was (lose, loose).

13. I really was left with no (alternative, alternate).

14. The guards (disbursed, dispersed) the crowds.

15. The house had (depreciated, deprecated) in value.

16. He died of a rare (disease, decease).

17. The (weather, whether) this summer was very bad.

18. She writes in her (dairy, diary) every night.

19. Some people make (elicit, illicit) whiskey.

20. She made the cake from a new (recipe, receipt).

<hr>

ACTIVITY 5

Choose the correct word for each of the phrases in the left column.

1. The head of a school   (principle, principal) ....

2. A prominent person   (imminent, eminent) ....

3. To quote from a book   (cite, sight) ....

4. A false statement about a person   (liable, libel) ....

5. Permission to do something   (aloud, allowed) ....

6. What hay is made into   (bale, bail) ....

7. Not fertile   (barren, baron) ....

8. A bed in a boat   (birth, berth) ....

9. A type of gun   (canon, cannon) ....

10. A clever device (ingenious, ingenuous) ....

11. To look for votes (canvas, canvass) ....

12. A hiding place for treasure (cash, cache) ....

13. To disagree (dissent, descent) ....

14. The yellow of an egg (yoke, yolk) ....

15. To forego a claim (wave, waive) ....

16. To praise (complement, compliment) ....

17. Go before (proceed, precede) ....

18. A problem that cannot be solved (insolvent, insoluble) ....

19. A wind coming through the door (draft, draught) ....

20. Further up the mountain (hire, higher) ....

21. It belongs to them (their, there) ....

22. A small part of a play (scene, seen) ....

23. To be diplomatic (discrete, discreet) ....

24. This is an offence (steal, steel) ....

25. To leave a country (immigrate, emigrate) ....

26. A large animal (guerilla, gorilla) ....

27. The principal city (capital, capitol) ....

BUSINESS TERMS

Every trade, profession and occupation has its own specialised terminology. It is evident that groups of specialists must use a special language among themselves so that they can speak and write accurately on their subjects. Technical language is often called jargon. Jargon is useful and is a vital aid to efficient communication. However, it is often looked on as a barrier to communication because people tend to use technical words even when speaking to people who have no knowledge of them. Jargon is a valuable and necessary part of the English language and it is vital for business employees to become familiar with the technical language of business. It would be useful to keep a dictionary of commercial terms. However, it is more efficient to be able to use the common language of business without having to refer to a dictionary. The following activities will help to increase your vocabulary of business terms.

Choose the word from the selection given on the right-hand side that most closely matches the definition on the left.

1. Payment of sum of money in the event of loss or damage to life
   (a) advance (b) insurance (c) asset (d) assurance

2. Gratuity to employees beyond their normal pay
   (a) discount (b) interest (c) bonus (d) rebate

3. Sum paid to author for copy of book sold
   (a) royalty (b) commission (c) drawings (d) lien

4. Amount by which sum drawn exceeds credit balance
   (a) loan (b) mortgage (c) overdraft (d) advance

5. One who buys in the stock exchange hoping to sell at a higher price
   (a) broker (b) bull (c) bear (d) stag

6. A list of goods sent
   (a) debenture (b) invoice (c) credit note (d) tare

7. Money contributed to keep down the price of commodities
   (a) subsidy (b) annuity (c) tariff (d) will

8. Agreement between parties for supply of goods or performance of work
   (a) trustee (b) contract (c) monopoly (d) partnership

9. Established custom or popularity of a business
   (a) endowment (b) return (c) goodwill (d) turnover

10. Companies coming together to agree on pricing policy
    (a) premium (b) actuary (c) usury (d) cartel

11. One who owes money
    (a) debtor (b) creditor (c) trustee (d) middleman

12. Sum payable as profit of joint stock company
    (a) requisition (b) share (c) dividend (d) annuity

13. Person who winds up, ascertains liabilities and apportions assets of a company
    (a) agent (b) receiver (c) liquidator (d) director

14. Instruction to bank to make regular payments
    (a) bank giro (b) standing order (c) credit note (d) blank cheque

15. Official examination of accounts
    (a) demurrage (b) search (c) audit (d) deed

FOREIGN PHRASES

English has borrowed extensively from other languages and occasionally you will come across words or phrases from other languages, especially Latin and French. Your dictionary will provide you with an exhaustive list of these words and phrases, so only the more frequently used ones are given here.

- *ad hoc*: for this special purpose. Used generally in regard to a meeting called to deal with a specific problem, e.g. an *ad hoc* meeting.

- *à la carte*: used in hotels to describe a menu where each item is priced separately.

- *table d'hôte*: the menus in hotels which have a fixed price for the complete meal.

- *rapport*: in sympathy with. 'He has great *rapport* with children.' He has a great relationship with children.

- *ex officio*: by virtue of office. 'The principal is a member of the board of management *ex officio*.' That means she is a member because she is the principal and if she ceased to be principal she would lose her position on the board.

- *in camera*: in private. 'The court proceedings were held *in camera* as children were involved.'

- *nem. con.*: This is used at meetings when a motion is passed unanimously. The words stand for *nemo contendere* and mean no one disputed the matter.

- *NB (nota bene)*: note well. It is often used at the end of letters or memos to add emphasis to a point.

- *post mortem*: an examination carried out to establish the cause of death.

- *sine die*: 'The meeting was postponed *sine die*.' It means the meeting was postponed indefinitely.

- *per annum*: yearly.

FIGURATIVE EXPRESSIONS

The English language is also rich in figurative expressions such as 'sticking out like a sore thumb', 'the tip of the iceberg' or 'straight from the horse's mouth'. The most common of these expressions are listed below, but you will find many more in your dictionary.

to buy a pig in a poke (bag)	to buy something without seeing it
a blind alley occupation	a job that has no prospects
a cock and bull story	a story made up to lead you astray
to be under a cloud	to be under suspicion
to cross swords with	to have a dispute with someone
to let the cat out of the bag	to reveal a secret
sour grapes	to be jealous
with a grain of salt	to treat something you heard with some disbelief
to call a spade a spade	to state in blunt terms. A person who is very blunt is sometimes said to call a spade a shovel
a square peg in a round hole	a person in a position that doesn't suit him
at sixes and sevens	to be confused
to bury the hatchet	to forget a grievance

ACTIVITY 7

Substitute foreign phrases or figurative expressions for the highlighted phrases.

1. The meeting was adjourned **indefinitely**.

2. He is the type of person who **speaks in very blunt terms**.

3. **An examination to establish the cause of death** was carried out on the victim.

4. Mary was **under suspicion** after the examination.

5. He was **not really suited to his new position**.

6. Liam and Garret decided to **forget their quarrel**.

7. The motion to ask for an increase in salary was passed **without opposition**.

8. The retired director is paid €10,000 **yearly**.

9. Iseult was advised **not to take the story she heard too seriously**.

10. When the child was in court, the proceedings were held **in private**.

REVIEW

1. What is the meaning of each of the following words?

exonerate	facet	denigrate	vulnerable
laconic	habitual	petulant	insinuate
inflation	countersign	uncouth	demurrage
demoniac	disburse	discern	ergonomics
flux	flummery	fudge	gumption

2. What is the meaning of each of the following business terms?

stagflation	deflation	inflation
dumping	share	index
preferential debts	merger	frozen assets
benefit-in-kind	arrears	

3. Find the meaning of the following words or expressions.

   (a) An *ad hominem* argument.

   (b) To be full of *bonhomie*.

   (c) A *coup d'état* took place.

   (d) A *gauche* person.

   (e) To be on tenterhooks.

   (f) Caught between the devil and the deep blue sea.

   (g) To be hand in glove with.

   (h) A chip off the old block.

   (i) To live in a fool's paradise.

   (j) To beat about the bush.

PITFALLS

won't wont

Won't comes from the words *will not*, e.g. I *won't* do it.

Wont means accustomed to doing something, e.g. As he was *wont* to say.

CONFUSING WORDS

calendar	calender	complacent	complaisant
candid	candied	concert	consort
cede	seed	confidant	confident
chance	chants	creak	creek
chord	cord	dam	damn

colour color

In Europe we spell colour c-o-l-o-u-r, in the US c-o-l-o-r. Find five other words where the spelling in the US differs from that in Europe.

SPELLINGS

The words most commonly misspelled are highlighted.

bachelor	barometer	benefit
bacteria	barren	**benefited**
baffle	barrister	beware
bagful	battalion	bewilderment
bail	beautiful	binary
bailiff	beauty	**breathe**
banal	bedevil	**breathing**
banana	**beginning**	budget
baneful	behaviour	**budgeted**
banquet	belief	bulletin
barbarous	**believed**	**bureau**
barbecue	belligerent	**bureaucracy**
bargain	**beneficial**	**business**

3

AND YET MORE POWER

PREFIXES

Prefixes are placed at the beginning of words. They are very important in word formation. The word *undress* is composed of *dress* and *un-* placed before it. The prefix varies the meaning of the root word, e.g. a *theist* is a person who believes in a god, but an *atheist* is a person who believes there is no god.

The commonly used prefixes are:

ante- (before) – antenatal, anteroom, antecedent, antedate

anti- (against) – anticlimax, antipathy, antidote

auto- (self) – automobile, automatic, autocratic

bene- (well) – benevolent, benefit, beneficial

bi- (two) – bicycle, bicentenary, bilingual

cent- (hundred) – century, centenary, centigrade

contra- (against) – contradict, contrary, contraband

di- (two) – dialogue, dichotomy

ex- (out) – exhale, exhaust

magna- (great) – magnificent, magnitude

mal- (bad) – malevolent, malicious

micro- (small) – microchip, microphone, microscope

mis- (wrong) – mistake, mishap

pan- (all) – pantheist, panacea

poly- (many) – polygon, polygamy

post- (after) – postpone, postgraduate, post mortem

pseudo- (sham) – pseudonym, pseudo-intellectual

quad- (four) – quadrangle, quadrilateral

retro- (back) – retrospective, retrograde

tri- (three) – triangle, trinity, tricycle

uni- (one) – uniform, unity, unilateral

Prefixes and spelling: be careful of spelling when using prefixes. Note 'disappoint' only has one 's', 'dissatisfy' has two; while 'unaided' has only one 'n' and 'unnecessary', two.

ACTIVITY I

1. Match the words in the right-hand column with the terms on the left.

(a) Antenatal	(a) Conversation between two people
(b) Post-mortem	(b) To breathe out
(c) Autocratic	(c) Having several spouses
(d) Contraband	(d) He doesn't know if God exists
(e) Dialogue	(e) Able to speak two languages
(f) Bisect	(f) Before birth
(g) Bigamy	(g) Smuggled goods
(h) Bilingual	(h) Having two spouses
(i) Malevolent	(i) An object having three legs
(j) Uniform	(j) To divide in two
(k) Exhale	(k) Car
(l) Benevolent	(l) An aversion to something
(m) Bicentenary	(m) Test to establish cause of death
(n) International	(n) Dictatorial
(o) Polygamy	(o) Evil
(p) Pantheism	(p) Generous
(q) Agnostic	(q) Between nations
(r) Antipathy	(r) Belief that God is everywhere
(s) Automobile	(s) Two hundredth anniversary
(t) Tripod	(t) Of the same

2. The prefix bi- means two. Match up the words on the left with their meaning on the right.

(a) Biannual	(a) For use by both ears
(b) Bilateral	(b) Having two axles

(c) Bimonthly	(c) Occurring twice each year
(d) Bifocal	(d) Occurring every two years
(e) Biennial	(e) Using both hands
(f) Binary	(f) Vehicle with two wheels
(g) Bimanual	(g) Occurring every two months
(h) Bicycle	(h) On both sides
(i) Biaxial	(i) Involving pairs
(j) Biaural	(j) Glasses combining distance and near vision

3. The prefix mis- means bad or wrong. Write the missing words, all beginning with mis-, in the spaces below.

(a) The guard said the man was .... in the street.

(b) The judge said the funds had been ....

(c) The accountant believed the totals had been ....

(d) The public felt it was a .... of justice.

(e) The actor was totally .... in the play.

(f) Most children are full of ....

(g) It was unfair of him to .... what I said.

(h) He should not have .... my statement.

(i) The judge found him guilty of a ....

(j) The dress is a total ....

(k) When I was driving the car I had a ....

(l) When taking the free shot he .... the ball.

(m) I found his speech a ....

(n) There is no doubt but that the solicitor .... him in court.

(o) You should try not to .... your words.

(p) I can't find it so I'm sure I .... it somewhere.

4. The prefix tri- means three. Supply words beginning with tri- for the following phrases.

(a) A flag with three colours ....

(b) A three-wheeled vehicle for children ....

(c) Three days of prayer ....

(d) Occurring every three years ....

(e) Having three spouses ....

(f) A group of three ....

(g) Having three sides ....

(h) Having three languages ....

(i) Figure bounded by three straight lines ....

(j) A three-legged stand ....

SUFFIXES

Suffixes are placed at the end of words. For example, if the suffix -*able* is added to *change*, we have the word *changeable*.

The commonly used suffixes are:

-cide (kill) – suicide, matricide, genocide

-ess (feminine) – abbess, mistress

-fold (times) – twofold, tenfold, a hundredfold

-ful (full) – helpful, beautiful, thankful

-hood (state) – boyhood, manhood

-less (without) – helpless, thankless, hopeless

-ology (study of) – sociology, psychology, biology

-man (person) – craftsman, swordsman, ploughman

-mania (craze for) – kleptomania, bibliomania

-monger (dealer) – ironmonger, fishmonger

-phobia (fear) – claustrophobia, hydrophobia

Suffixes and spelling: suffixes can cause problems in spelling. Note 'movable' but 'changeable'. Also note when to use 'full' and 'ful'.

ACTIVITY 2

1. Using the list of suffixes above, insert the missing word in the following sentences.

    (a) Many people are criminals because of their lost ....

    (b) Hitler was guilty of ....

    (c) The science of society is known as ....

(d) A fear of water is known as ....

(e) Some people just can't keep their hands off things; they are called ....

(f) If you are given a present, you should be ....

(g) A person who sells fish is called a ....

(h) The killing of one's mother is known as ....

(i) He is always collecting books; he is a real ....

(j) Many more students study .... than study chemistry.

2. Match the words ending in -ology on the left with their correct meaning on the right.

(a) Astrology	*(a) The study of God*
(b) Anthropology	*(b) The study of water*
(c) Archaeology	*(c) The study of language*
(d) Biology	*(d) The study of criminals*
(e) Criminology	*(e) The study of the stars and their influence on human affairs*
(f) Entomology	*(f) The study of insects*
(g) Gynaecology	*(g) The study of human antiquities*
(h) Genealogy	*(h) The study of the descent of families*
(i) Hydrology	*(i) The study of mankind*
(j) Meteorology	*(j) The study of climates*
(k) Philology	*(k) The study of life forms*
(l) Theology	*(l) The study of functions and diseases of women*

3. Write down the meaning of the following words ending in -phobia *and* -mania.

(a) Anglophobia ....

(b) Agoraphobia ....

(c) Claustrophobia ....

(d) Gynophobia ....

(e) Hydrophobia ....

(f) Zoophobia ....

(g) Bibliomania ....

(h) Kleptomania ....

(i) Megalomania ....

(j) Nymphomania ....

(k) Chronomania ....

(l) Ablutomania ....

PLURALS

The plural form of most words is very simple: just add *s* to the singular. There are some basic rules that will be of some help, but they do not cover all the eventualities.

Type 1: Add -*s* to the singular, e.g. girl, girls; boy, boys.

Type 2: Words ending in -*y* preceded by a consonant take -*ies* in the plural, e.g. lady, ladies; holy, holies; deputy, deputies; secretary, secretaries.

When the final *y* is preceded by a vowel, just add -*s*, e.g. holiday, holidays; donkey, donkeys.

Type 3: Words ending in -*o* take -*s* in the plural, but sometimes take -*es*, e.g. folio, folios; studio, studios; but be careful of cargo, cargoes; potato, potatoes.

Type 4: Some words ending in -*f* or -*fe* take -*ves* in the plural, e.g. half, halves; life, lives.

Type 5: Some words form plurals by changing the vowel, e.g. foot, feet; goose, geese.

Type 6: Compound words usually form the plural by changing or adding to the most important word, e.g. brother-in-law, brothers-in-law; looker-on, lookers-on.

Type 7: Some words are only used in the plural, e.g. trousers, spectacles.

Type 8: Some words have the same form in the singular as in the plural, e.g. sheep, salmon.

Type 9: Foreign words may form their plurals according to the rules of their original language. However, words in common usage may be allowed to form their plurals according to the rules of English, e.g. formula, formulas, though according to the rules of Latin it should be formulae.

FOREIGN WORDS

Singular	*Plural*
agenda	agenda, agendas
analysis	analyses
appendix	appendices, appendixes
axis	axes
basis	bases
bureau	bureaux, bureaus
circus	circuses
crisis	crises
criterion	criteria
curriculum	curricula
datum	data
dogma	dogmas
focus	foci, focuses
fungus	fungi, funguses
gymnasium	gymnasia, gymnasiums
hypothesis	hypotheses
ignoramus	ignoramuses
index	indices, indexes
medium	media (the press, radio and TV)
	mediums (those communicating with the dead)
memorandum	memoranda, memorandums
millennium	millennia, millenniums
nucleus	nuclei
oasis	oases
phenomenon	phenomena
plateau	plateaux, plateaus
radius	radii
series	series
species	species
stadium	stadia
stimulus	stimuli

stratum	strata
syllabus	syllabi, syllabuses
synthesis	syntheses
thesis	theses

ACTIVITY 3

1. Correct all the errors in the following sentences. Note that some of the sentences are correct. Ensure that singular nouns are followed by singular verbs and plural nouns are followed by plural verbs.

    Example: 'The media in Ireland has high standards.'

    This can be rendered as:

    'The media in Ireland have high standards.'

    (a) The students are working on their thesis.

    (b) RTÉ is a news medium.

    (c) Two court-martials were held this morning.

    (d) I always put two spoonfuls of sugar in my tea.

    (e) Powerful physique is one of the criterions for a good Kerry footballer.

    (f) Many people make jokes about mother-in-laws.

    (g) Most women do not have lady's-maids now.

    (h) We have too many good-for-nothings in society.

    (i) The company employs ten salesmen.

    (j) The child fell under the horse's hoofs.

    (k) The woman were delighted when they heard the news.

2. Turn the highlighted words in the following sentences into their plural form and ensure that the verbs are also plural.

    (a) A **lay-by** is useful on a busy road.

    (b) A **radio** is a help to pass the time.

    (c) Many houses have a **piano**.

    (d) What is a **hero**?

    (e) A **loaf** of bread will not go far.

    (f) **Life** is sacred.

    (g) The **thief** was caught.

*(h) Put on your **scarf**.*

*(i) The **staff** of the school was there.*

*(j) A rainbow is a beautiful **phenomenon**.*

*(k) The **thesis** was completed last year.*

*(l) I hear the **echo**.*

*(m) I saw the **dwarf**.*

*(n) Put it in the **safe**.*

From the right-hand side choose the word or phrase that corresponds most closely to the highlighted word on the left.

*(1) A literary **allusion*** (a) correct (b) indirect (c) reference (d) important

*(2) **Ambiguous** word* (a) difficult (b) strange (c) double meaning (d) observe

*(3) **Amenable** person* (a) criminal (b) foreign (c) responsive (d) silly

*(4) **Insipid** personality* (a) outgoing (b) dull (c) happy (d) introverted

*(5) **Bravura** performance* (a) hopeless (b) brilliant (c) uninspired (d) mediocre

*(6) **Alleviate** disaster* (a) relieve (b) increase (c) explain (d) report

*(7) **Blatant** disregard* (a) conscious (b) devious (c) strong (d) thoughtless

*(8) **Castigate** unfairly* (a) punish (b) reject (c) demote (d) acquire

*(9) **Dogmatic** personality* (a) logical (b) weak (c) illogical (d) forcing opinions on others

*(10) A **catalyst** for change* (a) facilitates (b) prevents (c) in favour (d) retards

*(11) **Denigrate** the proposal* (a) support (b) castigate (c) defame (d) second

*(12) A **cavalier** attitude* (a) bad (b) off-hand (c) proper (d) dangerous

*(13) **Concurrent** sentence* (a) long (b) at the same time (c) hard labour (d) complex

*(14) A **conciliatory** gesture*	*(a) open (b) aggressive (c) friendly (d) ambiguous*
*(15) An **audacious** suggestion*	*(a) daring (b) outrageous (c) stupid (d) impractical*
*(16) A **disproportionate** reaction*	*(a) timid (b) too large or small (c) over-zealous (d) criminal*
*(17) **Dissipate** your earnings*	*(a) increase (b) invest wisely (c) control (d) squander*
*(18) A **prevalent** attitude*	*(a) correct (b) widespread (c) immoral (d) dangerous*
*(19) A **prudent** suggestion*	*(a) foolish (b) wise (c) impractical (d) diplomatic*
*(20) Of **dubious** value*	*(a) great (b) precious (c) doubtful (d) useless*

ABBREVIATIONS

The use of abbreviations is common in all walks of life. It saves time and increases efficiency. You should be familiar with the following ones. If not, you will find some of them in your dictionary.

PAYE, GNP, a/c, ACCA, ACA, COD, PRSI, VAT, AA, BBC, EU, GMT, HMSO, PRO, VIP, SRN, RSVP, BComm, BA, BE, AMIEE, BSc, PhD, CIMA.

The following abbreviations are relevant to Ireland. You will find what they stand for in the IPA *Administration Yearbook & Diary.*

DCU, TCD, UL, NUI, NCAD, HEA, DIT, CAO, RIA, FÁS, ICMSA, IFA, TUI, INTO, ASTI, VEC, ICTU, IBOA, AIB, GAA, FAI, IRFU, IPA, ESB, IEI, IMI, FF, FG, PD, ICA, ESRI, FLAC, HEDCO, TD, MEP, MD, DG, SIPTU, IBEC, IMPACT, CCI, IT, COFORD, DEVCO, IBAR, INPC, OECD, RACO, TRBDI, USIT, HETAC, FETAC, NQAI

REVIEW

1. Find five words, other than the ones mentioned in this chapter, that have prefixes.
2. Find five words, other than the ones mentioned in this chapter, that have suffixes.

3. Find the word for a craze for animals.

4. Find the word for a fear of being alone.

5. Find the plural of the following:

   company, journey, man, child, deer, grouse, trout, fish, chateau, memento, halo, himself, sanatorium, stadium, sheaf, erratum, photo, motto, manifesto, tax.

6. Check that you understand the meaning of the following words:

   unequivocal, avaricious, cursory, opulent, gullible, subtle, invective, lethal, vicarious, tenuous, innocuous, strident, halcyon, derision, dearth, scurrilous, diffident, zenith, anticlimax, placate.

7. What do the following abbreviations stand for?

   RDS, B&I, SDLP, PSNI, FCA, USI, UN, NCH, BIM, VHI, PD.

PITFALLS

e.g. i.e.

e.g. means 'for example', from the Latin *exempli gratia*. It can be remembered in English as 'example given'. 'I will finish this chapter some day next week, e.g. Monday.'

i.e. means 'that is', from the Latin *id est.* 'I will finish the book in two weeks' time, i.e. the end of July.'

CONFUSING WORDS

lean	lien	main	mane
lends	lens	maize	maze
lineament	liniment	mantel	mantle
loath	loathe	marshal	martial
lose	loose	mean	mien

QUIZ

'The English,' said Oscar Wilde, 'have really everything in common with the Americans, except, of course, language.'

What is the meaning of the following American terms: band aid; billfold; diaper; closet?

SPELLINGS

The words most commonly misspelled are highlighted.

calendar
campaign
carpenter
casualties
catalogue
catastrophe
categories
category
cathedral
cautious
ceiling
cemetery

censure
census
centre
centred
centring
century
ceremony
changeable
chaos
character
chasm
chemistry

colleague
commemorate
committee
competent
concede
conscientious
conscious
consensus
convalescent
convenient

YOU MUST KNOW THE BASICS

SUBJECT AND PREDICATE

'A way a lone a last a loved a long the' (the ending of *Finnegans Wake* by James Joyce).

Words carry meaning, but to express our thoughts completely we use sentences. A sentence is a group of words which has a complete meaning. It begins with a capital letter and ends with a full stop, question mark or exclamation mark.

Example

Iseult goes to school.

This is a correct sentence. In all sentences two things are essential:

- *A subject.* The subject is the word or words which stand for the person or thing about which something is said. In our example, *Iseult* is the subject.
- *A predicate.* The predicate is the name given to the part of the sentence which tells you about the subject. In our example, *goes to school* is the predicate.

Sentences may be short or long, simple or complex, but they must have the two elements mentioned. Sometimes one of the elements may not be in the sentence but may be understood. If somebody snatches your money and you shout 'Stop', is that one word a sentence? Yes, it is. The predicate is 'Stop' and the subject 'you' is understood.

Examples

SUBJECT	PREDICATE
The office	opened at 9 a.m.
Conor	laughed.

You (understood)	halt!
You (understood)	put that down!
Tipperary	*is* (understood) the home of hurlers.

Question: Is the ending of *Finnegans Wake* at the beginning of this chapter a sentence?

ACTIVITY I

1. Decide which of the following are sentences and tick YES or NO in the column provided.

	YES	NO

    (a) The greatest scoundrel I ever met.

    (b) Careful!

    (c) Brown football boots.

    (d) In the evening.

    (e) Yours sincerely, Enda

    (f) See you tomorrow.

    (g) No parking.

    (h) Post early for Christmas.

    (i) Drifts of snow everywhere.

    (j) 'Nonsense!' said the mother.

2. Pick out the subject and predicate in the following.

    (a) A great man for jokes.

    (b) The manager called a meeting.

    (c) Be sure to keep accurate minutes.

    (d) We all complained.

    (e) A mighty man.

    (f) Please ask if the sales forecast is available.

    (g) It is surprising.

    (h) Don't mention that.

    (i) What a lovely day!

3. Add predicates to each of the following subjects to form complete sentences.

    (a) The river ....

(b) The setting sun ....

(c) The agenda ....

(d) The liquidator ....

(e) The receiver ....

(f) The view from the window ....

(g) Winter time ....

(h) Computers ....

(i) Silence ....

4. *Supply suitable subjects to the following predicates to form complete sentences.*

    (a) .... *entertained the audience.*

    (b) .... *decided to adjourn the meeting.*

    (c) .... *collapsed.*

    (d) .... *is a dangerous sport.*

    (e) .... *came to a stop.*

    (f) .... *flows into the sea.*

    (g) .... *are to receive an increase in wages.*

    (h) .... *reopen in September.*

    (i) .... *is a complete thought.*

    (j) .... *has a subject and a predicate.*

AGREEMENT

The most common error in sentences is lack of agreement. Agreement is concerned with the relationship between a subject and a verb. A verb is the word in the sentence that tells you what the subject does.

Iseult goes to school.

subject   verb

Subject and verb must agree, that is, they should both be singular or both be plural. In most cases this is obvious:

'Enda is in school' (subject and verb singular).

'The boys are in school' (subject and verb plural).

Be careful of the following types:

- *Type (i): two or more singular subjects joined by 'and'*
  When two or more singular subjects are joined by *and*, the verb is plural. For example:

  'The man and boy are in the car.'

  'The student and teacher are happy.'

- *Type (ii): each, every, any, either, neither*
  Each of these words takes a singular verb. For example:

  'Each of us should mind her own business.'

  'Everyone is going to the match.'

  'Either Iseult or Enda is in charge.'

  Sentences such as 'Everyone has their own opinion' might be recast as 'Everyone has a different opinion' to avoid the problem of trying to find the correct pronoun.

- *Type (iii): none*
  None can be looked upon as singular or plural. Strictly speaking it should be singular since *none* comes from the two words *not one*. Because of usage, however, the plural is now generally allowed. For example:

  'None of the troops was injured.'

  or

  'None of the troops were injured.'

- *Type (iv): subjects not joined by 'and'*
  Two or more subjects not joined by *and* take a singular verb. For example:

  'The ship, with its crew, was lost.'

  'John, with Emma, goes to school.'

- *Type (v): 'one of those who'*
  In sentences containing phrases such as *one of those who*, the following verb should be plural, agreeing with *who,* and not singular, agreeing with *one*. For example:

  'He is one of those judges who delight in putting people in prison.'

  'She is one of those managers who believe in punctuality.'

- *Type (vi): collective nouns*
  A collective noun is the name given to several persons or things of the same kind regarded as one group, e.g. crowd, school, team. Generally speaking,

collective nouns are singular and are followed by singular verbs. For example:

'The team is playing on Sunday.'

'The mob is very hostile.'

But it has now come to the point, through usage, that the plural may be used. So we can say the following, depending on whether we want to express the idea of the group or the individuals in the group:

'The committee has (or have) published its (or their) report.'

'The council intends (or intend) to refuse permission.'

NB The important thing is to be consistent in your use of the singular or plural. Consistency is the important rule. You should not write, for example, 'The class *is* requested to have *their* notes available' because *is* is singular and *their* is plural.

- *Type (vii): attraction*
  Many writers fall into what is called the *error of attraction*. For example:

  'A parcel of books were found' (incorrect).

  The subject is *parcel*, which is singular, hence the verb should be *was*. The verb is attracted by the plural word *books* and there is a tendency to use the plural verb. So it should be:

  'A parcel of books was found' (correct).

- *Type (viii): titles of books, articles and poems*
  The titles of books, articles and poems are singular and must take a singular verb. For example:

  '*The Grapes of Wrath* is excellent.'

  'Lamb's *Tales from Shakespeare* is enjoyable.'

  It must not be *are excellent* or *are enjoyable* because we are writing of just one book.

- *Type (ix): nouns with plural form*
  Certain nouns, although plural in form, are treated as singular, e.g. *means, physics, news* ('The news is good').

  Trousers, scissors and *shears* may be considered singular or plural. They are of course singular when preceded by *a pair of*. *Wages, riches* and *alms* are, however, considered plural. For example:

  'My wages are €65 a week.'

  Certain words may use the same form for singular or plural, e.g. *sheep, dozen, fish*.

Exception: when two singular nouns joined by *and* refer to the same person or thing, or are closely related in meaning, they take a singular verb. For example:

'Milk and sugar is provided.'

'The tumult and the shouting dies.'

1. Choose the correct verb in each of the following sentences.

    (a) Enda and Conor is/are going to the match.

    (b) Emma, with John, is/are going to school.

    (c) Bread and water is/are a good diet.

    (d) Shouting and roaring are/is forbidden.

    (e) Openness and frankness are/is expected from all the participants.

    (f) Great love and devotion is/are bestowed on children.

    (g) Hammer and chisel is/are on your desk.

    (h) Garret, with Emma, John, Patrick and Conor, is/are going to the theatre.

    (i) There is/are bacon and eggs for breakfast.

    (j) The size of the task, and its very complexity, lead/leads people to avoid it altogether.

2. Correct the errors you find in the following sentences. Note that not all the sentences contain errors.

    (a) Each of us must do our duty.

    (b) Each member of staff should park their car in the space provided.

    (c) Everyone has their own opinions.

    (d) Everyone is going to the concert.

    (e) Is there anyone there?

    (f) If anyone is going they would want to leave now.

    (g) Either Patrick or Garret are responsible.

    (h) Either Mary, Emma, Dermot or Tom is interested in the topic.

    (i) Is anyone going?

    (j) Neither I nor the stewards was aware of what was happening.

    (k) Neither I nor the steward was at the presentation.

    (l) Neither James nor Michael nor Mary is in a position to make a statement on the matter.

3. Explain why each verb is singular in the sentences below.

    (a) A series of ten questions was asked in the examination.

    (b) The value of your books, letters and notes is considerable.

(c) *A catalogue of descriptions, prices and reference numbers was found in the attic.*

(d) *A wide variety of apples, oranges and pears is available.*

(e) *What is the news?*

(f) *Every Tom, Dick and Harry is doing that.*

(g) *The scissors is in the drawer.*

(h) *Your trousers is on the line.*

(i) *Ten miles is a long distance to go home every evening.*

TENSES

The meaning of a sentence can be changed by the use of the wrong tense. The tense in which the verb is presented refers to the time period of the sentence and the time of a verb's action or being. The verb ending is changed (conjugated) to roughly show what time it is referring to. The English language uses two tenses for present and six tenses for the past. There are several different tenses used when referring to the future.

In order to get a clearer understanding of the structure of tenses, it helps to break them down by *time* and *action*.

Time can be divided into three periods – the present, past and future. The *action* of the tense can be simple, continuous and perfect.

- *Simple tenses* are used to refer to events which are permanent, occur regularly or occur once and never again. They do not refer to the continuous nature of the event.

- *Continuous tenses* are used when talking about a particular point in time.

- The *perfect tenses* are used when an action or situation in the present is linked to a moment in the past. It is often used to show things that have happened up to now but are not finished yet or to emphasise that something happened but is not true any more. They are never used for an event which occurred at a specific stated time, e.g. on 11 September.

The following is a brief outline of the five most commonly used tense forms: present simple, past simple, future simple, present perfect and present continuous. It is often possible to use more than one structure with the same meaning. It is important to remember that you should only change the tense when implying a change of time. If in doubt when writing a sentence, it is better to read it aloud and ask yourself what you are trying to write. Explore the sentence to see if an alternative meaning, other than the one you wish to convey, can be taken.

Present simple

- This tense is used when referring to things in general, e.g. 'Ireland is a member of the European Union.'
- It is also used to explain events that happen on a regular basis. It is not important when the action occurred, e.g. 'The earth goes around the sun.'
- The present simple tense is used when we say how often we do things, e.g. 'I go to the gym every weekend.'
- It is used for actions which are long term or permanent, e.g. 'I get up every morning.'

Present continuous

- This tense is used for an event that is happening at the time of speaking, e.g. 'It is raining now.'
- It is used to talk about present situations that are short term or temporary, e.g. 'I am staying with friends at the moment.'
- The present continuous tense may be used for future events or happenings, e.g. 'John is driving to Galway this evening.'

Past

Both the past simple and the past continuous refer to completed actions in the past. The past simple is the most commonly used.

- The past simple tense is used to refer to events or happenings in the past that are now finished, e.g. 'She wrote the essay last week.' A specific time may be stated, e.g. yesterday, in 1960.
- It is also used for a past habit, e.g. 'When he was a teenager he always went to Galway on holidays.'

Past continuous

- It is used for actions which continued for some length of time in the past. The exact nature and end of the action is not relevant.
- It is used to emphasise the continuity of the action, e.g. 'The firemen were battling the blaze all evening.'

Present perfect

- The present perfect is used when we want to look back at the past from the present, e.g. 'They have cancelled the match as a matter of respect.'

Future tenses

There are many different ways of referring to events or actions in the future.

- The future simple uses the verb 'will' or sometimes 'shall', e.g. 'I will see you tomorrow.'
- The present continuous can also be used to refer to the future when a specific time is mentioned in the sentence, e.g. 'I am meeting John next Tuesday.'
- By including the phrase 'going to' you can also refer to the future, e.g. 'I am going to e-mail all the documents to you.'

ACTIVITY 3

1. Put the verb into the correct form – present, present continuous, past or past continuous.
   - (a) Martin was busy when we (call) .... into the shop. He (talk to customer) .... We .... (not/want) to disturb him, so we .... (not stay) very long.
   - (b) When I first (hear) .... the news, I (not believe).............
   - (c) What speed .... (you travel at) when (you hit) .... the wall?
2. Using the present perfect, write a short report on a sporting event.
3. Write a short paragraph outlining your future career plans, using any aspect of the future tense you feel is appropriate.

REVIEW

1. What is a sentence?
2. What two elements must a sentence have?
3. How do you find the subject of a sentence?
4. How do you find the predicate of a sentence?
5. What is meant by saying that the subject may be understood?
6. Give two examples of sentences where subjects are understood.
7. What is known as 'the error of attraction'?
8. What is a collective noun, and should it be considered singular or plural?
9. 'None of us is going to class.' Is that sentence correct or incorrect? Give reasons for your answer.
10. 'Two fours is/are eight.' Should the verb be singular or plural?

PITFALLS

to too two

Examples: 'I will go *to* Dublin.'

'I will go there *too.*'

'The *two* of us will go there tomorrow.'

CONFUSING WORDS

miner	minor	nick	niche
moat	mote	oar	ore
naval	navel	oracle	auricle
nave	knave	packed	pact
neither	nether	pail	pale

QUIZ

In some parts of the country the following words are used. Do you know their meanings?

(a) bairn (b) lug (c) oxter

SPELLINGS

The words most commonly misspelled are highlighted.

dearth	derivation	**disappointed**
debris	derive	**disastrous**
debtor	descendent	discern
deceit	design	**discipline**
deceive	designation	**discrepancy**
decision	**desirable**	**dissatisfied**
defence	**desperate**	dissent
deferred	**deterrent**	dissipate
deficient	development	**distributor**
definite	disagree	**dossier**
definition	disagreement	draught
delicious	**disappeared**	

5

PUNCTUATION GIVES MEANING

INTRODUCTION

Punctuation is not used for ornamentation, but to help the reader understand a passage in the way in which the writer intended. A written text does not have expressions, gestures or vocal inflection to help convey meaning, so written English must depend on punctuation. The main purpose of punctuation is to help the writer convey his ideas clearly and without ambiguity, and to help the reader understand a passage without having to reread it. When we say 'Are you sad?', the pitch of the voice or its inflection shows that we are asking a question, which in writing is indicated by the question mark. All writers must decide what type of punctuation to use to convey their meaning.

Sample 1

'It was the best of times, it was the worst of times, it was the age of wisdom, it was the age of foolishness, it was the epoch of belief, it was the epoch of incredulity, it was the season of Light, it was the season of Darkness, it was the spring of hope, it was the winter of despair, we had everything before us, we had nothing before us, we were all going direct to Heaven, we were all going direct the other way – in short, the period was so far like the present period, that some of its noisiest authorities insisted on its being received, for good or for evil, in the superlative degree of comparison only.'

(Charles Dickens, *A Tale of Two Cities*, Heron Books, Centennial Edition)

Sample 2

'Studies serve for delight, for ornament, and for ability. Their chief use for delight, is in privateness and retiring; for ornament, is in discourse; and for ability, is in the judgment and disposition of business. For expert men can execute, and perhaps judge of particulars, one by one; but the general counsels, and the plots and marshalling of affairs, come best from those that are learned. To spend too much time in studies is sloth; to use them too much for ornament, is affectation; to make judgment wholly by their rules, is the humour of a scholar. They perfect nature, and are perfected by experience: for natural abilities are like natural plants, that need proyning by study; and study themselves do give forth directions too much at large, except they be bounded by experience.'

(Francis Bacon, 'Of Studies')

Sample 3

'Momentous day. The sun is shining. That in itself is not momentous – merely, for August, surprising.

The house sits sideways to the sea and facing south, so all the rooms are filled with sun. Judging by the haze on the horizon, almost like steam rising off the sea, the sun is shining everywhere, not just on this stretch of the east coast of Ireland, but in Cork, Skibbereen, Galway and Kilkenny; drying up the grass and causing anxiety to the farmers. Weather seems permanently to be causing anxiety to the farmers. Even in England, where I have never been, the sun is shining. We read this in the newspaper which arrives in time for breakfast every morning and keeps Aunt Mary occupied for half an hour or so.

If you climb up the hill at the back of the house, you can see Wales on a clear day. It's not really very exciting, just a grey lump in the distance, but it's somewhere else. Somewhere new. For the last two weeks there has been no sign of Wales at all, just that pale haze steaming gently up into the sky, shutting this island off from the rest of the world.

The morning trains from Dublin have been filled with people coming down from the city to sit on the beach, and paddle and throw stones into the sea, and shout at their children, who change as the hours go by from pale city children to fretful whiners grilled beyond endurance by the unexpected sun. They stay mainly up at the far end of the beach, near to the station and the two small cafés that sell fruit drinks and ice creams, and plates of biscuits and delicious cups of reviving tea. They don't in fact bother us over here at all. Two special trains have to be put on in the late afternoon to bring them back to town, as they don't all fit on the five-thirty from Wicklow. They leave an awful mess on the sand but the tide takes care of most of that. Poor Mr Carroll the stationmaster, however, has a terrible time keeping his station clean and tidy, and is the one person in the village to admit to being glad that heatwaves don't happen too often.

Momentous.

It is my eighteenth birthday.'

(Jennifer Johnston, The Old Jest, London: Hamish Hamilton Ltd, 1979)

Sample 4

'Yes because he never did a thing like that before as ask to get his breakfast in bed with a couple of eggs since the City Arms hotel when he used to be pretending to be laid up with a sick voice doing his highness to make himself interesting to that old faggot Mrs Riordan that he thought he had a great leg of and never left us a farthing all for masses for herself and her soul greatest miser ever was actually afraid to lay out 4d for her methylated spirits telling me all her ailments she had too much old chat in her about politics and earthquakes and the end of the world let us have a bit of fun first God help the world if all the women were her sort down on bathingsuits and lownecks of course nobody wanted her to wear I suppose she was pious because no man would look at her twice I hope Ill never be like her a wonder she didnt want us to cover our faces . . .'

(James Joyce, *Ulysses*, London: Vintage Books, 1961)

Discussion on four examples

Each of the four writers above uses punctuation not just to convey meaning, but also tone and emotion. Dickens begins with a very long sentence and rushes along from one short phrase to another using only commas. This gives the impression of confusion and turbulence. It is a passage full of feeling.

Bacon's 'Of Studies', on the other hand, is a short, concise, closely argued piece. It is an intellectual essay bereft of emotion, almost mathematical in its symmetry. There seem to be three reasons or three observations on everything. He uses a number of semi-colons to balance his arguments.

Jennifer Johnston once described herself as 'fairly handy with the comma'. This extract is written in very simple language and uses only the simplest punctuation. In it a young girl is talking to the reader and the simple words and the simple punctuation help to convey youth and freshness.

The final extract is very different from the others. It has no punctuation at all. In fact, the final forty pages of *Ulysses* have no punctuation except for the full stop at the end. Joyce is depicting Molly Bloom, thinking to herself, as she lies in her bed in Dublin on the night of 16 June 1904. When we think, we do not use punctuation marks but move from one thought to another and back again without maintaining any particular order. So Joyce, instead of putting in punctuation marks to give meaning, in fact dispenses with them.

But for the rest of us punctuation is very important. If you read the following sentences you will see why:

- The prisoner felt the judge was a danger to society.
- The prisoner, felt the judge, was a danger to society.

or

- Peter said the teacher is marvellous.
- 'Peter,' said the teacher, 'is marvellous.'

In both sentences the words and the word order are exactly the same, but there is a considerable difference between them. What has caused the difference? The answer is punctuation.

Punctuation makes the meaning of what we write clear to the reader. When we talk, the rise and fall of the voice and the pauses we use help to make our meaning clear, but in writing, we have no such aids. Instead we use punctuation.

EXPLANATION OF PUNCTUATION MARKS WITH EXAMPLES

Full stop (.)

- The full stop is used at the end of a complete sentence. For example:

  'I will go tomorrow.'

  'Carry it over there.'

  'I feel fine.'

- The full stop is used after abbreviations: e.g., etc., ave., Sept. It is also used after single letters standing for a word:

  'I can type 40 w.p.m.'

  'The car does 30 m.p.g.'

  However, modern usage allows you to omit the full stops in well-known abbreviations such as these.

  Abbreviations in common use do not require a full stop, e.g. per cent, memo, Mr, St, Dr. The full stop is also dropped from abbreviations that make a pronounceable word, e.g. FÁS.

- Full stops in a series are used to indicate the omission of words from a passage. Three are used if the omission is from the middle of a sentence, e.g. 'We are experiencing a literary breakdown . . . unlike anything I know of in the history of letters.' Four are used if the omission is from the end of a sentence, e.g. 'As Dickens wrote, "It was the best of times, it was the worst of times . . . ."'

The lights turned red. The car stopped.

The teacher is happy. Run quickly.

It started pouring rain. I never saw anything like it.

David is going to school in September. Gillian is still too young.

Capital letter

- A capital letter is used to begin every sentence, e.g. 'It was kind of you.'
- All proper nouns, proper adjectives and the first person singular pronoun begin with a capital letter, e.g. America, Tipperary, an Irish horse, I.
- People's titles and ranks are always introduced with capital letters, e.g. Professor Scully, Lord Mayor, Captain Kelly, President Douglas Hyde. But lower case should be used for those titles when applied in a general sense, e.g. 'a captain in the army'.
- The days of the week and months are introduced with capitals, but the seasons are not, e.g. Sunday, Tuesday, May, July, but spring, summer. However, in common usage the seasons are often capitalised.
- Buildings, well-known geographical regions and historical events begin with a capital, e.g. Leinster House, the North, the Irish Civil War.
- In titles of books, plays, films, etc., the first word always has a capital, but after that, conjunctions, prepositions and the words *the* and *a* are written in lower case, e.g. *An Only Child, The Lonely Passion of Judith Hearne, Lord of the Flies.*

Examples

Who is that?

How is Patricia?

I believe in God.

It is Friday.

The Taoiseach spoke at length.

The Anglo-Irish Agreement was signed.

The Minister for Finance attended.

Michael Collins was the Commander-in-Chief.

The North is in turmoil.

Comma (,)

- The comma is used to mark off a natural pause at the end of a phrase, e.g. 'When we had seen the fire, we went home.'
- The comma is also used to mark off phrases in the middle of sentences. For example:

  'The student, standing just outside the door, heard the teacher laughing.'

  'The enclosed book, which you may retain, is sent to you for your comments.'

- If a sentence contains two or more phrases or clauses linked by *and, but, for* or *nor*, then a comma precedes the linking word, e.g. 'He decided to do his lessons first, and then watch television.'
- Commas are used with words and phrases such as *at last, finally, however, of course, in fact, meanwhile, nevertheless.* Here are two examples:

  'However, we will do the best we can.'

  'It is clear, however, he was not telling the truth.'

- Commas are used to separate items in a list, e.g. 'The bag contains books, pencils, ink, paper and envelopes.'

It is not necessary to use a comma before the *and* separating the final two items unless not using it would cause ambiguity, as when one writes: 'At school I studied French, Biology, Physics, Irish, English and American History.' Did he study the subject English or was it English History? It would be clearer to write '. . . English, and American History' or '. . . English History and American History.'

Examples

The boy, with great expectation, waited for the result.

A loud, heavy bang was heard.

People of Westmeath, the famine is over.

The rain having stopped, all went home.

Every day, every week, every year, his mother worries about him.

Semi-colon (;)

The semi-colon is a longer stop than the comma. It is used in the following situations:

- If two sentences or main clauses are logically connected but not joined by a linking word, then they are separated by a semi-colon. For example:

'I went to their last production; it was not very good.'

'The product is selling well; I think it will continue to do so.'

'The firm is doing badly; it will close soon.'

Sometimes these same statements could be written in separate sentences, e.g. 'I went to their last production. It was not very good.'

- The semi-colon is also used to separate items in a list when these are phrases rather than single words, e.g. 'The weather was at its most wintry: dark, heavy clouds that rode quickly across the sky; gusts of wet wind that rattled the slates on the houses; the chill in the air that makes the body shiver.'

Examples

He is very happy; you should be also.

Go home; it would be better.

He was going out the door; otherwise I would not have seen him.

I refused to say what he asked me to say; I felt he had been misinformed.

ACTIVITY I

Punctuate the following.

1. go home

2. i will do it

3. carlow is a small county cork is a big one

4. the boys waited all night for the train it was very late

5. hurling is a great game i like playing it

6. when we got to the field we could not get in as we had forgotten our money

7. i dont like examinations yet they have to be faced

8. most schools in ireland now are modern not like years ago

9. the leaves on the trees are turning brown now what a pity

10. when i was young we kicked the dead leaves before us as we ran to school

11. the towns main streets are very narrow two cars can barely pass

12. people in general are fairly conscientious at their work i think

13. the all ireland football final is a great occasion for kerry people some others

arent all that interested

14. *there are many more female than male primary teachers is this a disturbing trend*

15. *vocational schools are governed by the vocational education act 1930*

16. *in ireland we have schools that are privately owned and schools that are in public ownership which gives parents a choice*

ACTIVITY 2

Punctuate the following.

1. *the organisation known as teagasc deals with agriculture*

2. *the gaa was founded in 1884 at hayes hotel thurles co tipperary*

3. *the firm is going to establish an o and m department*

4. *a car able to travel 60 mpg would be very useful*

5. *ireland has a great tradition in the short story russia has also*

6. *the ida tries to attract foreign firms to ireland with a package of attractive grants*

7. *when the school year finishes students look for work*

8. *it is always sad i think to remember the last summer of your childhood*

9. *somebody once said when youve seen one city youve seen them all*

10. *the enclosed form which you should complete as soon as possible will guarantee you entry*

11. *he went into the house and closed the door behind him*

12. *nuim dublin is now a university*

13. *did he cut his hand with a knife or did he fall*

14. *he stumbled but he didnt fall*

15. *ill be there tomorrow however dont expect me to be on time*

16. *according to you i should win easily*

17. *he did it yesterday in fact he might have done it the day before*

18. *never do that do you hear me as long as im around*

19. *i rushed into the room and i threw books papers pencils rulers and maps on the table*

20. *the enclosed book which you should read carefully and which youll find interesting was in fact written four years ago and then according to the best*

Colon (:)

The colon used to be looked on as a longer pause than a semi-colon. It is now rarely used in this way. It is now used to indicate that something is to follow.

- The colon is used to introduce a list of items, e.g. 'The bag contains the following: hurley, football, jerseys, first-aid kit, sweat bands and a whistle.'

- A quotation, if it is a long one, is also introduced by a colon, e.g. 'The President went to the platform and said: "I want to speak about a very serious matter . . . ."'

- The colon is also used to separate two statements in a sentence which are in sharp contrast to each other. For example:

  'If you join us you will succeed: if you do not, you will fail.'

  'Kings rule: subjects obey.'

Examples

Man proposes: God disposes.

Send me the following: a pen, a brush, a pencil and some ink.

Then the chairman stood up and said: 'I would like to welcome you all here this evening . . . .'

Good health gives happiness: there is none without it.

Parentheses ()

- Parentheses are used to separate words in a sentence which provide additional information or which explain something about certain words in the sentence, e.g. 'The subjects I like most are history (Irish history) and biology.'

- Parentheses are used to explain foreign words, e.g. 'My attitude is *de mortuis nil nisi bonum* (of the dead speak nothing but good).'

Examples

He gave all he had (it wasn't much) to the cause.

Be there on Wednesday (I'll be there myself) at 3 o'clock.

He'll be running in the Olympics (not that he has much of a chance) for the last time.

When he was at school (a long time ago) he did well.

Hyphen (-)

- A hyphen is a joining mark, e.g. brother-in-law, commander-in-chief, up-to-date.

- The hyphen is also used to divide a word at the end of a line, e.g. dis-appointed.

Examples

He is a very with-it person.

He looks very down-at-heel.

She had a hang-dog look.

The word has three syllables, for-mer-ly.

Dash (–)

- The dash is used to denote a strongly marked aside. For example:

  'Many countries – Ireland was not one of them – won gold medals at the Olympics.'

  'Complete the form – and don't forget to sign it – as soon as possible.'

- The dash is also used to bring together several subjects belonging to the same verb, e.g. 'If you buy this house, blinds, carpets and heaters – all will be included in the sale.'

Examples

Send down everything next week – this week if possible.

At the age of ninety – such is old age – he could remember nothing.

Last year – the date is uncertain – we bought it at discount.

Padraig was born in Perth, Australia today – I'm not sure what time.

Apostrophe (')

The rules for the apostrophe are very simple but cause endless trouble to students.

- The apostrophe is used to indicate omitted letters in contractions. It is placed where the omitted letter would appear if the word were written out in full, e.g. do not, *don't*; could not, *couldn't*; was not, *wasn't*; it is, *it's*; they are, *they're*.

- The apostrophe is also used to denote ownership, e.g. the boy's coat, cat's paw, table's leg. Here it is used in the singular.

  The *s* can still be used even when the possessor's name ends in an *s*, e.g. Keats's poems, Dickens's novels, St James's feast.

- The apostrophe without the *s* is used if three consecutive *s* sounds come together and make pronunciation difficult, e.g. Moses' Law, Jesus' disciples, St Francis' Day.
- An apostrophe is placed after the *s* in the possessive plural form, e.g. boys' coats, cats' paws, ladies' shoes.
- If the plural of a noun does not end in *s*, then *s* is added in the possessive form, e.g. men's coats, women's shoes, children's hats, sheep's clothing.
- Some possessive pronouns do not take an apostrophe, e.g. his, hers, yours, theirs, its, ours, mine.

The word *whose* does not take an apostrophe. However, note the word who's, which means who is, e.g. 'Who's there?'

Examples

I won't do it.

I don't like it.

The guard's helmet was knocked off.

Children's hour will begin soon.

Go to the players' entrance.

I'll be there.

It's got a great taste.

Question mark (?)

A question mark is used instead of a full stop when a direct question is asked, e.g. 'When are we going?'

A question mark is not used when the question is indirect, e.g. 'I asked when we were going.' Note the possibility of an indirect question embedded in another question, so that a question mark is needed, e.g. 'Can you tell me what time the next train leaves for Galway?'

Examples

Who's there?

What's the matter?

Are you going?

Exclamation mark (!)

An exclamation mark is used after an exclamatory expression, e.g. My God!, Well!, You don't say!

Examples

How the mighty have fallen!

Well, can you beat that!

I don't believe you!

Quotation marks (" ")

- It is fairly common practice now to use single quotation marks, e.g. He said: 'I will go to catch my train.'

- Double quotation marks are used for a quotation within a quotation, e.g. The father said to the boy: 'Did you tell him "Get lost" as you walked out the door?'

- Quotation marks are used instead of italics or underlining for titles of poems, articles in magazines, journals or collections, or individual stories in a collection, e.g. '"Night in Tunisia" is a good story.'

- Punctuation belonging to the quoted words should be placed within the quotation marks, e.g. He asked: 'Have you read the report?'

A separate paragraph is required for each new speaker in a quotation and every quotation begins with a capital letter, unless the quotation begins in the middle of a sentence, e.g. 'He said he was ". . . tired of life."'

Examples

'I agree,' said the chairman, 'but I still think it should be changed.'

'Put it over there,' she said.

'What did they do to you?' asked the girl.

'They gave me,' he said, 'strict orders, "Nobody to be let in without a ticket."'

'There it is!' shouted the boys.

'I'm not going,' said Mary.

'You'll go, or I'll give you something to think about,' said her mother.

'Did you say, "Why should I?"' she asked.

'Yes, I did,' said Conor, 'and why shouldn't I do it? I'm entitled to my own opinion. I have my rights.'

ACTIVITY 3

Punctuate the following.

1. *it should be marvellous go to it*

2. *down came the rain on went the coats*

3. out went the windows in came the snow

4. hes doing very poorly he wont last long

5. off with the coats get down to work

6. work never killed anyone many never recover from it

7. on the table are the following items money cheque books credit cards cancelled cheques and a bank statement

8. dont you think that i said to him going out the door is a very remarkable sky

9. put it over there she shouted or ill give you something to think about

10. i didnt say youre a fool did i

11. when were in company with other people am i to do nothing am i

12. the chairman said i now declare this meeting open

13. did you say go at two oclock or did you not

14. judges differ teams lose

15. the president began her speech thus it is a great honour to be here

16. have you seen that play by hugh leonard

17. if you say once more i knew it ill shout

18. it is a sound proverb never put all your eggs in the one basket

19. it is a very true saying that goes the evil that men do lives after them the good is oft interred with their bones

20. history is bunk said henry ford

Punctuate the following.

1. the thing i like best about living in ireland apart from the people is the mild climate

2. put it in the box the blue box when youre ready

3. youll find it in the warehouse the far corner be careful of it

4. the newsletter will be available on wednesday indeed on tuesday perhaps

5. the grapes of wrath now thats a good play novel i mean

6. did you really say to him get lost

7. didnt you say yesterday i like reading the irish times

8. when liam returned to work his father in law got to hear of it

9. the record book should be kept up to date and always available for the managers inspection

10. womens clothes are very fashionable mens are not

11. childrens personalities should be given free expression

12. his and hers boutique is on the far side of the street

13. it is theirs not mine

14. i asked her have you any money

15. did he say i have no money

16. put on your coat quickly or well never be on time

17. my favourite season is spring

18. who was known as the big fellow

19. the rich said f scott fitzgerald are different from you and me yes said hemingway they have money

20. have you ever been to the west of ireland

ACTIVITY 5

Punctuate the following.

1. fyodor dostoyevsky was born in moscow in 1821 he was the second of a physicians seven children from 1838 to 1843 he studied at the military engineering college in st petersburg graduating with officers rank he was sentenced to penal servitude in 1849 and spent much of this sentence at a convicts prison in omsk as he was a heavy gambler he often found himself in debt however his second wife whom he married in 1867 helped him to put his financial affairs on a firm footing

2. capital punishment is not a successful weapon against crime in countries where it has been practised regularly not a great reduction in crime has taken place in fact it has increased capital punishment tends to trigger even more violence to seek revenge on the government which inflicted capital punishment the present prison system is not what it should be the people in these houses of shame as oscar wilde called them require special treatment they certainly should not have to suffer the pain and misery that is sometimes inflicted upon them

3. the constitution of ireland came into effect in 1937 it is sometimes referred to as de valeras constitution it was of course voted on by the electorate and a majority was in favour the constitution provides for a president two houses of

the oireachtas known as the dail and the senate and also provides for the independence of the judiciary the president is commander in chief of the armed forces appoints judges and the members of the government the taoiseach must keep the president informed on all matters of state as far as is known this is not done very thoroughly one taoiseach said he met the president every now and then but their discussions were often about the cartoons in dublin opinion.

ACTIVITY 6

Punctuate the following.

1. a member of the house of commons once asked george stephenson supposing now one of these engines to be going along a railroad at the rate of nine or ten miles an hour and a cow were to stray upon the line and get in the way of the engine would that not be a very awkward circumstance it would indeed said george for the cow

2. well i met someone like you somewhere he said firmly and i have an hour to kill and i was wondering would you like to come and have a hamburger so that we can think where it was you look as if you have nothing to do either you could read the evening paper i said because i am so extremely kind i would never hurt anyones feelings i wouldnt tell him to get lost that he was an inoffensive bore ive read the evening paper i said i was silent well make up your mind he said its starting to rain do we have a hamburger or dont we its stupid standing here getting wet

(Maeve Binchy, 'My First Book', The Irish Times)

3. finally on 31 march i set out to meet cardinal dalton of armagh he was a pleasant withdrawn scholarly looking man our conversation was stilted formal and with the exception of one brief period banal and inconsequential the cardinal gave the impression that he was politely wondering what on earth he was doing sharing his luncheon table with this odd earnest young man who was clearly preoccupied with an abstruse and awkward health problem the sole gain for me was the pleasant hock with the fish at luncheon which i had arrived just in time to share with the cardinal i suspect that he accepted the ordeal and decided to offer it up as did i there was but one reference by me and none by him to the mother and child service

(Noel Browne, Against the Tide, Dublin: Gill & Macmillan, 1986)

4. and when he came to himself he said how many hired servants of my fathers have bread enough to spare and i perish with hunger i will arise and go to my father and will say unto him father i have sinned against heaven and before thee and am no more worthy to be called thy son

REVIEW

1. 'Quotation marks ("quotes") or inverted commas are the most troublesome marks in punctuation; and the irony of the thing is that we could easily do without them. In fact, we did until the end of the eighteenth century.'

   (G.H. Vallins, *Good English*, London: Pan, 1951)

   What do you think?

2. James Joyce in *A Portrait of the Artist as a Young Man* used no quotation marks. Use quotation marks to punctuate this passage from it.

   – Well, my little man, said the rector, what is it?

   Stephen swallowed down the thing in his throat and said:

   – I broke my glasses, sir.

   The rector opened his mouth and said:

   – O!

   Then he smiled and said:

   – Well, if we broke our glasses we must write home for a new pair.

   – I wrote home, sir, said Stephen, and Father Arnall said I am not to study till they come.

   – Quite right! said the rector.

   Stephen swallowed down the thing again and tried to keep his legs and voice from shaking.

   – But, sir . . .

   – Yes?

   – Father Dolan came in today and pandied me because I was not writing my theme.

   The rector looked at him in silence and he could feel the blood rising to his face and the tears about to rise to his eyes.

   The rector said:

   – Your name is Dedalus, isn't it?

   (James Joyce, *A Portrait of the Artist as a Young Man*, London: Viking Press, 1956)

3. See if you can punctuate Activity 6, #4 in the manner in which James Joyce used punctuation in *A Portrait of the Artist as a Young Man*.

PITFALLS

prescribe proscribe

Prescribe means to lay down or impose authoritatively, e.g. to prescribe a drug for a patient.

Proscribe comes from the Latin words *pro*, meaning 'before', and *scribere*, meaning 'to write'. It has now come to mean to ban something. The government might proscribe certain organisations.

CONFUSING WORDS

mitten	mittimus	momentous	momentum
motto	mottle	mugger	muggins
nape	napery	mumps	munch
natter	natty	moil	moiety

QUIZ

So now you are very good at punctuation? Then try the sentence below. It can be done.

'That that is is that that is not is not but that that is not is not that that is nor is that that is that that is not.'

SPELLINGS

The words most commonly misspelled are highlighted.

eccentric	encyclopaedia	exceedingly
efficiency	endeavour	**excellent**
eight	enormous	exceptional
eighteenth	**enthusiasm**	excessive
eighty	epidemic	exchequer
elapse	**equipment**	excitable
electricity	**equipped**	exclamation
elegance	**erroneous**	**exercise**
eliminate	**especially**	**exhausted**
embarrass	**essential**	exhibit
emigrated	establishment	expedite
eminent	etiquette	**expense**
emphasise	eventually	**extremely**
encouragement	**exaggerated**	

6

PERSONAL WRITING

INTRODUCTION

As a student taking a communications module, you may be required to present a piece of personal writing. This may vary from a letter to a short story, a review or even a poem. In deciding what to write, view the task with an open mind. Listen, use your senses and draw on your personal experiences. Always bear in mind the profile of your audience, as this will have an impact on the language and experiences you may use. In order to build up your confidence and develop ideas, it is important to read. Newspapers and the written media are full of examples of personal writing, e.g. the player's view of the championship match, the columnist's opinions on the latest government initiative. You will find ideas everywhere. Finally, while it is your personal experience, do remember to plan and structure the piece.

REVIEWS

In writing a review, always approach the film or book with an open mind.

1   Identify your audience or readership.

2   Decide on its length.

3   Adopt an approach style for the audience.

4   Make notes as you read the book or watch the film, ensuring that they are detailed enough for inclusion in your piece.

5   After watching the film or reading the novel, jot down your immediate impressions and views. This will be of great importance when you actually sit down to write the piece.

6   Plan what you want to say. Whatever you review is, it is important to present your views in a structured manner. Examine the work more closely and try to go into detail about the many ideas contained in it. As in any piece of writing, it is important to decide

what you want to highlight and include and what you dismiss as irrelevant.

7   Many reviewers omit a full account of the plot, instead giving a brief synopsis of the film or book. It is a review of the work, not a summary of the plot.

8   In structuring the review, you could state opinions early on in the piece and then support them with examples from the work under review. Avoid giving away too much detail. Your aim is to make the audience want to finish the article.

9   If you are reviewing a film, examine the contribution of the cast, director and producer. Look in detail at the role special effects, location or music plays in the film, as soundtracks and scenery are important elements in films. *The Sound of Music* is remembered for the Austrian scenery and numerous songs, while the Scottish castle portrayed in *Braveheart* was actually Trim Castle. Key components in James Cameron's *Titantic* were the lavish set and the soundtrack.

10   When reviewing a book, compare it with previous work published by the author. Examine the complexity or otherwise of the plot and the presentation of the characters.

11   Highlight what you enjoyed and remembered from the images and ideas presented in the film or portrayed in the book.

12   Finally, remember that your review could be the deciding factor in whether or not the reader actually goes to see the film or reads the book themselves. If you really enjoyed it or really hated it, make it clear. Even though your article should show from the start what your opinions are, at the end of the piece you should give a conclusion that strongly states what you thought.

STARTING A LETTER

The ability to write a good letter is a skill essential to all office administrators and junior business executives. The letter is an important means used by a firm to keep in touch with customers and suppliers. It has been truly said that a firm's letters are its ambassadors. Customers form an impression of a firm from the layout, content and tone of the letters it sends out. If a bank were to send out letters poorly typed, poorly constructed and containing spelling and grammatical errors, clients would soon lose confidence in its efficiency. Letters should be written on good-quality paper, the letterhead should be attractive and the address on the envelope should be neatly and correctly typed.

Address labels can now be used on envelopes using recent versions of Microsoft Word, a word processing program. An Post asks the public to put the sender's name and address on the front of the envelope.

In every letter:

- spelling must be perfect
- grammar must be perfect
- punctuation must be perfect
- typing and layout must be perfect.

Always proofread your letter.

There are a number of different layouts for letters. We will use the fully blocked style, as it is the one most commonly used in the modern world. When you go out to work you will, of course, adopt whichever layout your company uses.

ELEMENTS OF A LETTER

References

Spaces for references are usually provided for in a letterhead. When replying to a letter it is discourteous and inefficient not to quote the reference on the letter with which you are dealing. The reference will enable your correspondent to locate the appropriate file quickly. Sometimes the initials of the person signing the letter and the typist's initials are used as the reference.

Date

The date should always be written or typed in full, e.g. 5 July 2006. It is not necessary to put *th* after the 5. Never write the date in figures, e.g. 5/7/06. This is discourteous, as it gives the impression that you are in a hurry. It can also be confusing, as in the US the order of the date is month, day and year, whereas we follow a different order – day, month, year.

For the attention of

Some companies adopt the rule that all correspondence should be addressed to the company and not to individual persons by name. The sender of a letter may wish it to reach a particular person. This can be achieved by using FOR THE ATTENTION OF at the left-hand margin and two single spaces below the date. No punctuation is necessary. To type it in capitals and not underline is the modern way of doing it.

FIG. I — FULLY BLOCKED STYLE

In the fully blocked style everything begins at the left-hand margin.

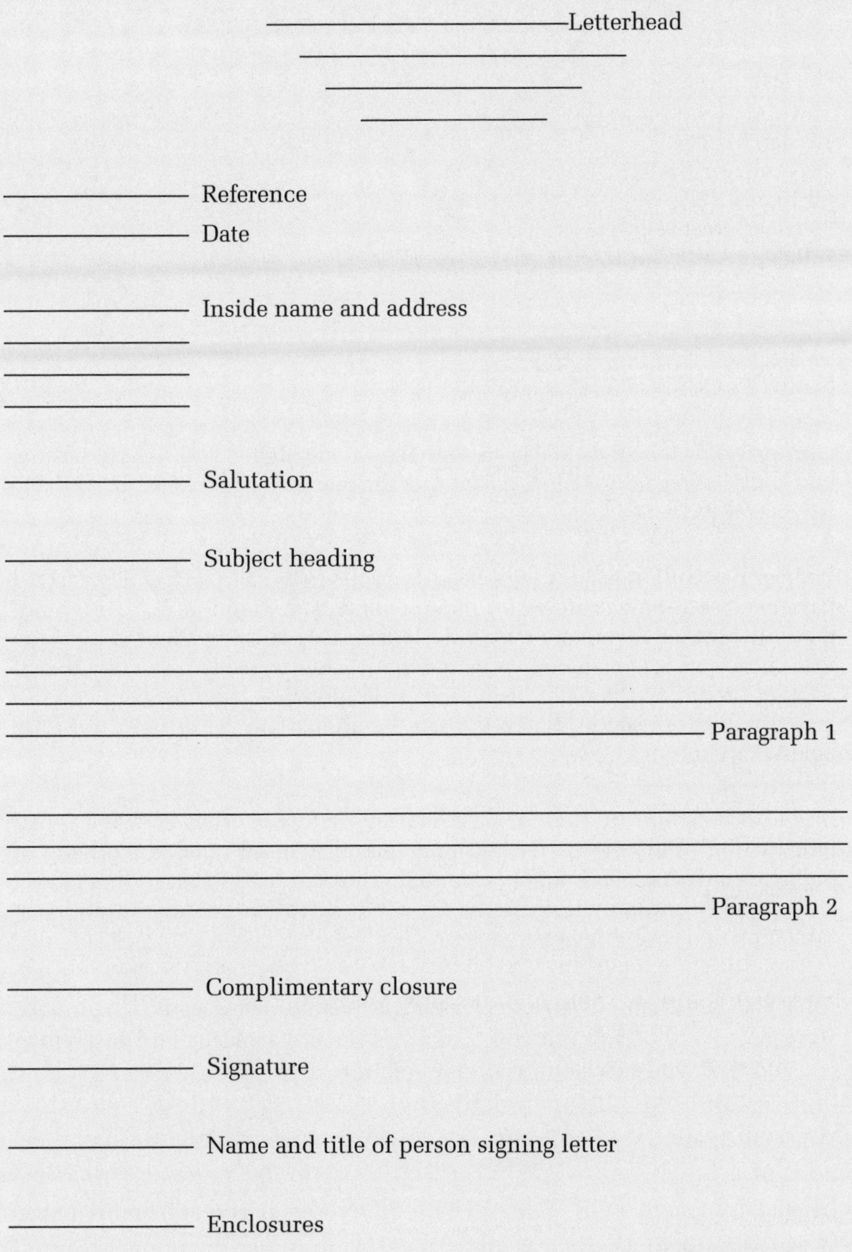

—————————————————Letterhead

————————— Reference
————————— Date

————————— Inside name and address

————————— Salutation

————————— Subject heading

————————————————————————— Paragraph 1

————————————————————————— Paragraph 2

————————— Complimentary closure

————————— Signature

————————— Name and title of person signing letter

————————— Enclosures

FIG. 2 — FULLY BLOCKED LAYOUT

S & SK MARKETING
Kilmeany
Carlow
Telephone (0503) 32507, Fax (0503) 07235

Our Ref: e. mc/sk

18 March 2006

Mr Ruairi Kelly
35 High Street
Kilkenny

Dear Mr Kelly

FULLY BLOCKED LETTER STYLE

I am sorry for the slight delay in replying to your letter of 9 March, but the unusually heavy fall of snow meant that the electricity had been unavailable for several days.

We can certainly design a letterhead for your new company and, in fact, I have enclosed some samples for your comments. I would advise you to use the fully blocked layout style for your letters, as it is being adopted by many firms now and is considered very modern. It simply means that every line of a letter, including the date, inside name and address, headings and complimentary closure, begins at the left-hand margin. This letter is in the fully blocked style.

It is also common in modern business letters to use what is called 'open punctuation'. This means that no punctuation is used outside the body of the letter unless it is absolutely essential. You will notice that in this letter I have used no punctuation marks in the date, inside name and address, salutation and complimentary closure.

After you have had a chance to look at the sample letterheads, I will make arrangements to call to see you to discuss them. I look forward to helping you and wish you success in your new venture.

Yours sincerely

Emma McGrane
Works Manager
Enc.

Inside name and address

Place the inside name and address two single spaces after FOR THE ATTENTION OF or two single spaces after the date if there is no FOR THE ATTENTION OF.

Salutation

Every letter begins with a greeting. If you are writing for the first time to the secretary of a company, you should begin your letter with 'Dear Sir/Madam'. Your correspondent's first name should be used only if you know the person well. If in doubt about the form of salutation, it is always best to err on the side of formality. A woman may be addressed as 'Dear Miss Connolly', 'Dear Mrs Connolly', 'Dear Ms Connolly' or 'Dear Madam', depending on the situation. In a circular letter, 'Dear Sirs' or 'A Chara' may be used.

The message

The message should be brief and to the point. If the information to be conveyed can be given in three sentences, then there is no need to write four.

Complimentary closure

The complimentary closure used will again depend upon the relationship with the person to whom you are writing. Only two complimentary closures are in present use. The rule to follow is simple. If the letter begins with 'Dear Sir' or 'Dear Madam', it should end with 'Yours faithfully'. If it begins with the name of the person, e.g. 'Dear Mr Gallagher', end it with 'Yours sincerely'. The initial *f* of 'Yours faithfully' and the *s* of 'Yours sincerely' should not be in capitals.

Dear Sir or Madam ⟶	Yours faithfully
Dear Mr Gallagher ⟶	Yours sincerely

Signature

The letter should be signed under the complimentary closure. Always use the same signature. Do not sign yourself 'Catherine Lonergan' on one letter and 'Mary C. Lonergan' on another. As a general rule, a title is not used in a signature. For example, to sign oneself 'Doctor Michael Hogan' is incorrect.

Name of signatory

Type the name of the person to sign the letter under the signature.

Designation

The official position of the person signing the letter should be placed below his or her name.

Enclosures

Two single spaces after the designation, type 'Enc.', or 'Encs' if more than one paper or document is to be enclosed with the letter.

Open punctuation

All letters should be punctuated in the normal manner. However, many firms now use what is called 'open punctuation'. The sample letters in this chapter are examples of this. No punctuation is used in the reference, date, inside name and address, salutation and complimentary closure.

Commercialese

Avoid the use of what is called 'commercialese' – language such as Re your letter of, Your letter to hand, We beg to inform you, as per your instructions, etc.

Summary
- Careful layout: attention to every detail.
- Content: brief and to the point.
- Vocabulary: keep it simple and clear.
- Expression: avoid the overuse of jargon.
- Tone: adopt a tone suitable to the subject matter.
- Sentence structure: short sentences are preferable to long, rambling ones.
- Accuracy: be careful of spelling and punctuation.
- Style: your style should reinforce the message and present a professional image.
- Use good-quality paper.
- Check for damage, ink stains, etc. after printing.
- Always proofread.
- Ensure address on envelope is correct.

1. The following phrases are sometimes referred to as 'commercialese'. Rewrite them in acceptable English.

    Re your letter of 15 inst., We beg to inform you, We beg to acknowledge, Your letter to hand, As per instruction, We are in receipt of, We have to acknowledge, The favour of an early reply will oblige.

2. In the following letter you are required to (a) lay it out in fully blocked style (b) rewrite the body of the letter to make it more understandable and (c) correct any other errors you find.

    International Insurance Company Ltd
    14–17 Dawson Street, Dublin.
    Telephone 01-6765322

    Ref. gs/ms   Date: 22/3/06
    Mr Oliver McGrane
    22 Oaklawns
    Terenure
    Dublin

                    Re: Motor Insurance No. AC 105/23/45676

    Dear Mr McGrane

        I have pleasure to enclose herewith the above numbered Certificate to renewal date, duly prepared as per your instructions and trust you will find same in order.

        I appreciate your valued support for which I thank you and shall look forward with confidence to a continuation of this as well as your further valued business which will receive prompt personal attention.

        Always at your service, I remain,

                                        Yours faithfully

                                        James Mackey
                                        Claims Manager

    Enc.

3. Rewrite the following impersonal sentences in a more personal form.

    (a) It is pointed out that registration will conclude at 5.00 p.m.

    (b) Delivery of goods will be accepted next Wednesday.

    (c) It is regretted that this mistake occurred.

    (d) Sincerest apologies are offered for this unfortunate incident.

    (e) Enclosed is a copy of our prospectus.

    (f) Ensure that payment is made before the end of the month.

    (g) All regulations must be observed.

    (h) Payment of all outstanding debts would be appreciated.

    (i) The Company extends thanks for orders received on 20 March 2006.

PERSONAL LETTERS

Personal letter writing is not as popular as it used to be. However, occasions still do arise when you may be called upon to send a letter of congratulations, sympathy or thanks. The fear most people have is what to say. Often they postpone the deed or may substitute the letter with a card, a quick phone call or even an e-mail. However, good manners require a short written note.

General tips for personal letters

Handwritten letters are more personal than word processed, since they imply that the sender has taken the time to craft a personalised message as opposed to generating a standard one that will do for all types of letters.

As with any correspondence, check all details before sending, including the spelling, grammar, punctuation, titles and address details. You should never use text language or abbreviation. Keep it short and simple.

Letters of congratulations

Express your delight at hearing the news. Wish the person well on their promotion, their marriage, their new baby, etc. If you are offering congratulations on promotion, aim to write a plain, straightforward letter that cannot be misinterpreted or viewed in any way other than a genuine statement of congratulations.

Letters of sympathy or condolence

Even if you select an appropriate card, it is important to craft a few lines to express your sympathy. If you do decide to write a letter, then it is important to keep it short and simple; this is not the time for a novel on your experiences with the deceased. Express you regret at what occurred. If appropriate, mention your regard for the deceased or any personal memories you may have of them. A letter of condolence should aim to strike a careful balance between its deeply personal nature and a formal letter expressing your regret.

In reply to a letter or card of sympathy, it is important to acknowledge the sentiments expressed. Briefly thank the sender for their kindness and thoughtfulness in taking the time to think of you.

Thank you letters

The art of sitting down and sending a note of thanks for a gift or an invitation is dying. The late Princess Diana always wrote a note of thanks to her hosts on returning from an event. Thank you cards are not just a task for completion following your wedding. They should form a regular part of your personal and business life. Thank you letters or notes strengthen your relationship with the sender or host. A letter of thanks does not need to be long or detailed. Express sincere appreciation for the efforts of the host or sender. Mention details of the event or the usefulness of the gift. Do not send a generic letter or card that could be to or from anyone.

Letters to the media

If writing to the media, always remember that your letter may be published, thus be careful of making libelous statements. In order to ensure publication, keep your letter short and to the point, make your point in the opening paragraph and support it with a clear argument, facts or experience, and conclude. If you are responding to an article or letter to the editor, state the details of the article, e.g. the publication date, the journalist and the title of the article.

ACTIVITY 2

1. Your best friend's father just died. You were unable to attend the funeral. Send a letter of sympathy to her and her family.

2. Your bank has just announced that it is rationalising its services and plans to close its offices in your local town. Send a letter to The Irish Times outlining your views on the planned closure.

3. You object to plans to build a waste disposal facility in your local area. Send a letter to the local newspaper outlining your views.

4. Prepare a letter of thanks to the manager of the local hotel where you held your wedding reception.

REVIEW

1. What are the advantages of arranging a letter in the fully blocked style?
2. What is the purpose of a reference on a letter?
3. Why should the date always be written in full?
4. What is open punctuation?
5. What is the purpose of having an inside name and address?
6. '"Except of me, Mary, my dear, as your valentine and think over what I've said.

   My dear Mary, I will now conclude."

   That's all,' said Sam.

'That's rather a sudden pull up, ain't it, Sammy?' inquired Mr. Weller.

'Not a bit on it,' said Sam, 'she'll wish there was more, and that's the great art o' letter writing.' (Charles Dickens, *Pickwick Papers*)

What do you think of this advice from the point of view of business letters?

PITFALLS

In 1976 the *Daily Telegraph* drew attention to a notice in a Dublin laundrette that read: Please remove your clothes as soon as all the lights are out.

CONFUSING WORDS

persecute	prosecute	observance	observation
expedient	expeditious	flaunt	flout
perspicacity	perspicuity	erotic	esoteric
statue	statute	stature	status

QUIZ

'Men used to be children.'

When the Abbey Theatre put on *The Great Hunger* by Tom MacIntyre in Leningrad, this is how the phrase 'Ahah, the men's the boys' was translated for the Russian audience.

What do you think it means?

SPELLINGS

The words most commonly misspelled are highlighted.

facsimile	festivity	fourth
fallacy	fierce	fraud
familiar	fiercely	fraudulent
fascinate	**financial**	**friend**
fatality	forcible	fugitive
fatigue	**foreign**	fulfil
favourable	foretell	**fulfilled**
feasible	forfeit	fulfilling
February	forgotten	**fulfilment**
feign	**forty**	fullness
ferocious	fought	funeral

7

TYPES OF LETTERS

INTRODUCTION

In this chapter we will give examples of the common types of letters you may have to write when you work in an organisation. No matter what type of letter you have to write, the principles of good letter-writing are the same. It is sometimes useful to consider letters as printed conversations. You should imagine yourself speaking to your reader face to face. You will probably not use all the words in the conversation, but you will catch the spirit of the conversation in the written word.

Though a conversational tone and style is desirable, a letter differs significantly from the actual words used in a conversation. Letters are more organised than conversations. Sentences flow smoothly without the stops, starts and repetitions of conversations.

There is another important difference between conversation and letters. Due to the fact that business letters are printed in a permanent form, they can be considered a legal document. Anything you promise might be considered an informal contract obliging your employers to fulfil that promise. The words you write on company stationery create lasting impressions of the company and of you. It is important, therefore, that your business letters are written very carefully.

There are many types of business letters. In this chapter we will give examples of:

- letters seeking to collect money outstanding
- letters asking to vary the terms of payment
- letters of complaint.

Step-by-step process of collecting money

FIG. 1 – LETTER ORDERING GOODS

Michael Branagan & Sons Ltd
Builders
75 Main Street
Donnybrook
Dublin 4
Tel 01-4941327

Ref. mc/mb

29 September 2006

Kevin Byrne & Sons
Builders Providers
Lower Churchtown Road
Dublin 14

Dear Mr Byrne

I wish to order 10 tons of cement and would ask that it be delivered immediately to Castletroy where I am building at the moment. Turn right on the Tipperary/Limerick road and the site is about a quarter of a mile from Castletroy Golf Club on the right side of the road.

Yours sincerely

Michael Branagan

This order could also be taken over the phone.

Step 1: End-of-month statement

Most firms will give thirty days' credit, so at the end of October Mr Branagan will simply get a statement of his account.

FIG. 2 – END-OF-MONTH STATEMENT

Kevin Byrne & Sons
Builders Providers
Lower Churchtown Road
Dublin 14
Tel 01-4896543
Fax 01-4678534

Customer

Mr Michael Branagan
(Builders)
75 Main Street
Donnybrook
Dublin 4

First statement   Date 31/10/2006

Order No.	Quantity	Description	Unit Price	Total
11570	10 tons	Cement	€15	€3,000
			Discount 5%	150
		Amount outstanding		€2,850

30 days		60 days	90 days
€2,850		nil	nil

Step 2: Second end-of-month statement

If the outstanding amount is not paid during November, another statement is sent at the end of the month.

FIG. 3 – SECOND END-OF-MONTH STATEMENT

Kevin Byrne & Sons
Builders Providers
Lower Churchtown Road
Dublin 14
Tel 01-4896543
Fax 01-4678534

Customer

Mr Michael Branagan
(Builders)
75 Main Street
Donnybrook
Dublin 4

Second statement   Date 30/11/2006

Order No.	Quantity	Description	Unit Price	Total
11570	10 tons	Cement	€15	€3,000
			Discount 5%	150
		Amount outstanding		€2,850

30 days	60 days	90 days
€2,850	€2,850	nil

Step 3: First collection letter

If the amount is still not paid, a first collection letter must be sent. This will simply state the amount owed and ask for payment.

FIG. 4 — FIRST COLLECTION LETTER

Kevin Byrne & Sons
Builders Providers
Lower Churchtown Road
Dublin 14
Tel 01-4896543
Fax 01-4678534

Ref. kb/js

5 December 2006

Mr Michael Branagan
(Builders)
75 Main Street
Donnybrook
Dublin 4

Dear Mr Branagan

ACCOUNT NO. 11570

On checking our records we notice that the above account of 29 September 2006 has not been settled. The enclosed statement shows the outstanding balance to be €2,850.

We look forward to an early payment of this amount and also to receiving your next order.

Yours sincerely

Kevin Byrne
Manager

Enc.

Step 4: Second collection letter

If no reply has been received to your first collection letter, a second, firmer in tone, must be sent. It would, of course, be unusual for a reputable builder to have no contact whatsoever with his supplier over a three-month period. It must be remembered that most people pay their debts, otherwise business could not continue to operate.

The second collection letter should be sent about two weeks after the first one. Adopt the following procedure:

- firm tone, but polite
- refer to previous applications for payment
- ask if there is some reason for delay
- ask for payment.

FIG. 5 – SECOND COLLECTION LETTER

Kevin Byrne & Sons
Builders Providers
Lower Churchtown Road
Dublin 14
Tel 01-48965/Fax 01-4678534

Ref. kb/js

16 December 2006

Mr Michael Branagan
(Builders)
75 Main Street
Donnybrook
Dublin 4

Dear Mr Branagan

ACCOUNT NO 11570

We do not seem to have received a reply to our letter of 5 December requesting payment for the above account. The amount outstanding is €2,850.

We cannot continue to offer our very competitive prices and generous discounts unless our customers settle their accounts within the agreed time limits. Perhaps there is some explanation for non-payment. If so, you should contact us immediately.

We look forward to receiving your remittance without delay.

Yours sincerely

Kevin Byrne
Manager

Step 5: Third collection letter

If no payment is received and no reply or contact of any kind is made after your second collection letter, another letter must be sent. Some firms at this stage might make a personal visit to the holder of the outstanding debt. A personal visit is much more persuasive than a letter, and an explanation for non-payment can be obtained there and then.

In the third collection letter you must make it clear that you intend to pursue the matter with urgency and point out the steps you intend to take to collect the money. The letter should include the following:

- detail earlier efforts to collect payment
- use a fair and reasonable tone
- set a reasonable deadline for payment
- state further action if request is ignored
- regret the necessity for the letter.

FIG. 6 – THIRD COLLECTION LETTER

Kevin Byrne & Sons
Builders Providers
Lower Churchtown Road
Dublin 14
Tel 01-4896543
Fax 01-4678534

Ref. kb/js

3 January 2007

Mr Michael Branagan
(Builders)
75 Main Street
Donnybrook
Dublin 4

Dear Mr Branagan

ACCOUNT NO 11570

You ordered 10 tons of cement from us on 29 September 2006. We delivered your order immediately. It is now over three months since the cement left our premises, and we have still not been paid. We wrote to you on 5 December and 16 December requesting payment of the outstanding amount, which is €2,850. We have received no reply to either of our letters.

This matter has gone on so long that we must now press for immediate payment. We cannot offer our keen prices and credit facilities if customers do not settle their accounts within the specified time limits.

We must point out, therefore, that if the account is not settled by 20 January we will have no choice but to place the matter with our legal advisers.

Yours sincerely

Kevin Byrne

Manager

Step 6: Final collection letter

If no reply is received to this third collection letter, it is reasonable to assume that the customer either cannot, or will not, clear his account. A brief letter informing him of the action taken should be sent out.

FIG. 7 – FINAL COLLECTION LETTER

Kevin Byrne & Sons
Builders Providers
Lower Churchtown Road
Dublin 14
Tel 01-4896543
Fax 01-4678534

Ref. kb/js

23 January 2007

Mr Michael Branagan
(Builders)
75 Main Street
Donnybrook
Dublin 4

Dear Mr Branagan

ACCOUNT NO 11570

We have not received a reply to our letter of 3 January requesting payment of your outstanding debt. The amount owing is €2,850.

We stated in that letter that if payment was not received by 20 January we would be forced to hand the matter over to our legal advisers. We have now taken that action and they will be dealing with this matter.

Yours sincerely

Kevin Byrne

Manager

We have now seen the complete process that a firm might go through in attempting to collect an outstanding debt. As has been pointed out before, this is just one method of collection and must not be taken as the only way.

1. One of your best customers, who has always paid you promptly, now has an account of €1,230, overdue for two months. Write a letter requesting payment.

2. Three weeks have gone by and your customer with €1,230 overdue still has not settled his account. Write him a second letter.

3. You receive an immediate reply to your letter concerning the €1,230. Your customer tells you that he will not be able to pay for about eight weeks. Write him a letter granting him the extended credit.

4. A customer of the firm for which you work owes €2,450. Several letters have been written to him requesting payment. He always replies and promises to pay as soon as possible. However, payment has not arrived. You are now asked to write a final letter telling him that if he does not pay within ten days, you will be forced to place the matter with your solicitor.

5. Your customer who owes €2,450 has replied to your letter and promised to pay his outstanding debt. However, within the ten days his payment has not arrived. You are to write him a letter informing him that the matter has now been placed with your solicitor.

6. Write a letter to one of your customers who has a small debt outstanding but is making no effort to pay it. The collection of such a small debt is not important, but the manager feels there is a principle involved.

7. You sell goods on the understanding that payment will be made within thirty days. A new customer bought goods six weeks ago but payment has not been received. Write her a letter setting out your terms for payment.

8. Mealy & Lanigan, who have been good customers of A.D. Electronics for a number of years, now owe €9,380. This sum has not been paid within the usual trade terms and a standard reminder has brought no results. As accounts manager of A.D. Electronics, write a tactful letter dealing with the situation.

9. A good customer has an outstanding debt of €13,800. Despite a number of reminders she has not settled her account. Now she has placed a new order for goods worth €2,500. Write a letter asking her to come to your premises for a discussion of her outstanding debt before deciding to fill the new order.

10. Reply to the following letter:

Michael Ryan & Co. Ltd
The Square
Ballylanders
Co. Limerick
062-72124

8 October 2006

Peter Looby & Sons Ltd
Galbally
Co. Limerick

Dear Mr Looby

I was annoyed to receive your letter of 3 October threatening to hand over my outstanding account to your solicitor.

You must surely know that my wife had been very ill and died just two weeks ago. It is surely beyond the bounds of common humanity that you should send such a letter at such a time. Words can scarcely express my feelings about your action.

I demand an immediate apology.

Yours sincerely

Michael Ryan
Manager

11. *A customer in Germany, who has always paid his account by banker's draft, has not sent his latest payment. It is ten weeks overdue. You wrote to him a month ago but received no reply. Write him another letter requesting payment.*

VARYING THE TERMS OF PAYMENT

When a customer does not, or cannot, meet the terms of payment he may request that the terms of payment be changed. This request would have to be accompanied by strong reasons for the present difficulties and a commitment to pay by a definite date.

FIG. 8 – REQUEST TO DEFER PAYMENT

O'Connell & Scully Ltd
13 Davis Street
Clonmel
Co. Tipperary
Tel. 052-31442

Ref. bs/ps

15 October 2006

James Keating & Co.
Dublin Road
New Inn
Co. Tipperary

Dear Mr Keating

With reference to your letter of 1 October asking for payment of €14,500 which is still outstanding on our account with you, I would ask you if I could defer payment for two months.

We are not experiencing any special difficulties here at the moment, but a fairly large tax liability had to be discharged recently and this has meant that we have had to defer certain payments which we would normally make immediately. This tax liability will not be as large in the future and so should cause no problems next year.

I hope that you can see your way to granting my request to defer payment for two months.

Yours sincerely

Patrick Scully

Manager

FIG. 9 — GRANTING DEFERMENT OF PAYMENT

James Keating & Co.
Dublin Road
New Inn
Co. Tipperary
Tel. 062-72114

Ref. cd/jk

20 October 2006

Mr Patrick Scully
Manager
O'Connell & Scully Ltd
13 Davis Street
Clonmel
Co. Tipperary

Dear Mr Scully

Your letter of 15 October requests deferment of payment for two months of €14,500, which is outstanding on your account.

While we appreciate your difficulties, we feel that to defer the full payment is not the appropriate action to take, since the goods supplied to you were given at a very keen discount. This action would also damage your good credit reputation.

We would suggest the following:

1. Pay €4,000 immediately.
2. Pay €4,000 on 20 November.
3. Pay the balance of €6,500 on 15 December.

Any deferment of payment beyond the schedule suggested above would not meet with our approval.

I look forward to receiving your cheque for €4,000 within the next few days.

Yours sincerely

James Keating
Manager

ACTIVITY 2

1. A good customer has an outstanding debt of €2,500. Every effort has been made to collect it, but it seems he is short of money. In his last letter he

suggests that he will pay €620 now and try to pay another €620 in two months. Write a letter to him stating whether you will accept his suggestion or place the matter with your solicitors.

2. *A customer has a very small debt of €200. Every month or six weeks he comes in and pays €9. It will take about two years to clear this small debt if this continues. Write him a letter asking him to clear this account immediately.*

3. *One of your customers who was paying off a large debt in monthly instalments has stopped doing so. Write her a letter asking the reason for non-payment.*

4. *A customer has deducted 5 per cent from his final payment. Write a letter to him pointing out that the amount must still be paid.*

5. *You have bought goods from your regular supplier. You owe €5,000. You now find that you are unable to pay this amount when it falls due. Write a letter to your supplier asking her to vary the terms of payment.*

6. *One of your customers has the habit of always deducting a few pounds when settling his account. The amount involved is not significant, but he has always been given the full discount. What action will you take?*

7. *A customer had an outstanding debt of €3,000. He says he cannot pay. He suggests that you take his racing bike, which he purchased a few months ago, in lieu of payment. Write a letter to him dealing with this matter.*

8. *A customer who has always paid her account has now run into financial difficulties. She has written to you to point out that she sees no prospect of being able to pay her outstanding debt of €6,500. She is very apologetic about this and asks you to understand her position. Write her a letter dealing with her situation.*

LETTERS OF COMPLAINT

Letters of complaint call for tact and diplomacy. The reason for writing a letter of complaint is so that the matter may be corrected. Most people do not complain just for the sake of complaining. Many complaints are genuine, for example:

- the end-of-month statement may be incorrect
- the wrong goods may have been sent
- the goods may have been delivered late
- the goods may have been damaged in transit
- the quality of the goods supplied may have been less than expected.

When writing a letter of complaint, though you may feel angry, this should not appear in your letter. Your supplier may not be responsible for whatever happened.

Writing a letter of complaint

When writing a letter of complaint, the following rules should be observed:

- Always make your complaint at once, as delay weakens your case.
- Begin by regretting the need to complain.
- Give all the details, such as order number, date, quantity, etc.
- Give precise details of your complaint.
- Explain why you are dissatisfied and point out the inconvenience caused.
- If possible, suggest how the matter can be rectified. Ask for a repair, refund or replacement.
- Do not try to place the blame; it is up to your supplier to investigate the complaint.
- Assume that your supplier will want to put matters right.
- Never be unreasonable or rude as you may create ill-will.

FIG. 10 – SAMPLE LETTER OF COMPLAINT

New City Secondary School
Shannon
Co. Clare
Tel. 065-21248

Ref. Account No. 05431423

6 April 2006

The Editor
Longford Publications Ltd
Main Street
Longford

Dear Sir

Your representative, Mr Edmund O'Donnell, came to our school at the end of February to display your new school books for the coming year.

I expressed an interest in examining three books which I might adopt for my classes in the coming year. Mr O'Donnell agreed to send me the three books, and I was under the impression that these books would be considered complimentary copies. The books

(i) *English for the New Junior Certificate*, J. K. McArdle, €12.00

(ii) *Bookkeeping for the New Junior Certificate*, John Hinds, €14.00

(iii) *A New Approach to English*, Patrick Lonergan, €11.00

arrived on 16 March.

However, I have just today received a bill of €31 for the books in question. If I am to retain these books, I will have to buy them personally as there are no funds in our school for such purchases. However, I would again emphasise that Mr O'Donnell told me they would be considered complimentary copies.

I regret to have to complain about this matter, but this is the *third* time this same difficulty has arisen with your company. I would ask you therefore to cancel the bill in question.

Yours faithfully

Siobhan Doyle
English Teacher

Replying to letter of complaint

Suppliers should be glad to hear from customers who have complaints because it provides an opportunity to rectify them. It gives them a chance to retain the customer's goodwill and it highlights weaknesses in the product or service.

When replying to a letter of complaint, adhere to the following guidelines:

- Assume that the customer *may* be right.

- Always acknowledge the complaint promptly and assure your customer that the matter is being investigated.

- If the customer made a mistake and the complaint is not in order, point this out politely.

- If you are to blame, accept responsibility, explain why the problem occurred, apologise for the inconvenience caused and promise to put matters right immediately.

- Establish a friendly, co-operative tone in your letter.

- Provide the customer with the necessary details in order for them to avail of the solution offered.

FIG. 11 — SAMPLE REPLY ACCEPTING COMPLAINT

Longford Publications Ltd
Main Street
Longford
Tel 043-46582   Fax 043-39921

Ref. Account No. 05431423

9 April 2006

Ms Siobhan Doyle
New City Secondary School
Shannon
Co. Clare

Dear Ms Doyle

Thank you for your letter of 6 April. Your understanding of what our representative, Mr O'Donnell, said to you is quite correct. The three books in question are indeed complimentary copies, therefore, there is no charge to you.

We have had some difficulty with the program which we are using on our computer. It has been issuing bills to everybody who receives books, even people like yourself who are sent complimentary copies. This problem has been rectified in the past week and, we hope, will not occur again.

We would appreciate your comments on the three books you received, and hope that you will be adopting them for your courses next year.

I apologise for the inconvenience which this matter has caused, and enclose an end-of-month statement which shows your account to be clear.

Yours sincerely

Michael Hanly
Managing Editor

Enc. 1

You may sometimes have to reject a complaint. If it is necessary, do so briefly and politely and retain a friendly, co-operative tone. While rejecting a complaint, you must still retain the customer's goodwill so that she will do business with you again. Point out gently that the customer is wrong, or that there has been some misunderstanding.

FIG. 12 – SAMPLE REPLY REJECTING COMPLAINT

Longford Publications Ltd
Main Street
Longford
Tel 043-46582   Fax 043-39921

Ref. Account No. 05431423

9 April 2006

Ms Siobhan Doyle
New City Secondary School
Shannon
Co. Clare

Dear Ms Doyle

Thank you for your letter of 6 April.

There seems to have been some misunderstanding between yourself and our representative, Mr O'Donnell. Copies of books are supplied to teachers on the understanding that they may be retained free of charge if at least twelve copies of the book are ordered for class purposes. This is stated on the invoice which is enclosed with the books.

If you intend to adopt the books for your course next year, you may retain the copies free of charge. Fill in the enclosed form stating where you will be placing your order. The same rules apply in regard to the other books for which you have been charged. If, however, you are not adopting a particular book at the present time but would like to retain it for yourself, you are entitled to the special teachers' discount of 25%.

When you have had a chance to read the books I would be very pleased to have your views on them. A form for this purpose is enclosed with this letter.

I apologise for any inconvenience caused and look forward to your comments on our texts.

Yours sincerely

Michael Hanly
Managing Editor

Enc. 1

OTHER BUSINESS LETTERS

Letters announcing business or personal news

Letters to colleagues informing them of a change in your status should be straightforward and concise.

If your letter is regarding your successful promotion, your tone should aim to motivate and continue good relationships. Such letters can often be used to build morale and instill confidence, loyalty and goodwill. Make sure to thank colleagues for their support in your current position/business. Avoid making negative statements or using the opportunity to criticise your employer.

If you are announcing bad news, then do not hedge the news – make a direct, no-nonsense statement. You should ensure that all relevant information is contained in the letter with a considerate tone.

Letters concerning employment

In business, you may be required to draft letters concerning employment. For letters of application, see Chapter 20.

Invitations to interview

Letters inviting applicants for interview should thank the applicant for their application. State that you are pleased to invite them for interview. Give them all the relevant details, including the date, time and venue. It may also include details of any presentations that applicants are required to make. You should include details of the equipment that will be made available to applicants for the delivery of their presentation. Some public authorities also include a statement that they are not liable for any expenses incurred by applicants in attending the interview. Finally, you should conclude the letter with a request that the applicant confirm their attendance.

Letters offering employment

Letters offering employment should congratulate the applicant and include all relevant details, the job title and the commencement date. You may also wish to request that the applicant forward proof of qualifications and references. It is important to state that the offer is conditional on receipt of such documents. The letter should also request that the applicant confirm their acceptance in writing by a certain date. Remember, the letter is the first step in the hiring of an individual, so be careful to avoid making any commitments that you may not be able to fulfil. Additional details about responsibilities, job location and starting salary may be listed in the employment contract which may be included with the letter.

Accepting an offer of employment

Acknowledge the offer of the specific position and thank the employer. State whether or not you wish to accept the position. If accepting, state that you are looking forward to taking up your new position.

Letters of rejection

Letters to unsuccessful applicants should thank them for their interest in the position and for attending an interview. If appropriate, acknowledge that there were a substantial number of applicants, that the standard was very high, that short listing occurred and that they were unsuccessful. If it is company policy, assure them that their CV will be kept on file should a suitable position arise.

Letters requesting a letter of reference

The letter must be courteous, since asking for such a letter is an imposition on someone else's time. Include details of the nature of the position that you have applied for and when they may expect contact from prospective employers. In order to assist them in writing a reference, enclose a copy of your CV or application form. This will ensure that they have all the necessary information to write a suitable letter of recommendation. Invite the person to contact you if he or she has any questions or concerns, and thank him or her for taking the time to consider your request.

ACTIVITY **3**

1. Reply to the following letter.

Midland Bank Ltd
Holburn Place
Mullingar
Co. Westmeath
Tel 044-29844   Fax 044-29438

Ref. Ac No 33211765

16 September 2006

Mr Michael Boland
South Swan Circle
Mullingar
Co. Westmeath

Dear Mr Boland

We observe that your account (No 33211765) is currently operating in an irregular fashion. Your overdraft limit is €1,000 (one thousand euros) and at present your account is in debit €2,000. The Bank cannot allow you to operate your account in this fashion. When you exceed your overdraft limit, the Bank automatically operates a surcharge. However, customers are expected to operate their accounts within the terms freely agreed with the Bank.

Perhaps you would be kind enough to explain why your account is being operated in this fashion, and what steps you propose to take to reduce your overdraft.

Yours sincerely

Kevin Mahon
Accounts Officer

2. You have received a consignment of typing paper, but as the boxes were damaged in transit, most of the paper is wet and dirty. Write to your supplier informing him of this and asking him what he proposes to do to rectify the matter.

3. You are working for the company that received the letter of complaint in question 2 above. You have investigated the complaint and discovered that the boxes were sent by rail and arrived safely at the station in your customer's town. The paper was collected by an employee of your customer. It seems the damage must have taken place between the station and your customer's premises. Write a letter to your customer tactfully explaining that the blame does not lie with your company.

4. You ordered twenty football jerseys from a supplier but only fifteen arrived. Write a letter of complaint to your supplier.

5. You have received the letter of complaint in question 4 above. Write the reply you would send accepting the responsibility.

6. A customer has complained that your telephonist is curt and unfriendly when dealing with enquiries. Write a letter to the customer attempting to retain his goodwill.

7. A customer has complained that the previous three letters she has received contained several errors in basic English. She does not criticise your secretary, but criticises you for signing and sending out such letters. Write a letter of explanation to your customer. Remember you cannot blame your secretary; if he is a poor secretary, you should not have employed him.

8. You have two customers with the same surname and, in error, you have sent a large bill owed by one to the other. Write a letter of explanation to the offended person apologising for the error.

9. *Your automatic washing machine has been serviced twice in the past three months but it is still not working properly. Write a letter to the company involved.*

10. *You have received the complaint in question 9 above. Write the reply.*

11. *Reply to the following letter, rejecting the complaint.*

United Manufacturers Ltd
The Green
Clonmel
Co. Tipperary
Tel. 02-71271   Fax 02-71216

Ref. N6538

16 August 2006

The Editor
The Midland Star
Bianconi Drive
Clonmel
Co. Tipperary

Dear Sir

I wish to protest in the strongest possible terms at a news report in your issue of 23 May. You allege that my company is responsible for pollution of the River Suir. We have always been conscious of our obligations to the environment and my plant has been built to the highest standards possible. Every effort is made to ensure that no damage is caused to the river.

I am a member of the Clonmel Tidy Towns Committee which indicates my concern about the environment. Last year my company donated €500 to the Tidy Towns Committee. You can hardly imagine that I would donate money to make the town a better place and at the same time pollute the river.

You have put forward no credible scientific evidence for your allegations, and I would ask you to display a prominent withdrawal statement in your next issue.

Yours faithfully

Enda Walsh
Manager

12. *A customer has written a complaint about the unreliability of your milk delivery service. You have contracted the delivery of milk to a delivery company. Write two letters: (a) a reply to the customer (b) a letter of complaint to the delivery company.*

13. You were promised delivery of insulation for your attic within ten days of placing the order. It is now over three weeks later and it has still not arrived. Write a letter of complaint to the suppliers.

14. You receive a reply from the suppliers of the insulation saying that the order is held up because of a dock strike. It has to be imported. However, when you ordered it you were told they had it in stock. Write a letter pointing out that they misled you when you ordered it.

15. As personnel manager, draft a letter of offer to the successful candidate for a position as receptionist. Also prepare letters of rejection for the other candidates.

REVIEW

1. What are the two aims of collection letters?

2. Why are firms reluctant to take court action against customers who do not pay outstanding debts?

3. 'It is much better to visit a person who does not pay his bills than to send letters.' Discuss.

4. One way to avoid outstanding debts is to demand cash for every transaction. Why do many firms not demand cash, and indeed, extend generous credit facilities?

5. 'Collection letters should always be polite and courteous.' Why should you be polite and courteous when someone has refused to pay you what he owes?

6. Why is it always wise to assume that there is a valid reason for non-payment?

7. In what circumstances might letters of complaint be genuine?

8. Why should you use a restrained tone in letters of complaint?

9. Rewrite the following in a restrained tone:

    (a) I am outraged at your treatment of me.

    (b) I demand that you rectify the matter immediately.

    (c) I am amazed that your company is still in business since you treat your customers so poorly.

    (d) How could your company be so stupid?

PITFALLS

quite

Quite means completely, entirely, absolutely. *Quite* is an adverb, e.g. 'He is *quite* a hero.' You should not write '*Quite* a number of people were present.' The word *quite* is not an adverb in that sentence. You must say 'A large number of people . . .' or 'A great many people . . .'.

It is true that *quite* is sometimes used colloquially to mean 'to a large extent'.

CONFUSING WORDS

requisite	requisition	superficial	superfluous
resume	resumé	temperate	temporary
social	sociable	ultimate	ultimatum
spacious	specious	unsatisfied	dissatisfied
stimulant	stimulus	memoir	memorandum

QUIZ

There are two words in English that contain the five vowels (a, e, i, o, u) once in their alphabetical order. What are they?

SPELLINGS

The words most commonly misspelled are highlighted.

gaiety	gigantic	grieve
gaily	glacier	grievous
garage	glossary	grotesque
gauge	gorgeous	grudge
generosity	gossiping	guarantee
generous	govern	**guard**
genius	**government**	**guardian**
genteel	governor	guess
genuine	gracious	guest
geography	**grammar**	guidance
gesture	grandeur	guide
ghastly	gratitude	gymnastics
ghost	grief	
giant	**grievance**	

8

MEMO, NOTICE, NEWS RELEASE

INTRODUCTION

The letter is the best-known means of communication in business, but when you go to work you will discover that there are several other methods of written communication which are commonly used. Some of these are used for internal communication, such as the memo; some for external communication, such as the press release; and others, such as the notice, may be used for either.

THE MEMO

The memo, or memorandum, is the chief method of written communication within an organisation. It is frequently a hurried, handwritten message from one department or worker to another department or worker. A more formal memo may be typed. A memo may be sent by just one person to another or by several people to one person. In a firm, a manager may send a memo addressed to 'All Staff'. *Memos are usually brief.*

Memos are used to:

- confirm arrangements made

- issue instructions

- convey information that has been requested.

Many firms have printed memo slips which are available to anyone who will have occasion to use them. These slips measure about 20 cm × 12 cm. Since these slips are so small, the message must be concise.

Microsoft Word has several different layouts for memos, such as 'contemporary memo', 'elegant memo' and 'professional memo'. It also has a 'memo wizard', which will take you through the various steps in composing a memo. Fig. 1 is an example of the contemporary memo. This template can be found in Microsoft Word.

FIG. 1 — MEMORANDUM

To:	[Click **here** and type name]
CC:	[Click **here** and type name]
From:	[Click **here** and type name]
Date:	7 May 2006
Re:	[Click **here** and type subject]

How to use this memo template

Select text you would like to replace, and type your memo. Use styles such as Heading 1–3 and Body Text in the Style control on the Formatting toolbar.

To delete the background elements, such as the circle, rectangles or return address frames, click on the boundary border to highlight the 'handles' and press Delete. To replace the picture in this template with a different one, first click on the picture. Then, on the Insert menu, point to Picture, and click From File. Locate the folder that contains the picture you want to insert, then double-click the picture.

To save changes to this template for future use, choose Save As from the File menu. In the Save As Type box, choose Document Template. Next time you want to use it, choose New from the File menu, and then double-click your template.

FIG. 2 — SAMPLE MEMO LAYOUT

MEMORANDUM   Bondonno Manufacturing Company

To:	Lyn Martin (Head of Administration)
From:	Hannah Scully (General Manager)
Date:	24 March 2006
Subject:	Flexible hours

Following our meeting last Wednesday with regard to the introduction of flexible working hours, I would be grateful if you could gauge the reaction of the staff in your section to this matter. Perhaps at our meeting next Wednesday we could evaluate their objections to the proposal.

Writing a memo

- A memo should confine itself to one major point. If you wish to deal with two separate topics, send two memos.
- The language of a memo is usually somewhat informal.
- Every memo should be dated.
- Be concise and direct in your writing. Remember, a memo contains no salutation or complimentary closure.
- Use an appropriate tone and always be courteous.
- Memos need not be signed or initialled, but more formal memos are usually signed. Job titles may be used instead of, or as well as, names.
- Titles such as Mr, Mrs, Ms are generally not used.
- A reference is sometimes used.

Fig. 3 – Sample memo

MEMORANDUM	Bondonno Manufacturing Company

To: Michael McCabe

From: Aidan Moran

Date: 7 May 2006

Ref.: am/sk

Subject: Video equipment

I wonder if you could look at the video equipment in room 504 and supply me with a list of the items that are obsolete so that we can dispose of them.

If the memo is somewhat long, it may be useful to use headings rather like what one might use in a report.

FIG. 4 – SAMPLE MEMO WITH HEADING

MEMORANDUM   **Bondonno Manufacturing Company**

To: All production staff

From: Stephen Hogan (Head of Production)

Date: 19 February 2006

Subject: Borrowing of computers

Staff are allowed to borrow computers for use at home under certain conditions.

1. Conditions

(a) Computers may be borrowed only when not required at the plant.

(b) They may not be borrowed for more than one week at any one time.

(c) The borrower is responsible for the computer during the time it is in his/her custody.

2. Borrowing Procedure

(a) Obtain form from secretary and complete.

(b) Have form signed by Head of Dept.

(c) Obtain computer from Computer Technician.

3. Returning Computer

(a) Return computer to Computer Technician.

(b) Have form initialled by Computer Technician.

(c) Bring form to Head of Dept for signature.

Stephen Hogan

E-MAIL

E-mail is quickly replacing the memo. Firstly, transmission is much faster. It is much easier to send the same information to several people in the same organisation, as it entails simply entering the various people's names in the 'To:' section. E-mail also makes it easier to respond, as you will already have the e-mail address of the person who sent the message. You can also include the original message in your reply.

Sample e-mail

From: Ann Smith <annsmith@yahoo.com>
To: eimearsherwin@eircom.net
Subject: **Re: Meeting**
Date: Thursday, 30 June 2006 07:57:52

Hi Eimear,

Just to confirm that I will be attending the meeting on Friday. However, I will be unable to stay for lunch. Thank you for your invitation and I look forward to meeting you on Friday.

Kind regards,

Ann

ACTIVITY I

1. You work for a large company where the manager is concerned at the haphazard parking around the building. Instead of using the car park provided, some employees park close to the entrance on double yellow lines and thus limit access for delivery vans. Draft a memo to all members of staff informing them that the manager has decided that, in future, cars parked on double yellow lines will have a sticker put on the windscreen with the words 'Parked incorrectly' written on it. Cars which receive a second sticker will be towed to the Garda compound.

2. The personnel officer has received the above memo and having investigated the matter discovers that the car parking facilities are inadequate. She has asked you, her assistant, to draft a memo to be sent to the manager informing him of this and requesting him to defer measures suggested as they may cause displeasure among staff.

3. As manager of an office, send a memo to all your staff informing them that punctuality is not as good as you expect.

4. As the company accountant, draft a memo to all divisional managers informing them that no further requests for money can be entertained as the company's bank account is overdrawn.

5. As the switchboard operator in your company, send a memo to your boss explaining that your switchboard is constantly unable to deal with the volume of incoming calls.

6. Type a memo on your computer using the memo wizard. The memo is to the personnel officer, and you are enquiring about the pension scheme offered by your company.

THE NOTICE

A notice should be short, simple, designed in such a way that it attracts attention to itself and placed in a central and easily accessible position.

It differs from a memo in that:

- it is not directed at a specific individual
- it is posted on a notice board or other conspicuous place
- it does not normally demand a written reply
- it need not be signed unless knowledge of the source or transmitter is relevant.

If the notice is informal (see Fig. 5) a variety of means may be employed to attract attention and make it more dramatic. Use of unusual design, bright colouring, large lettering, drawings and cartoons will attract the readers' attention. Most computers are capable of designing very attractive notices.

Size, colour and the use of clip art

The size of a notice depends on the distance from it of the people for whom it is intended. It should be large enough to attract attention.

Choosing appropriate colours for the notice requires careful thought. For example:

- browns and oranges give a sense of mildness and warmth
- gold and silver convey a sense of luxury
- bright reds and yellows tend to 'shout' at the audience.

Do not be over-ostentatious in your use of typefaces. Over-ornamentation, allied to the use of colours, can sometimes make a notice difficult to read.

Clip art (so called because you can 'clip' it to size and paste it electronically onto notices) is made up of all sorts of drawings, borders, signs and symbols to give the notice visual appeal. Clip art provides visual appeal in notices but should not dominate the notice by being out of proportion and should relate quickly and easily to the message of the notice.

FIG. 5 – SAMPLE NOTICE

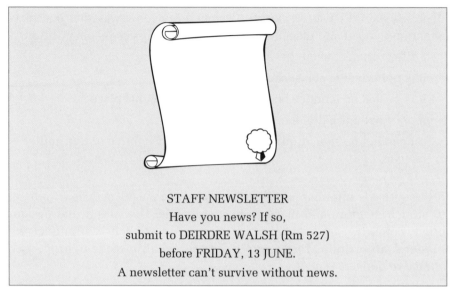

STAFF NEWSLETTER
Have you news? If so,
submit to DEIRDRE WALSH (Rm 527)
before FRIDAY, 13 JUNE.
A newsletter can't survive without news.

More formal notices (Fig. 6) need not be quite so dramatic and may use a more restrained tone. These may also be signed.

FIG. 6 – SAMPLE NOTICE

LIBRARY BOOKS

All library books borrowed by staff should be returned before the start of summer holidays on 20 June.

Each member of staff is allowed to check out six (6) books for the duration of the holidays.

If this number is insufficient, please discuss the matter with me.

Signed: Date: 1 June 2006

    Brendan Crosse
    Librarian

ACTIVITY 2

1. Draft a notice reminding all staff that cars may be parked only in assigned spaces in the staff car park.

2. Draw up a notice bringing to the attention of all staff that the 11.00 a.m. break runs from 11.00 to 11.15. Many of the staff are still on break at 11.30.

3. Design a notice encouraging students to use the waste bins in the classrooms.

4. Pay cheques for staff will not be available for collection until 5.30 p.m. They have usually been available at 3.00 p.m. Write a notice informing staff of the change.

5. A social club is to be formed in your firm. Draft a notice for the notice board giving details of the arrangements for a preliminary meeting.

THE NEWS RELEASE

Most firms are now very conscious of their public or corporate image. They need to keep their image before the public as often as possible. This is often done through the use of the news release.

A news release is sent to the media with information on the company. It may be about:

- a new person joining the board
- a new investment programme
- installation of new equipment
- opening of a new factory
- sponsorship of some activity.

News releases are useful to the media as they set out the facts of whatever is taking place without the necessity of a journalist coming to interview someone.

Writing a news release

- It should be adapted to the media that are to receive it. Some news releases are only of use to local newspapers or local radio. To a certain extent it is just common sense to know the type of information the various media will be interested in.
- State the date and time for release of the information, e.g. 'Not for publication before 10.00 a.m. 16 July 2006.' If the information is to be published immediately, put 'For immediate release' on it.
- Put a headline on every news release. This should sum up the contents. The sub-editor may change this.
- Emphasis should be on factual information. What happened? When did it happen? Where? Who was involved? Why did it happen?
- Use a simple, plain, direct style.
- The essentials of the story should be contained in the first paragraph.

- Use direct quotes from people involved if possible. These will add variety and colour to the piece. Make sure you state their title, e.g. chief executive officer.
- Keep press releases short.
- Always provide the name and telephone number of a contact at the end.

Layout of news releases
- Always use company notepaper.
- Use double spacing and wide margins. This allows the sub-editor to make changes.
- Type 'News Release' on top.
- Each continuation page should have 'more follows' or 'm f' typed at the bottom.
- Number each page and put the title of the press release on each page also.
- Type 'ends' at the end of the document.

The final three guidelines are particularly important if the news release is being sent by fax.

FIG. 7 – NEWS RELEASE

Arravale Manufacturing Company
Mooncoin, Co. Kilkenny
Telephone 056-81231
Fax 056-82214

NEWS RELEASE

(For immediate release) Date: 27 June 2006

NEW MARKET FOR KILKENNY COMPANY

A new market, worth €1,000,000. This was the good news announced today by Mr Michael Finn, Managing Director of Arravale Manufacturing Company in Mooncoin, Co. Kilkenny. His company has secured a three-year contract to supply Phlemco, a French farm machinery company, with blades for their harvesters.

Announcing the good news, Mr Finn said that the contract will secure the jobs of the 250 employees and the new technology recently installed will enable the company to fulfil the new order without engaging in an expansion programme.

'We won the order against very stiff competition,' said Mr Finn. 'A very big factor was our ability to meet deadlines and our very high level of quality control.'

The French company visited the Mooncoin plant recently and were very impressed with the skills of the employees and the high level of technology available. The first consignments to France will be leaving towards the end of October.

Mr Finn said this success encourages his company to seek further markets in Europe and he himself will be visiting Germany soon to seek new opportunities for Arravale.

ENDS

For further information contact

James Deering

Telephone: Business 062-81231   Home 062-83435   Mobile 087-2575960

ACTIVITY 3

1. Write a news release on the official opening of a new school by the Minister for Education and Science on Monday, 23 January 2006.

2. Reynella Manufacturing Company is extending its plant and will be recruiting 100 skilled employees. Invent the details and write the news release. It is not for publication until Thursday, 9 February 2006.

3. North Midlands Business College will launch their new website on Wednesday, 6 December 2006. The website was designed by Killulagh Web Studio. Write the appropriate press release.

REVIEW

1. What is the difference between a memo and a notice?
2. In what circumstances should a notice be signed?
3. Give three situations in which you would write a memo.
4. Give three situations in which you would write a notice.
5. Give three advantages of a news release from the point of view of the company issuing it.
6. Give three advantages of a news release from the point of view of the media which receive it.
7. Why should press releases always give a contact name and telephone number?
8. Should the same news release be sent to several media, or should it be adapted to suit each medium?

PITFALLS

Dutch auction

Sometimes when a general election is being held the political parties are accused by the media of turning it into a *Dutch auction* for the votes of the people.

This use of the term *Dutch auction* implies that the political parties are making higher and higher bids for the votes of the people. This is an incorrect use of the phrase. A *Dutch auction* is applied to a situation in which the price is reduced step by step, as opposed to the usual kind of auction, where the price is increased.

CONFUSING WORDS

arc	ark	ail	ale
alley	ally	hail	hale
annalist	analyst	banded	bandied
ante	anti	beau	bow

QUIZ

What is the answer to this riddle?

He went to the wood and caught it,
He sat down and sought it.
Because he could not find it
Home with him he brought it.

SPELLINGS

The words most commonly misspelled are highlighted.

harassed	hesitation	humanity
harassing	hideous	humiliation
having	hoist	**humorous**
healthiness	honest	**humour**
hearth	**honorary**	hungry
heather	honour	**hurriedly**
height	honourable	hymn
heighten	horizon	**hypocrisy**
heir	horizontal	hypocrite
hereditary	**horrendous**	**hypothesis**
heroes	hospital	

9

REPORTS

INTRODUCTION

A report is an objective and orderly presentation of factual information drawn up to meet a specific need. It may be a record of work completed, an account of an accident at work or the results of a specific investigation which would include conclusions and possibly recommendations based on findings.

We are concerned here with written reports, but the writer may often be requested to present it orally at a meeting.

There are three main types of reports:

- routine reports
- special reports
- long reports.

ROUTINE REPORTS

Routine reports are written at regular intervals and are brief, using a simple format. Some routine reports may just involve completing a report form provided.

Fig. 1 – Routine report on form provided

Routine Insurance Company Ltd

Accident Form

Name of person involved in accident: _____

Address: _____

Age: _____ Number of years in your employment: _____

Date of accident: _____ Time of accident: _____

Location of accident: _____ (attach map if necessary)

Circumstances of accident: _____

_____

_____

Witnesses to accident: _____

_____

_____

Injuries received: _____

_____

Name of doctor called: _____

Signed: _____

(to be signed by manager of department where accident occurred)

Return completed form to:

Routine Insurance Company

21 Patrick Street

Cork

A typical routine report is the weekly summary of work completed by a department. This may be done in the form of a memo. If so, it is then called a memo report.

Fig. 2 – Routine report

To: James Connolly

From: Conor Ashe

Subject: Report of Sales Department

for week of

17 July 2006 to 24 July 2006

1. Sales

The total sales recorded for the week were €15,600. This is a 15% increase on the figure for the same week last year. Confirmation of a large order from Video Equipment was received on Tuesday.

---

2. Notice of Intention to Leave

Our sales representative for the western region, Gerard O'Connor, is leaving to take up employment with Ballycrogue Company Ltd in Nenagh, Co. Tipperary. His last day with the firm will be 25 August 2006.

3. Complaint

Annacarty Manufacturing Company has complained that its order of 5 June (Order No. 1756043) has still not been delivered. Reply has been sent explaining the problem with the new machine and promising delivery in two weeks.

Signed: _____   Date: 24 July 2006

Conor Ashe

ACTIVITY **I**

1. You have been in charge of the student shop at your college for the past week. Prepare a routine report on the week's activities.

2. The public telephone in your factory has been damaged and the contents of the cash box stolen. Prepare a report for the managing director.

3. At your college one of the students has been injured while playing for the official college team. Prepare a report of the accident which will be sent to the insurance company using a standard accident form as in the example in Fig. 1.

4. You are assistant to the personnel officer. Your boss has been sick for the past week. He will return on Monday. Prepare a report for him on the week's work. Invent the details you need.

5. A video recorder is missing from your department. Prepare a report on the circumstances of its disappearance.

SPECIAL REPORTS

Special reports are sometimes called for to respond to particular situations in a firm. The person requiring the special report states, usually in writing, the terms of reference, i.e. the exact purpose of the report. The terms of reference should be clear, precise and unambiguous.

A special report may be drawn up under the following headings:

• *Terms of reference*: the subject and limits of your report are precisely stated. If you are expected to make recommendations, the terms of reference will state this.

- *Method of procedure*: under this heading you indicate in detail the steps taken to collect the necessary information. The worth of a report can be measured against the relevance, significance and comprehensiveness of the steps taken. Where the method of procedure is careless, findings will be suspect.
- *Findings*: all items discovered relevant to the terms of reference are noted here. Great care should be taken to ascertain the facts.

The special report should contain conclusions and may contain recommendations.

- *Conclusions*: conclusions should be numbered and arranged in descending order of importance. They must be based on the findings. One person looking at findings may arrive at different conclusions from another person looking at the same findings.
- *Recommendations*: recommendations should be numbered and arranged in descending order of importance. To be of any benefit they must be capable of implementation. Different people working from the same findings and conclusions may make different recommendations.

All reports should be written in an objective style, e.g. 'It was discovered that . . .'.

All reports should be signed and dated.

FIG. 3 – SPECIAL REPORT (FORMAL)

Report on Parking Facilities

at

Mullingar Business College

1. **Terms of Reference**

   'To investigate the adequacy of the parking facilities at the College and to make any necessary recommendations.'

2. **Method of Procedure**

   2.1 The car parks in the College were visited on three occasions each day at different times over a period of three weeks.

   2.2 Staff and student registers were consulted to ascertain the number and type of vehicles requiring parking facilities.

   2.3 Over a three-week period a register was maintained to record the number of visitors who required parking.

   2.4 Caretaker who is responsible for removing cars improperly parked was interviewed.

3. Findings

3.1 Present Position

    3.1.1   There are four separate car parks in the College, containing 500 parking spaces in total.

    3.1.2   200 staff members and 350 students have a vehicle to park each day.

    3.1.3   Car park near back gate is never completely filled.

    3.1.4   Car park near front door is always the most crowded.

3.2 Difficulties with Present Situation

    3.2.1   There are no facilities for bicycles and motorcycles.

    3.2.2   Some spaces are not properly utilised as just one motorcycle may be parked in it.

    3.2.3   Parking on double yellow lines is frequent.

    3.2.4   Usually it is the same cars which are parked on double yellow lines.

    3.2.5   There is usually no parking space available for visitors' cars.

4. Conclusions

4.1 The number of parking spaces available is inadequate.

4.2 Most people wish to park near the front door so the rear car park is under-utilised.

4.3 Some people are parking incorrectly even when spaces are available.

5. Recommendations

5.1 Provide separate parking facilities for bicycles and motorcycles.

5.2 Reserve ten parking spaces in front car park for visitors.

5.3 Owners of cars repeatedly parked incorrectly should be written to by the principal.

Emma McGrane: Date: 10 October 2006

Chief Clerk

Special reports need not always conform to the layout in Fig. 3. Special reports which are not as formal as the type just considered may have any layout that suits the topic being investigated. A common layout for a less formal special report follows.

FIG. 4 – SPECIAL REPORT (INFORMAL)

Report on Care of Grounds

at

Rathduff Manufacturing Company

1. The Problem

1.1 Concern was expressed at the Board of Directors' last meeting on 25 July 2006 on the general untidiness and lack of care of the grounds. The managing director has asked me to carry out a report on the extent of the problem and to suggest means by which it can be solved.

2. Discussion of the Problem

2.1 Present State of Grounds

The grounds to be maintained consists of four acres, of which one acre is covered by paths, driveways and shrubs, while the remaining three acres is in lawn.

2.2 Maintenance of Grounds

The difficult time for maintenance is during spring and summer when growth is strong. Cutting of grass, weeding and tending to shrubbery are the main tasks. At present, a caretaker spends two days a week during spring and summer tending the grounds, and one day a week during the rest of the year. This person has no special training in such work and the equipment available to him is old.

3. Conclusions

3.1 It is necessary for a person to spend more time tending the grounds, but this is not possible because of internal duties for the caretaker.

3.2 During spring and summer it is necessary to have one person working on the grounds full-time.

3.3 New equipment needs to be purchased, especially a good lawnmower.

3.4 It may be possible to contract out maintenance of the grounds.

3.5 A further and more detailed report would need to be carried out on which is the more cost-effective way of getting the work done, i.e. putting the work out to contract or replacing old equipment and assigning more of our manpower to the task.

Signed: _____   Date: 1 August 2006

James Doyle

Chargehand

ACTIVITY 2

1. *The general manager of your place of employment is concerned about security of the premises. She has asked you to draw up a report on the subject and to make recommendations.*

2. During the summer, while the college is closed, local children are allowed to use the tennis courts. The nets on all three courts and the wire fencing around the courts have been damaged. Prepare a report for the principal on the extent of the damage.

3. The new managing director has asked you to prepare a report on best practices in serving the customer.

4. The tea break in your factory is to last ten minutes. However, employees seem to be absent from their machines for between twelve and sixteen minutes. Employees who were asked about extending the tea break mentioned such reasons as overcrowding, tea not ready on time and milk running short. You are asked to draw up a report on the problem of the extended tea break and to make recommendations.

LONG REPORTS

A firm reviewing its normal procedures and strategies may occasionally need a detailed, in-depth exploration of itself and its markets. As well as studying itself, the firm may wish to know how similar firms are progressing. In this type of report it may be necessary to give background information and to detail the present state of research in the area before dealing specifically with the firm itself. A long report may have the following layout:

- *Title page*: this will contain (i) the title of the report (ii) author's name (iii) name of department authorising the report (iv) date report was presented and (v) may state whether report is confidential or not.

- *Circulation list*: if the report is intended for a small number of readers, a list of these will appear on the title page. If the circulation is longer, it will appear on a separate page.

- *Acknowledgments*: on this page, the author will thank the individuals and organisations who helped in the compilation of the report.

- *Table of contents*: this will include the major headings of the report in the order in which they appear. Sub-headings may also be given. Too much detail here may be confusing and intimidating to the reader. Word processing programs on a computer will do a table of contents for you.

- *Terms of reference*: the precise statement of the problem being investigated is given. This should appear in quotation marks.

- *Executive summary*: in this very brief section, the main conclusions should be stated. This will accommodate the reader who is interested in the study but does not need, or does not have time, to read the whole report.

- *Method of procedure*: this section details the various means used to collect, analyse and interpret the findings.

- *Introduction*: this section will explain why the present study is being undertaken and give some background information.

- *Findings*: the findings are presented here. This will be the longest section in the report. Sub-headings should be used to facilitate understanding.

- *Conclusions*: the conclusions, based on the findings, should be presented in descending order of importance. Every effort should be made to avoid prejudice in reaching conclusions.

- *Recommendations*: recommendations are proposals for future actions. These should be presented in descending order of importance. Avoid prejudice and personal interest. Recommendations should be capable of implementation.

- *Appendices*: the appendices present tables, graphs, charts, drawings, photographs and other relevant materials omitted elsewhere in the report. The writer will have to make a decision as to whether he should use appendices. Appendices should be used to present relevant information which, if included in the main body of the text, would deflect the reader from the main thrust of the report.

- *Bibliography*: this is a list of books, pamphlets, articles, etc., both published and unpublished, which are relevant to the report.

- *Index*: the index is an alphabetical list of names, subjects, etc. mentioned in the report. It is more detailed than the table of contents. It helps the reader find specific data quickly by indicating the page and/or paragraph number of every reference to the name or subject listed in the index. For example, if Michael Argyle is mentioned four times in the report, the index will show an entry similar to the following:

Argyle, Michael, 2.3, 4.6, 10.1, 10.8

Word processing programs on a computer will do an index for you.

FIG. 5 – TITLE PAGE

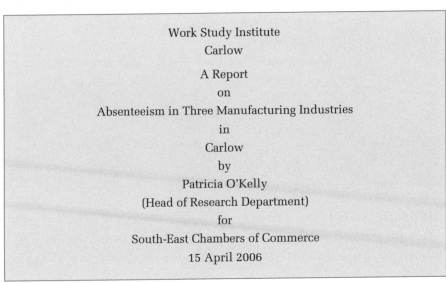

Work Study Institute
Carlow

A Report

on

Absenteeism in Three Manufacturing Industries

in

Carlow

by

Patricia O'Kelly

(Head of Research Department)

for

South-East Chambers of Commerce

15 April 2006

FIG. 6 – SAMPLE TABLE OF CONTENTS

Table of Contents

FIG. 7 – SAMPLE BIBLIOGRAPHY

BIBLIOGRAPHY

Books

Boyle, Martin, *Absenteeism – Its Causes*, Dublin: New Book Publishers, 1988.

Boyle, Martin, *Absenteeism – Another Look*, Dublin: Old Gate Publishers, 1989.

Articles

Allen, Michael, 'Alcoholism and Absenteeism', *Irish Work Study Weekly*, July 1987, pp. 12–18.

Planning the long report

The most difficult part of drawing up a report is its initial planning and organising. This is time-consuming but necessary, and should not be rushed.

FIG. 8 – PROCEDURE FOR DRAWING UP A LONG REPORT

1. **Planning**
   Clarify terms of reference
   Prepare an outline plan of work
   Decide on method of procedure
   List people and organisations that may have to be contacted
   Establish a timetable for the work
2. **Research**
   Do background research
   Obtain information from relevant people and organisations
   Evaluate data obtained
   Organise data
   Decide layout
3. **Writing**
   Write first draft
   Give to colleagues for comments
   Write second draft
   Type
   Proofread
   Retype
   Proofread again
   Make copies and bind

The terms of reference

You need to be quite clear on the aims, extent and limitations of your report, so before you begin, precisely establish your terms of reference. Ideally these should be given in written form and should appear in quotation marks in your report. Insist, if necessary, on a meeting with the person who requires the report. If the terms of reference are given to you orally, they should be written down and submitted to your client for approval.

In addition to the precise terms of reference, you need to know:

- The purpose of the report. Is it a preliminary report or is it one upon which important decisions are going to be based?
- The amount of detail necessary. For example, is it necessary to go into precise costings of various operations?
- Who the report is intended for. This information will enable you to decide what assumptions you can make about the prior knowledge of your readers. It will determine the language and tone you will use.
- Length of report. You can only gauge the approximate length.
- Date for completion of report. This will influence your plan of work.

WRITING A REPORT

- Begin with the body or the main part of the report and divide it into logical sections using headings and subheadings.
- Jot down in note form what will come under each heading and subheading.
- Write clearly, concisely and simply.
- Use an objective, unemotional style. Write 'It was discovered' rather than 'I discovered'.
- It is a good idea to have a balance between text and illustrations. A report consisting completely of text may be very off-putting to read. Graphs, charts, illustrations and clip art will add interest and variety to your report.
- Make sure the conclusions you reach are valid.
- Use a suitable numbering system for each section and subsection. Automatic numbering systems are available on most word processing programs on your computer. There are basically two systems, the letter numbering system and the decimal numbering system.

LETTER NUMBERING SYSTEM	DECIMAL NUMBERING SYSTEM
I	1.0
A	1.1
1	1.1.1
a	1.1.1.1
(i)	1.1.1.2
(ii)	1.1.1.3
b	1.1.2
(i)	1.1.2.1
(ii)	1.1.2.2
2	1.2
a	1.2.1
(i)	1.2.1.1
(ii)	1.2.1.2
b	1.2.2
(i)	1.2.2.1
(ii)	1.2.2.2
II	2.0
A	2.1
1	2.1.1
a	2.1.1.1

REVISING AND PROOFREADING

Your report may need one or two full revisions. It is a good idea to give your first draft to someone to read and then consider their suggestions in your revisions.

Always proofread. Again, it is a good idea to get a friend to proofread.

REVIEW

1. What is the difference between a report and a memo?
2. How does a report differ from a letter?
3. What are the three main types of reports and how do you distinguish between them?
4. What is a memo report?
5. How do you distinguish between conclusions and recommendations?

6. What is meant by terms of reference?

7. Why is it important to clarify your terms of reference before beginning your report?

8. Explain what is meant by method of procedure.

PITFALLS

same

The word *same* is frequently used incorrectly, e.g. 'Your tender has not been accepted, so I am returning *same* to you.' Or 'I received your letter this morning and am forwarding *same* to the manager.'

In each of these sentences *same* is used as a pronoun, which it is not. The pronoun *it* should have been used in each sentence. 'Your tender has not been accepted, so I am returning *it* to you.' 'I received your letter this morning and am forwarding *it* to the manager.'

CONFUSING WORDS

there	their	its	it's
too	two	flair	flare
right	write	feint	faint
there	they're	stationary	stationery
canvas	canvass	hair	hare
due	dew	bare	bea

QUIZ

What is the meaning of the word *floccinaucinihilipilification*?

SPELLINGS

The words most commonly misspelled are highlighted.

identify
idiot
idiotic
ignorance
illegal
illegible
illustrious
image
imaginable
imaginary
imagination
immediately
immense
immigrate
immovable
impartial
impatient
imperative
impertinent
impetuous
impetus
impossibility
imprudence
imprudent

impulsive
inaccessible
incapacity
incense
incidentally
incipient
include
incompetent
inconvenient
incredible
incurred
indelible
independent
indignant
indispensable
indolent
industrious
inferior
influential
influenza
ingenious
inheritance
inimitable
initial

injurious
inoculate
inoculation
insensible
inseparable
install
instalment
intelligence
intelligible
intercede
interference
interior
interrupt
invincible
invitation
irregular
irrelevant
irreparable
irresistible
irresponsible
irritate
ivory

PART

ORAL

COMMUNICATION

SKILLS

10

TALK, TALK, TALK

INTRODUCTION

(a) 'Fourscore and seven years ago our fathers brought forth on this continent a new nation conceived in liberty and dedicated to the proposition that all men are created equal. Now we are engaged in a great civil war testing whether that nation, or any nation so conceived and so dedicated, can long endure. We are met on a great battlefield of that war.'

(Abraham Lincoln, 'Gettysburg Address')

(b) 'The title I have chosen for my talk, as most of you know, is "The Camel's Nose is Under the Tent". The expression comes from an old Arabian fable, and to an Arab it spells trouble and disaster. The fable of the Arab and his camel goes something like this:

One cold night, as an Arab sat in his tent, a camel gently thrust his nose under the flap and looked in.

"Master," he said, "let me put my nose in your tent, for it is cold and stormy out here."

"By all means, and welcome," said the Arab, and turned over and went to sleep. A little later he awoke and found that the camel had not only put his nose in the tent but his head and neck, as well.

The camel, who had been turning his head from side to side, said, "I will take but little more room if I place my forelegs within the tent. It is difficult standing without."

"You may also plant your forelegs within," said the Arab, moving a little to make room, for the tent was small.

Finally the camel said, "May I not stand wholly within? I keep the tent open by standing as I do."

"Yes, yes," said the Arab. "Come wholly inside. Perhaps it will be better for both of us." So the camel crowded in.

The Arab with difficulty in the crowded quarters again went to sleep.

The next time he woke up he was outside in the cold and the camel had the tent to himself.

Independent of how he got there, the important point is that the camel of government control now has his nose under the tent of free competitive industry and is crowding in. We will all have to watch him or he will take over the tent . . .'

(W. R. Gondin, E. W. Mammen and J. Dodding, The Art of Speaking Made Simple, London: W. H. Allen, 1967)

(c) 'It's not often I get a chance to do this. I know when I was getting married there was no presentation made to me. It says something about the great esteem in which I was held! However, Michael is held in great esteem, not only by his colleagues, as evidenced by the great number of you who came to this presentation,, but also by me. I found that I could always depend on Michael. It is good to have highly organised people like Michael on the staff. Enough of us are disorganised – such as myself – so we need people like Michael who are constant as the Northern Star. I'm becoming poetical now. Was it Shakespeare said that?'

(Manager making presentation to staff member who is getting married)

These are three quite different speeches: the first very formal and dignified; the second making a serious point in a somewhat lighthearted fashion; and the third very informal and simple, as befits the occasion.

There are different types of writing for different occasions, and the same holds for speeches. Speech is, after all, the most normal method of expression. Speech comes before writing. The business of life depends on speech. No business organisation could function without it. The higher you climb in the business world, the more you will use speech to communicate.

SPEAKING

Speaking differs from writing in:

- use of language
- importance of non-verbal elements
- speed
- immediate feedback
- flexibility.

Use of language

The type of language used in speeches tends to be less formal than that used in writing. Some speeches can use formal language, as in Lincoln's 'Gettysburg Address', but in general, there is a tendency towards informal constructions and simple vocabulary. The degree of formality used will depend on the situation; the more important the situation, the more formal will the language be.

Non-verbal elements

'You look terrible, what happened?'

'I knew by the look in his eyes that he was telling a cock-and-bull story.'

'With that sort of voice, sure you couldn't believe anything he says!'

'You can't go dressed in that rig-out!'

'When he walked away he looked a beaten man.'

We have all heard some, if not all, of the previous statements. They refer to non-verbal aspects of communication. This is one of the most important aspects of speech. The speaker can use a variety of non-verbal elements to support his message. These may include (a) gesture (b) appearance (c) dress (d) posture (e) facial expression (f) eye contact (g) orientation.

- *Gestures*: it is difficult to speak without using gestures. We tend to use our hands to make emphasis. Some cultures use gesture more than others. When a person is speaking, watch his gestures to see what sort of emphasis it adds to the speech.

- *Appearance*: how you look will have a bearing on how seriously you will be taken. A middle-aged man wearing the hairstyle of a teenager will have difficulty in holding attention when he gets up to speak.

- *Dress*: people make judgments on us according to how we dress. Your dress is determined by your age, position, sex, personality and the occasion.

- *Posture*: when giving a speech, much communication has taken place before you begin to use words. Do you sit or stand? Do you stand up straight or slouch? Do you lean on the table or stand free with no props?

- *Facial expressions*: the face is very expressive. Some people have very interesting faces; others have faces that are blank. We look pale when sick, blush when embarrassed and perspire when angry. We only have to look at people's faces to see if they are happy, sad, depressed, anxious or annoyed.

- *Eye contact:* the eyes are very powerful communicators. Teachers keep attention through eye contact. We look at people in different ways. Do you stare, glance, gaze or 'stick someone to the floor' with a look? Our culture determines how long you may look at a person. Children are told not to stare. Staring makes people uncomfortable.

- *Orientation*: this refers to how close or how far away we place ourselves in relation to others. You place yourself close to your friends. You can use space in this way to strengthen your position. Speakers sometimes stand on a raised platform to enhance their position. The spotlight on stage performs a similar function. In the work situation a person may use a big, heavy desk to add to her power and importance.

Speed

Oral communication is quick. If the person is available to you there is no need to find pen, paper or computer. Because you can use many non-verbal elements with speech, it is likely to be more successful.

Immediate feedback

In oral communication the response from your listener is immediate. There is no need to wait for a letter or memo.

Flexibility

When communicating orally, you can alter the presentation of your message as you proceed depending on the feedback you are getting from your listener. This feedback need not be verbal. Watch the person's eyes and facial expressions.

ACTIVITY I

1. What do the following gestures mean: (a) clapping hands (b) scratching head (c) hand over mouth (d) putting hand up in the air (e) folding arms (f) drumming fingers on table?

2. What gestures do people use to express the following types of behaviour: (a) happiness (b) tiredness (c) annoyance (d) self-consciousness?

3. What type of dress do the following people adopt: (a) solicitors (b) doctors (c) nurses (d) teenagers (e) artists?

4. What type of clothes do the following males wear: (a) aged 9–12 (b) aged 16–18 (c) aged 20–30 (d) aged 35–50 (e) aged 50–70?

5. What type of clothes do the following females wear: (a) aged 9-12 (b) aged 16-18 (c) aged 20-30 (d) aged 35-50 (e) aged 50-70?

6. *Choose five different hairstyles for women and indicate what type of person would wear each one.*

7. *What is the significance of wearing a tie?*

8. *Study the following drawings of people and indicate what emotional state each face suggests.*

9. *Find ten pictures from newspapers or magazines and write a few sentences on each, indicating which emotion each person is feeling and which elements of the picture tell you the person's emotional state.*

10. *Draw a manager's office with the furniture arranged in various ways (desk, chair, visitor's chair, etc.) and say how communication is affected by the various arrangements.*

11. *Find ten pictures from newspapers or magazines showing groups in conversation. Study the composition of the groups and indicate whether they are friendly, uncivil, aggressive, etc.*

12. *Describe four types of bodily contact, e.g. shaking hands, backslapping, and indicate what each type says about the relationships between the individuals.*

WHAT MAKES AN EFFECTIVE SPEAKER?

An effective speaker:

- can be *heard*
- has something *interesting* to say
- is *clear*
- is *logical*
- uses a *variety* of expression, tone, pace and language.

The aim of speech is to communicate ideas, opinions and feelings. It will be effective if the speaker:

- considers her audience
- knows what she wants to say
- is sincere
- takes steps to retain interest
- is well prepared.

THE FIVE Ps OF SPEAKING

Preparation
- What type of audience are you dealing with?
- Do your background research and write your notes.
- Rehearse your speech.
- Check visual aids you will use.
- Check the venue.

Purpose
- What is the main aim of your speech? What are you attempting to accomplish?
- Grab the audience's attention.
- Explain who you are.
- Establish your credibility.
- What tone will you use? Serious? Humorous? Discursive? Explanatory?

Presence
Command attention by your presence. Part of your presence will be your appearance, enthusiasm, punctuality and general liveliness.

Passion
The audience should feel your enthusiasm for your topic. Even boring material can be made interesting if the audience knows why you feel so strongly about the subject. If you do not feel strongly about your subject, why should the audience listen to you?

Personality
Your personality should shine through as you deliver your speech. Sometimes a person who is trying to control their nervousness leaves vital parts of their personality outside the door, and their presentation becomes bland and colourless.

PRESENTATION AIDS

Presentation aids can help to get your message across. Use them as appropriate to enhance your message, not just to display the variety of equipment available.

The type of aids used can be classified by their complexity, from low to medium to high.

Low	Medium	High
Hand-outs	Slide projector	Computer graphics projector
Flip chart	Overhead projector	Large-screen projector
Whiteboard	Tape-recorder	Laser pointer
Display of products	Videos	Mobile display

Why use presentation aids?

Presentation aids:

- enhance understanding of the topic
- add authenticity
- add variety
- help the speech to have a lasting impact.

Using presentation aids effectively:

- Make sure the presentation aids are integrated into your speech.
- Plan the placement of aids before you begin.
- Ensure that electronic equipment is working and that you know how to operate it.
- Do not stand directly in front of an aid. Stand to the side and face the audience as much as possible.
- Turn off all equipment when it is not in use.
- Do not distribute material during your speech, as your audience will be reading it rather than listening to you.

TYPES OF TALKS

There are basically three types of talks:

- talks that compliment

- talks that explain
- talks that persuade.

Talks that compliment

The occasion may be that you are a special guest at a function, representing the firm at a prize-giving or thanking a speaker at a local function. On such occasions:

- be brief
- congratulate, do not criticise
- be polite and diplomatic
- be sincere.

Talks that explain

An expository talk may be called for when describing your firm's product to a group of visitors, representing your firm at a conference or explaining the financial affairs of the company to shareholders. On such occasions:

- know your audience
- be certain of the facts
- be aware of any time limit
- be clear about objectives
- make sure there is time for questions.

Talks that persuade

This type of talk may be given to an audience of potential customers, or to staff on certain occasions. On such occasions:

- be frank
- be positive
- be sincere
- answer objections honestly
- be enthusiastic.

PREPARING YOUR SPEECH

Advance preparation

1. As early as possible, find out all you can about the circumstances in which the speech is to be delivered, such as:

   - audience
   - time of day
   - time allowed for speech
   - situation – will others speak before you, after you?

2. Allow the topic to germinate in your mind for a while. Have some small cards with you at all times so that when a good idea strikes you it can be noted.

3. If the opportunity presents itself, discuss the topic with friends and colleagues.

A speech has an introduction, body and conclusion. Begin the preparation with the body of the speech, as the introduction and conclusion will depend on the main contents.

Main part of speech

Spread out the cards with notes on them before you. Eliminate the ones which do not advance the aim of your speech.

If your speech is on 'Absenteeism' and the aim is to encourage staff in your firm to be absent less often, cards might contain notes such as the following:

(1)	Extent of absenteeism in country as a whole.
(2)	Trends in absenteeism in past five years.
(3)	Extent of absenteeism in own firm.
(4)	Effects of absenteeism.
(5)	Absenteeism in your firm according to age, skills, sex, etc.
(6)	Days when absenteeism is highest.
(7)	Days when absenteeism is lowest.
(8)	Periods of year when absenteeism is highest.
(9)	Periods of year when absenteeism is lowest.

(10)   **Suggestions for improvement.**

(11)   **Causes of absenteeism.**

These cards should now be arranged in a logical sequence. Some may be eliminated. Points should now be developed, e.g. card 4.

Effects of absenteeism:

(a) **More work for colleagues**

(b) **Leads to inefficiency in firm**

(c) **Affects motivation**

(d) **Causes firm to be less competitive**

Introduction

The introduction must:

- catch the audience's attention immediately
- lead logically into the subject.

The audience's attention can be caught by using:

- rhetorical questions, e.g. 'Do you realise that one out of every three people does not have enough to eat?'
- personal incidents, e.g. 'Last week I was talking to a man from London . . .'
- stories, e.g. 'When George B. Shaw was asked . . .'
- humour – should not be used for its own sake. If you think it will divert the audience, omit it.

Conclusion

Conclusions of speeches should be brief, crisp and delivered with spirit. *Do not allow your speech to die painfully.* A conclusion usually consists of:

- summary of main points
- urging audience to action.

HOW WILL YOU GIVE YOUR SPEECH?

Types of delivery

There are several methods of delivery. The speaker must choose the method most appropriate for the occasion and the audience.

- *Impromptu speech* (delivered without preparation):

  Only fairly accomplished speakers can handle this situation. If called upon, say a few sentences appropriate to the situation, such as, 'Mary Woods has been one of the most conscientious secretaries we've had and I am sorry to see her leave.'

- *Memorised speech* (memorised completely and then delivered):

  Stage fright affects the memory and part of the speech may be forgotten. Memorisation also affects the delivery, as one is so intent on delivering the speech word perfect that the audience tends to be forgotten.

- *Written speech or prepared statement* (written out and then read to the audience):

  This method is sometimes necessary for people in positions where their every word will be analysed. It is not recommended in most business situations. Written style is much more formal than oral style and a speech delivered like this can sound like an essay. Also, few people today have much experience of reading aloud. Eye contact, a very important aspect of public speaking, is lost.

- *Speech delivered from notes* (prepared in content and structure but not in exact wording):

  This is the most popular method. The speaker has jotted down the main points on cards but chooses the exact words while on her feet. Advantages include:

  - less risk of forgetting
  - allows for more spontaneity and flexibility
  - allows eye contact
  - enables speaker to have greater rapport with audience.

HELPFUL HINTS

- *Posture*: take up a comfortable position. Avoid stiffness and exaggerations.
- *Hands*: concentrate on what you are saying and the hands will move naturally. Keep them out of your pockets and avoid fiddling with keys or money.

- *Gestures*: do not overuse.
- *Movement*: avoid the extremes of standing stock-still and of pacing back and forth.
- *Mannerisms*: can be extremely irritating. Ask your friends about yours.
- *Style*: depends on topic and audience. Older people may not like too casual an approach.
- *Slang*: if it is the best word, use it. However, remember some audiences may resent it.
- *Vulgarity*: never!
- *Audience reaction*: try to anticipate reactions and take them into account.
- *Diction*:

  Major – 'I do not.'

  Minor – 'I don't.'

  Always use the minor unless you want to be emphatic.
- *Dress*: appropriate for the occasion. Anything which might take the audience's attention from your speech should be avoided.
- *Sitting or standing*: depends on the size of audience and atmosphere you want to create.
- *Rehearsal*: rehearse your speech the night before delivery and the following morning. Be rested and in good form.
- *Nerves*: it is natural to be nervous before giving a speech. Everyone is somewhat nervous, though some may conceal it better than others. It is, in fact, good to be a little nervous. This shows you consider the occasion important. Your nervousness will mean that you will think faster and your body will be ready to react faster than usual. If you were not a little nervous, it would be unusual. So, to be a little nervous is good. This will also mean that you will prepare well, and good preparation will give you confidence.

FIG. I – SELF-EVALUATION SHEET FOR SPEECHES

(1) Name:	_____
(2) Title of speech:	_____
(3) Duration:	_____

A. Content

(4) Was aim of speech clear? _____

(5) Was body of speech stimulating and interesting? _____

(6) Was it logical and coherent? _____

(7) Was the content suitable to this type of audience? _____

(8) Did the speaker know his/her subject? _____

Grade for content: A,B,C,D,E,F. _____

B. Introduction and conclusion

(9) Did the introduction get audience's attention? _____

(10) Did conclusion follow logically from body of speech? _____

(11) Was conclusion successful? _____

Grade: introduction A,B,C,D,E,F; grade: conclusion A,B,C,D,E,F. _____

C. Delivery

(12) Did speaker use enough variety in voice? _____

(13) Was speaker's voice pleasant to listen to? _____

(14) Were gestures and movements effective? _____

(15) Did speaker's conviction come across? _____

(16) Did speaker establish contact with audience? _____

Grade: A,B,C,D,E,F. _____

D. Language

(17) Was the speaker's language suitable to his/her audience? _____

(18) Was the speaker's language suitable to his/her subject? _____

(19) Did the speaker use rhetorical questions and were they successful?

_____

Grade: A,B,C,D,E,F. _____

E. Questions

(20) Did the speaker encourage questions? _____

(21) How well did speaker answer questions? _____

Grade: A,B,C,D,E,F. _____

F. Overall

(22) Did speaker use words effectively? _____

(23) What were the three most positive aspects of the speech?

(a) _____

(b) _____

(c) _____

(24) What were the three aspects of the speech which need to be improved?

(a) _____

(b) _____

(c) _____

Overall grade for speech: A,B,C,D,E,F. _____

GROUP ACTIVITY

Speakers' corner

Divide the class into groups of about five. Write three topics on some cards (one card for each group) and place the cards face down on the table. The first person in group 1 picks up a card and chooses one of the topics. He speaks on it for three minutes. The second person in the group takes a different aspect of the topic for the same length of time and so on until the whole group has spoken. Each speaker must disagree with the previous speaker. Continue with the other groups in the class. This is very good practice and forces students to 'think on their feet'.

To make it a little easier you may allow the first speaker of each group a minute to prepare.

Topics for speakers' corner

Emigration	Books	Work
Anger	Humour	Banks
Unions	Money	History
Courage	Love	Hate
Hair	Smoking	Sun
Fitness	Roads	Music
Holidays	Marriage	Teenagers

ACTIVITY 2

1. In the following oral exercise, pay particular attention to the final consonants. For example, in (a) make sure you pronounce the 't' of get and the 't' of it.

   (a) Go and get it.

   (b) I did not do it.

(c) I got it.

(d) Get off the board.

(e) Wait until I see a bit of it.

(f) Around about that time I went.

(g) The party was tip-top.

(h) I kept it.

(i) It is better but a little bitter.

(j) I cannot meet him tonight.

(k) That is quite all right.

(l) Has Peter the strength to lift it?

(m) I doubt it.

(n) When did you send that letter?

(o) I sent it last Thursday.

(p) Is the criminal still at large?

(q) He is, according to the British news of this morning.

2. *Some people have difficulty pronouncing 'th'. Practise the following words:*

   this, that, these, those, thigh, though, then, thoroughly, mother, father, thunder, thin, thick, path, author, myth, bath, depth, either, width, length, thistle, their.

Variety

An effective speaker varies the pitch, tone, pace, even the volume of her voice. All of this is done to attract and hold the audience's attention. Much will depend on the speaker's vitality and enthusiasm.

3. *(i)   Recall a speaker who conveyed ideas effectively. Compare her techniques with a speaker who was ineffective.*

   (ii)   Show how it is possible to communicate different meanings in each of the following sentences depending upon the word stressed:

   (a) I saw you going there.

   (b) I want you to get the book.

   (c) I fixed the car yesterday.

   (iii)   Watch a programme on television or listen to one on radio and decide which speaker involved was the most effective. What made him more effective than the other?

4. *(i)   Compose and deliver a one-minute talk for the following situations:*

   (a) thanking a visiting speaker

(b) complimenting the committee that organised an annual function

(c) praising students on graduation day

(d) complimenting the retiring secretary of a voluntary organisation for her service

(e) wishing a retiring employee a happy future.

(ii) Compose and deliver a short talk on:

(a) the most economical means of duplicating material

(b) how a particular piece of new equipment should be operated

(c) how flexible working hours operate

(d) how your college or firm is organised.

(iii) Compose and deliver a short talk:

(a) on why your firm should introduce flexible working hours

(b) to a group of customers on why they should buy your product.

5. Arrange cards for a speech on punctuality in logical order.

6. Prepare an introduction and conclusion for the same speech.

7. Borrow a book from your local library containing the speeches of some well-known person and analyse the introductions to them under the following headings: (a) Does it arouse interest? (b) What devices are used?

8. Analyse the conclusions of the speeches under the following headings: (a) Are the conclusions successful? Why? Why not? (b) What devices are used?

9. List four typical situations in which you might have to give a speech, and in each situation: (a) analyse the composition of the audience (b) write down the aim of your speech.

10. What is the topic on which you have to speak most frequently?

(a) Write down the main points of that topic.

(b) Arrange them in logical order.

11. Topics for speeches:

Alcohol; The best book I ever read; Why read newspapers?; Life is marvellous?; Teenage music; The songs of my parents; Equality; What is a fair wage?; Sport is a waste of time; Jails should be abolished; Capital punishment; Betting should be banned; Our politicians should be paid more; TV; Roads; What I hate most; Food; Grandparents; When I was sick; Businessmen; Women in business; Money; Retirement; Make-up; Strikes; Dole; House design; Prejudice; The army; Students; The Gardaí; Charity; Violence; College life; Pollution.

REVIEW

1. In what way does speaking differ from writing?
2. Which type of communication is more successful, oral or written?
3. 'The apparel doth oft proclaim the man.' How important is this quotation from the point of view of giving a speech?
4. What is meant by flexibility in oral communication?
5. What are the characteristics of an effective speaker?
6. How can you make the introduction to your speech interesting?
7. Discuss the use of humour in a speech.
8. What are the disadvantages of reading a speech?
9. What is the danger of memorising a speech?
10. What is a rhetorical question? Why are rhetorical questions useful in speeches?

PITFALLS

between among

The words *between* and *among* are often used incorrectly.

Between is used when two people or things are involved, e.g. 'I divided the sweets *between* Iseult and David.'

Among is used when three or more are concerned, e.g. 'I divided the sweets *among* Iseult, David and Una.'

CONFUSING WORDS

impassable	impassible	judicious	judicial
personal	personnel	aggravate	arrogate
artifact	artifice	average	averment

QUIZ

What is a 'Goldwynism'? Here are three examples:

(1) He bit the hand that laid the golden egg.

(2) Include me out.

(3) A gentleman's agreement is not worth the paper it's written on.

Who was Goldwyn?

SPELLINGS

The words most commonly misspelled are highlighted.

January
Japanese
jargon
jaunty
jealous
jealousy
jeopardy
jersey
jester
jewel
jeweller
jewellery

jocose
jocular
jostle
journal
journalist
journey
journeys
jubilee
judge
judiciary
judicious
juice

juicy
jumble
junction
jungle
junior
junket
junta
justice
justification
justify
juvenile

11

MEETINGS

INTRODUCTION

'I have to attend a meeting.'

'I'm off to a meeting now.'

'I have an important meeting.'

'Not another meeting, and all the work I have to do.'

How often have we heard these phrases? People often consider meetings as an interruption to their normal work. They resent the enormous amount of time spent at them and are often irritated at how little seems to be achieved. They become frustrated with the procedures, the rambling discussions, high-handed chairpersons and internal disputes. Some people get so frustrated that they try to avoid meetings altogether. But there is no way of avoiding meetings. For the smooth running of an organisation, people must meet and discuss issues and problems. Meetings should be useful and stimulating and should be seen to make progress. In order for this to happen, it is important to understand how meetings should be conducted. The rules for holding and conducting meetings are there to ensure that they are efficient. It is impossible to participate effectively unless you understand procedures at meetings.

A meeting has been defined as 'an assembly of people for a lawful purpose'. The implication of this definition is that a meeting must have more than one person (case of Sharp and Dawes 1826). There are some exceptions in the context of company meetings where a single person may be treated as a meeting. The word 'assembly' implied that the people should be gathered in one place. However, with modern technology it is now possible to hold meetings without everyone being gathered in the same place.

TYPES OF MEETINGS

- *Public meeting*: anyone may attend, e.g. a political meeting in the town square.

- *Private meeting*: membership is restricted. The Dáil is a private meeting. The public attend as observers but cannot participate. The meetings we are concerned with are private meetings.

- *Formal*: conducted according to rules and regulations such as constitution, standing orders or articles of association.

- *Informal*: conducted according to no definite set of rules. This type of meeting is not very common. A group meeting with any frequency will build up rules, regulations and customs over time.

- *Ordinary*: a regular meeting held each week or month.

- *Extraordinary (special)*: a meeting held to deal with one specific important issue that must be decided before the next ordinary meeting. It may deal with a complex issue that demands the sort of time that cannot be devoted at an ordinary meeting because of routine business.

- *General*: all members may attend.

- *Committee*: a small group acting on behalf of the general membership of the organisation.

- *Annual general meeting (AGM)*: held once a year to review the work of the year and elect new officers.

PURPOSE OF MEETINGS

Meetings may also be classified according to the purpose they serve:

- to give information

- to receive information

- to solve a problem

- to boost morale

- to allow people to relieve their frustrations

- to reach decisions.

Many meetings might do a number of the above at the same time.

WHAT IS A VALID MEETING?

For a meeting to be valid, a number of requirements must be fulfilled.

- It must be properly convened. It can be held on regular specified days, e.g. the first Monday of every month. If this is not the case, a notice must be issued. The notice must indicate where and when the meeting is to be held and give some indication of the agenda to be covered.

- It must be properly constituted. This means that the proper person must take the chair. It may also be that a certain number of members may have to be present before the meeting can take place. This is called the quorum.

- It must be conducted according to the rules and regulations of the group. These are often referred to as the constitution or the standing orders.

- A proper record of the proceedings must be kept. These are known as the minutes.

ROLE OF THE CHAIRPERSON

The success or otherwise of the meeting depends to a great extent on the chairperson. To carry out her role effectively, she must understand her duties and powers. But as well as understanding these, she needs to know when to be flexible.

Duties of the chairperson

- Ensure that the meeting is properly convened.

- Ensure that it is properly constituted.

- Maintain order.

- Draw up an agenda with the secretary..

- Guide the meeting through its business.

- Permit an adequate amount of discussion..

- Deal with questions about procedure (points of order).

- Ascertain the sense of the meeting by conducting a vote or summing up the discussion.

Powers of the chairperson

The chairperson's powers come from the general rules for conducting meetings and from the standing orders or constitution of the particular group of which she is the chairperson. If a group does not have standing orders or a constitution, then the chairperson derives her authority from custom and practice. The chairperson's powers allow her to:

- maintain order

- decide points of procedure

- decide order of speakers

- adjourn the meeting if it becomes impossible to maintain order.

The chairperson's real power comes from her careful preparation for meetings, her knowledge of the rules, regulations and procedures, and especially her fair and impartial dealings with members. *The chairperson must deal impartially with all members.*

ROLE OF THE SECRETARY

Before the meeting

- Draw up an agenda with the chairperson.

- Send out notice and agenda to members.

- Prepare any necessary documents for the meeting.

- Prepare the room.

At the meeting

- Take a record of attendance.

- Read the minutes of the last meeting.

- Read correspondence.

- Give the secretary's report.

- Take notes for minutes.

- Assist the chairperson.

After the meeting

- Write up minutes.

- Act on decisions taken.

MOTIONS AND AMENDMENTS

Motions

'I want to propose a motion . . .' Those who attend meetings regularly will be familiar with that phrase. At meetings which are run along very formal lines, the chairperson will not allow discussion unless there is a motion proposed and seconded.

A motion is a proposal to take some action or to decide some policy issue, e.g. I propose 'that the annual subscription be raised from €7 to €10.50'.

All motions must:

* be proposed

* be seconded

* begin with the word 'that'

* be positive rather than negative

* be unambiguous

* be within the scope of the meeting as indicated in the agenda.

When a motion is passed or carried, it is called a *resolution*.

Amendments

An amendment is a proposal to alter a motion which has been put before the meeting but has not been voted upon.

All amendments must:

* be proposed

* be seconded

* begin with the word 'that'

* be relevant to the original motion

* be positive rather than negative

* be in character with the original motion. The chairperson will have to use her judgment here as to whether it is in character or not.

Amendments may:

* Add words to a motion. For example (with reference to the motion: I propose 'that the annual subscription be raised from €7 to €10.50'): I propose 'that after €10.50 add "and no further increase to take place for at least three years"'.

- Delete words from the original motion. For example: I propose 'that the ".50" after €10 be deleted'.

- Replace part of a motion with different words. For example: I propose 'that €10 be deleted and replaced by €12'.

Always vote on the amendments first. If some amendments are carried, then vote on the original motion as amended. If, for example, the third amendment above was carried, the original motion would then read 'that the annual subscription be raised from €10 to €12'. You must then vote on that amended motion. An amended motion is called a substantive motion.

Procedural motions

Procedural motions may be put forward in order to facilitate or regulate the business of a meeting. A procedural motion cannot be amended.

The meeting may decide that it has heard enough discussion on a particular topic. A procedural motion can be put forward to cut short the debate.

The following are the types of procedural motions:

- *The closure*: 'I propose that the question be now put' or 'I propose that a vote be now taken.' If carried, the vote on the original motion is taken immediately. If lost, the debate continues.

- *The previous question*: 'I propose that the question be not now put' or 'I propose that the vote be not now taken.' If carried, the debate on the original motion is ended without a vote. If lost, the original motion is immediately put to a vote.

- *Next business*: 'I propose that the meeting proceed to the next business.' If carried, the meeting drops the matter under discussion without a vote and moves on to the next item.

- *Adjourn debate*: 'I propose that the debate be adjourned.' If a debate is getting very heated, this can be a good idea, or if sufficient information is not available to make a decision.

- *Adjourn meeting*: 'I propose that the meeting be adjourned.' The meeting may adjourn simply because people must leave. When a meeting is resumed after an adjournment, it is treated as a continuation of the earlier session.

OTHER TERMS USED AT MEETINGS

(a) Quorum

A quorum is the smallest number of people who must be present at a meeting in order for business to be transacted. The number to make up a quorum is usually written into the constitution or standing orders of an organisation. The quorum should be big enough to represent a range of viewpoints but not so large that it would be difficult to have enough persons present to hold a meeting.

(b) Point of order

When a member questions the chairperson as to whether proper procedures are being followed, it is called a point of order. The chairperson must always answer a point of order.

(c) Casting vote

The chairperson, as well as having a vote just like every other member of the organisation (called the deliberative vote), usually has a casting vote which can be used in the event of a tie. The chairperson should avoid using her ordinary or deliberative vote to retain her impartiality. How she should use her casting vote depends on the circumstances.

(d) Voting

It is not necessary to vote on every matter. The chairperson may say 'Are we all agreed?' and members may nod assent. At meetings, voting is usually by show of hands or by secret ballot.

A person at a meeting has three choices when it comes to voting. They may vote in favour of the motion, they may vote against the motion or they may abstain. To abstain means not to vote for or against the motion. To abstain from voting is sometimes looked on as sitting on the fence and not coming to a decision on a matter, but it can be a valid option. A person may feel they do not have sufficient information on the matter to arrive at a decision. Or, despite having plenty of information, they may not be able to arrive at a decision. They may not want to offend people on either side of the discussion and so decide to abstain, though this option can have the effect of offending everyone.

(e) *Sine die*

If a meeting adjourns without setting a date to meet again, it is said to have adjourned *sine die*.

(f) *Nem. con.*

If a motion or amendment is passed unanimously, it is said to have been carried *nem. con.*

BUSINESS MEETINGS

Many meetings which take place daily in businesses do not necessarily have all the formality described in the previous pages. The meeting may be called to allow people to air their views, to give their reactions to a plan or to discuss a problem. An element of formality, however, is necessary at all meetings if they are to be productive. The chairperson of such a meeting must:

- decide who is to attend

- plan carefully

- control the discussion

- cope with difficult members.

Who is to attend?

Sociologists who have studied the efficiency of groups recommend that the most effective group contains about seven members. Meetings should, then, be confined to small groups if possible. Restricting the number has obvious advantages: the shy person is more likely to contribute; the specialist has greater possibility of explaining difficult concepts; the leader is in a better position to lead and guide the discussion.

Plan

Effective meetings are the product of careful planning and sensitive leadership. A skilled chairperson devises a plan in advance of the meeting but is prepared to modify, adjust or even change it if the 'feel' of the meeting so directs.

The meeting room should be clean, bright and comfortable. It should be arranged to promote maximum participation in the discussion. Classroom-style arrangement discourages this. A circular arrangement will encourage discussion and allow the leader to merge more with the group.

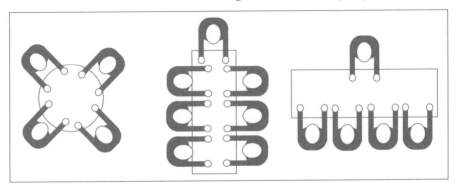

Chairpersons develop their own style, but the following formula may be a useful basis to work from:

- inform members of the purpose of the meeting
- state the precise topic or problem to be dealt with
- indicate the procedure you intend to adopt and the proposed duration of the meeting
- allow for, and indeed encourage, free-flow participation from everyone
- sum up the progress of the discussion at suitable intervals
- summarise conclusions and decisions reached at the close of the meeting
- suggest future actions for adoption related to decisions taken.

FIG. I — SAMPLE OUTLINE

Purpose of meeting: to deal with the problem of unpunctuality.

Aim: to reduce the problem of unpunctuality among employees at all levels.

Introductory remarks:

- gives bad image to company
- shows lack of interest in work
- problem must be eased if it is not to get completely out of hand.

Consequences of unpunctuality:

- lack of punctuality creeping in at all levels
- customers on telephone at 9.05 a.m. and no one to answer it
- machines being underutilised
- production falling off
- costs increasing
- losing goodwill.

Rules for discussion:

1. Consider the following points:

- lack of punctuality in the morning
- lack of punctuality in returning from tea breaks
- lack of punctuality in returning from lunch.

2. Reasons for lack of punctuality:

- traffic problems
- buses late
- lack of interest in job.

3. Possible solutions to problems:

- introduce flexible working hours
- circular to all employees emphasising the extent of the problem
- supervisors and foremen to keep details of chronic offenders for future action.

Forward plan: further meeting two weeks hence to assess progress.

Controlling the discussion

The skilled group leader creates an atmosphere which encourages maximum participation. She will stimulate the discussion by injecting questions calculated to draw shy members into the discussion and to encourage members with needed specialist knowledge to contribute at appropriate points.

The types of questions used by the leader may be divided into five categories.

1. *The open-ended question*
This is a question which cannot be answered by a simple yes or no, e.g. 'What do you think are the chief reasons for lack of punctuality in the mornings?' This will allow a member to give an expanded answer.

2. *The closed question*
This should be used sparingly as it allows only a yes or no answer, e.g. 'Is lack of punctuality having a bad effect on morale?'

3. *The overhead question*
This can be usefully employed in stimulating the discussion and in getting everyone's attention. It is not directed at anybody in particular, e.g. 'Could I have your suggestions on how big the sample should be for this survey?' It is a mistake to put the question to one person first, as it allows all other members to relax.

4. *The direct question*
This is directed at a specific individual. It is a useful means of drawing a

quiet member into a discussion. However, it should be a simple question that he can answer, otherwise he may be reluctant to contribute in the future. It is also used for eliciting knowledge from an expert member.

5. *The leading question*

For example: 'You will agree, I'm sure, that we should postpone action until next week?' This type of question encourages members to agree with the questioner. It is not useful when the leader is seeking an open exchange of views.

Coping with difficult members

1. *The chatterer*

This person knows everything and scatters his wisdom indiscriminately. He can be stopped by a searching question which requires real and detailed knowledge or with a polite comment: 'We've just heard from you. Perhaps we could hear the views of Mr Ryan, who didn't have an opportunity yet?'

2. *The rambler*

He wanders off the topic completely. Summarise the relevant part of his contribution to get back to the topic.

3. *The thunderer*

Do not invite him to the meeting if possible. If this is unavoidable, try to find merit in some of his contributions and then move on. Keep your temper.

4. *The mumbler*

Ask him to repeat his contribution or summarise his points.

5. *The silent member*

Ask him a direct question.

6. *Member with persecution complex*

This member feels that some wrong was done to him at some time and he brings it up at every opportunity. Point out to him that the business of this particular meeting does not include his point. Indicate pressure of time.

7. *Member who engages in side conversation*

Ask him a direct question. A look of displeasure may suffice.

8. *The superior type*

This person acts as if he is above all of this and considers most of the other members beneath him. Challenge his contributions every now and then to bring him down to earth.

9. *Member who always quotes the rules*

This member constantly calls for points of order and highlights infringements of the rules. Answer each point of order with patience and always be familiar with the standing orders and rules for conducting meetings.

10. *Member with little to contribute but comes to hear himself talk*

When not speaking directly to the topic under discussion, rule this type of person out of order.

ACTIVITY I

1. Your organisation is electing a new treasurer at your AGM. How would you conduct the voting and why?

2. What is the difference between a motion and a resolution?

3. Give some suggestions for formulating motions.

4. Write down a sample motion.

5. Write three different types of amendments to the motion you wrote in question 4.

6. If amendments no. 1 and 3 above were carried and no. 2 was lost, how would the amended motion read?

7. Why should organisations have a quorum for meetings?

8. Why might a member at a meeting propose the closure of the meeting?

9. What type of seating arrangement should be used at a meeting where the chairperson wishes to encourage discussion?

REVIEW

1. Why do many people dislike going to meetings?

2. What requirements must be fulfilled for a meeting to be valid?

3. What is the difference between an ordinary and an extraordinary meeting?

4. Should the chairperson just referee the debates at meetings or should she provide leadership?

5. What is the role of the secretary (a) before the meeting (b) at the meeting (c) after the meeting?

6. What power has a chairperson at a meeting?
7. Define (a) motion (b) amendment.
8. Why are motions sometimes amended?
9. What are procedural motions and how should they be dealt with by the chairperson?
10. How should the chairperson use her casting vote?

PITFALLS

Comparatives and superlatives

Adjectives describe, or qualify, nouns and pronouns, e.g. 'the clever man'. Adverbs qualify verbs, adjectives and other adverbs, e.g. 'The machine moved very quickly.'

Adjectives can be used to make comparisons:

- *Positive*: 'Their service is *good*' (no comparisons made).
- *Comparative*: 'Their service is *better* than the other company's' (comparing two persons or things).
- *Superlative*: 'Their service is the *best* available' (comparing more than two persons or things).

Adverbs can also be used in this way:

- This van brakes quickly.
- This van brakes *more* quickly than the old one.
- This van brakes the *most* quickly.

CONFUSING WORDS

accept	affect	effect
access	aggravate	annoy
adapt	alter	altar
adverse	alternate	alternative
advise	allusion	illusion

QUIZ

Can you explain the following excerpt from the Income Tax Act 1967, section 507?

'For the purposes of the Part, a person shall be deemed not to have failed to do anything required to be done within a limited time if he did it within such further time, if any, as the commissioners or officer concerned may have allowed; and where a person had a reasonable excuse for not doing anything required to be done, he shall be deemed not to have failed to do it if he did it without unreasonable delay after the excuse had ceased.'

SPELLINGS

The words most commonly misspelled are highlighted.

kangaroo	**kidnapper**	knave
karate	kidney	knead
keen	kilogram	knight
keenness	kilometre	knitting
keepsake	**kindliness**	knot
kennel	kindly	know-all
ketchup	kindred	know-how
keyboard	kitchen	**knowledge**
keyhole	kleptomaniac	knuckle
khaki	knapsack	

12

DOCUMENTS FOR MEETINGS

NOTICE AND AGENDA

There are two main ways of calling a meeting:

- The meeting is held at pre-arranged times and always in the same place, e.g. the meetings are held on the first Tuesday of every month in the staff common room. If this is the practice it is not necessary to issue a notice for each meeting. However, some bodies such as local authorities issue notices and agendas even though their meetings are held at regular times.

- Issue a notice of each meeting. Notice could be issued by telephone, e-mail, letter or word of mouth or could be put in a newspaper for an AGM. The notice should be issued by the proper authority, usually the secretary in consultation with the chairperson.

A notice should:

- be issued by the proper authority
- observe the minimum period of notice
- state where and when the meeting is to be held
- be accompanied by an agenda
- be sent to all individuals entitled to receive it.

The minimum period of notice is often taken as 'seven clear days'. For company meetings the period of notice is fixed by law. The 'clear days' begin when the notice is delivered at the correct address or after an interval specified in the standing orders, e.g. forty-eight hours after posting.

The agenda is drawn up by the secretary with the approval of the chairperson. The secretary should:

- consult the chairperson
- keep a folder of items which colleagues want on the agenda

- refer to minutes of previous meetings to bring forward any items which were deferred.

The usual order for an agenda is:

- preliminary business, e.g. apologies for absence, minutes of last meeting, matters arising from minutes
- ordinary business, e.g. treasurer's report
- new business, e.g. proposal for new projects
- closing items, e.g. any other business, date of next meeting.

FIG. 1 – NOTICE OF MEETING INCORPORATING THE AGENDA

STAFF SOCIAL CLUB

2 June 2006

The next meeting of the Staff Social Club will be held on Wednesday, 14 June at 8.00 p.m. in the Staff Common Room.

Signed: Kate McGrane
      (Secretary)

Agenda

The agenda will include the following:

1. Apologies for absence
2. Minutes of last meeting
3. Matters arising from minutes
4. Correspondence
5. Treasurer's report
6. Snooker tournament
7. Trip to All-Ireland hurling final
8. Any other business

SECRETARY'S AGENDA

At a meeting, the secretary need not be writing furiously all the time, trying to take down everything that is said. He should have a copy of the agenda and just make brief notes opposite the various items to help in writing the minutes. This will allow the secretary to assist the chairperson and participate at the meeting.

FIG. 2 – SECRETARY'S AGENDA

STAFF SOCIAL CLUB

14/6/06 at 8.00 p.m.

Chair – K. Kenny   Secretary – K. McGrane

Present: P. Ryan (Treasurer), O. Dunphy, G. Carr, T. Hearne, P. Meehan, M. Murray.

Agenda   *Notes*

1. Apologies for absence

2. Minutes of last meeting

3. Matters arising

4. Correspondence

5. Treasurer's report

6. Snooker tournament

7. Trip to All-Ireland hurling final

8. Any other business

CHAIRPERSON'S AGENDA

Before the meeting begins, the chairperson needs to study the agenda and make notes on it to help him run the meeting. These will usually be very brief. He might put down times opposite items to indicate the rate at which the meeting should progress.

FIG. 3 – CHAIRPERSON'S AGENDA

STAFF SOCIAL CLUB

14/6/06   8.00 p.m.

Agenda   *Notes*

1. Apologies for absence

2. Minutes of last meeting

3. Matters arising

---

4. Correspondence	»	8.15
5. Treasurer's report		
6. Snooker tournament		
7. Trip to All-Ireland hurling final	»	People who have not paid for last year's tickets cannot paticipate until debt is cleared.
8. Any other business		

MINUTES

The minutes are a brief, accurate record of the business transacted at a meeting. They should contain the following:

- name of organisation
- place, date and time of meeting
- names of chairperson and secretary
- names of other members present
- all motions and amendments, no matter how they may have fared
- names of movers and seconders of all motions and amendments
- results of voting.

Minutes should be:

- concise but sufficiently detailed to make the sense of the meeting clear
- precise and unambiguous
- impersonal and impartial
- written in the past tense
- numbered in ascending order from one meeting to another. In our sample minutes (Fig. 4), the first minute is numbered 149. The last minute of the previous meeting was 148.

Fig. 4 — Sample minutes

STAFF SOCIAL CLUB

Minutes of the meeting of the Staff Social Club held on 14 June 2006 at 8.00 p.m. in the Staff Common Room.

Chairperson: Kevin Kenny

Secretary: Kate McGrane

Present: P. Ryan, O. Dunphy, G. Carr, T. Hearne, P. Meehan, M. Murray

149 – Apologies for Absence

The Secretary reported that N. Doyle and P. Foran sent apologies for being unable to attend.

150 – Minutes of Meeting of 12 May 2006

The Minutes of the meeting of 12 May 2006 were read, approved on the proposal of P. Ryan, seconded by G. Carr, and signed by the Chairperson.

151 – Decorating Staff Common Room

The Secretary read a letter from the Manager proposing the redecoration of the Staff Common Room and requesting the Social Club's views.

Proposed P. Ryan, seconded O. Dunphy

'that a committee be appointed consisting of G. Carr, P. Meehan and T. Hearne to make recommendations for the redecorating of the Common Room and to report to the next meeting.'

Result – Carried unanimously

152 – Treasurer's Report

The Treasurer reported that the Club is €200 in credit. However, some subscriptions are still outstanding. The Chairperson urged the Treasurer to attempt to collect outstanding subscriptions.

153 – Snooker Tournament

Proposed T. Hearne, seconded P. Meehan

'that the Secretary be assisted by O. Dunphy and M. Murray in making arrangements for the autumn snooker tournament.'

Result – Carried: 6 for, 1 against, 1 abstention.

154 – Trip to All-Ireland Hurling Final

It was agreed that the Secretary should write to Croke Park immediately for ten tickets and book a minibus for the trip. To participate in the draw for tickets, all outstanding debts must be paid.

Next Meeting: 13 August 2006

Meeting concluded at 9.10 p.m.

Signed: _____ (Chairperson)   Signed: _____ (Secretary)

Date: _____   Date: _____

The minutes should be approved at the next meeting. The secretary should read the minutes and then the chairperson should ask if they are a fair and accurate record of the last meeting. If the meeting agrees, the chairperson should sign them. If the meeting approves an alteration to the minutes, the secretary should make the alteration and the chairperson initial it. If the alteration is substantial, it may be necessary to rewrite the minutes.

When the minutes are being approved, the chairperson should not allow questions that have been decided to be reopened again.

STANDING ORDERS

Standing orders are the rules by which an organisation decides to run its affairs.

Fig. 5 – Standing orders

STAFF SOCIAL CLUB

Standing Orders for Meetings

1. At each meeting of the club the chair shall be taken at the time for which the meeting is convened and business immediately proceeded with. At all meetings the chairperson (or deputy chairperson) shall take the chair, or in his/her absence, the secretary, or failing both, a chairperson from the meeting shall be elected.

2. (a) The order of business for ordinary meetings shall be as follows:

   (i)   Minutes of last meeting

   (ii)   Matters arising from the minutes

   (iii) Correspondence

   (iv)   Minutes of special meetings

   (v)   Treasurer's report

   (vi)   Elections

   (vii) Motions

   (viii) Any other business.

   (b) The order of business for the annual general meeting shall be as follows:

   (i)   Minutes of previous AGM

   (ii)   Chairperson's report

   (iii) Secretary's report

      (iv) Elections of chairperson, secretary, treasurer and committee members.

3. Speaking rights:

    (a) No speech shall be permitted which is not strictly to a distinct and competent motion or amendment or to a point of order or information.

    (b) A motion or amendment shall not be discussed by anyone except the mover, put to the meeting, or entered on the minutes until the same shall have been seconded. On a motion being ruled out of order, no further discussion on it may take place at the meeting.

    (c) The proposer of any motion, or of an amendment to a motion, shall have the right to make a proposing speech on such motion or amendment and to reply before it is put to a vote. The seconder of such motion or amendment, and any other member called upon by the chairperson, shall be entitled to speak on the motion or amendment.

    (d) The proposer of an original motion shall have the right to speak immediately after the proposer of an amendment which has not been accepted by him/her. If an amendment which has not been accepted by the proposer of the original motion is carried, the proposer of such amendment shall be deemed, for all purposes, to be the proposer of the motion.

    (e) No ordinary member can speak more than once on the same motion.

4. Points of order: points of order must be strictly to questions relating to rules of debate. No member may speak until the chairperson has ruled on the point of order.

5. Points of information:

    (a) A member, when asking or giving information on matters referred to by any member, may do so only with the consent of the chairperson.

    (b) No point of information shall be made in a speech of reply by the proposer of a motion or amendment.

6. Questions: members may ask questions arising out of the business before the meeting. Any member who wishes to put a question to the chairperson of any committee as to the general work or procedure of that committee not included in a report submitted for approval, shall forward it in writing to the chairperson of the meeting. Such questions shall be answered by the chairperson of the committee at that meeting if possible. No other speech or discussions shall be allowed on any question so put.

7. Amendments: when a motion is under debate at any meeting of the club, a further motion shall not be received, except the following:

    (a) to amend the motion

(b) that the meeting be adjourned

(c) that the debate be adjourned

(d) that the question be now put

(e) that the meeting proceed to next business

(f) that the question be not now put.

When amendment (a) is on the floor, any of amendments (b) to (f) may be moved. Subject to this, there shall not be two amendments on the floor at the same time. A member shall not move an amendment without the permission of the chairperson if s/he has previously spoken to the motion, or move more than one amendment to the motion.

8. An amendment must be germane. It must not merely negate the motion, and it must not be inconsistent with anything already agreed upon at the same meeting.

   If an amendment be carried, the motion as amended shall take the place of the original motion and shall become the question upon which any further amendment shall be moved.

9. Motion (f) must be seconded. The proposer of the motion must speak and the proposer of any substantive motion on the floor may oppose it. The motion will then be put.

10. Should disorder arise, the chairperson shall be entitled to adjourn the meeting and quit the chair and on doing so the meeting shall be held to be, *ipso facto*, immediately adjourned. The chairperson shall give his/her reasons at the following meeting of the club, and there shall be no discussion thereon.

11. The club by a two-thirds majority of those present at a meeting may suspend standing orders.

12. Suspension of members:

    (a) In the event of any member at a meeting of the club disregarding the authority of the chairperson or being guilty of obstructive or offensive behaviour, the club may, on a motion duly moved and seconded by a resolution of at least two-thirds of the members present, suspend such a member for the remainder of the meeting, and may in addition order the suspension to continue until submission of apology by the offending member. The motion to suspend shall be put without discussion.

    (b) The motion to suspend may be put at any time during the meeting and it shall be put to a vote immediately on being proposed.

13. Voting powers of chairperson: at all meetings of the club the chairperson shall have a deliberative vote. In cases of equality of votes, s/he may give the casting vote.

1. Write a notice and agenda for a meeting of any organisation of which you are a member.

2. Prepare the chairperson's agenda for the conduct of the same meeting.

3. Also prepare the secretary's agenda and make the appropriate notes which would be made during the conduct of the meeting.

4. Write the minutes for the meeting from your notes on the secretary's agenda.

5. Draw up a chairperson's agenda for the canteen committee of the students' union. The meeting is to discuss (a) space (b) seating (c) slow service (d) provision of health foods.

6. You are secretary of the students' union social committee. Write the minutes of the last meeting from the notes on the agenda below.

STUDENTS' UNION SOCIAL COMMITTEE

Meeting 28 January 2006 at 7.00 at the Social Club.

Attendance: L. Ahearn, R. Foran, J. Fogarty, T. Delaney, T. Doyle (Chairperson), D. McDonough (Secretary).

Agenda		Notes
1. Apologies	»	Róisín Foran
2. Minutes of last meeting	»	OK
3. Matters arising	»	none
4. Correspondence	»	none
5. Treasurer's report	»	€600 in bank, some subs due (Liam Ahearn)
6. Rag Week gigs	»	No gig to cost more than €7 – proposed, J. Fogarty seconded, T. Delaney
7. Cleanliness of rooms		
8. Any other business	»	None. Next meeting 17 February.

7. Find the original meaning of the word 'minute'.

8. Why is it a good idea not to include what people said in the minutes?

9. Minute the following items from the secretary's agenda:

Secretary's Agenda

Agenda	Notes
1. Apologies	None
2. Minutes	OK
3. Matters arising	Every member expected to sell 20 tickets for €100 draw.
	Prop. B. Scully
	Sec. D. Finn

ACTIVITY 2

Preparing for the meeting

You are secretary of the Golden Dramatic Society and you have met the chairperson to discuss the agenda for the August meeting.

Chairperson: 'What do you think of having the next meeting on Tuesday? That night usually suits everyone. It's sort of traditional.'

Secretary: 'Well, we decided at the last meeting to have it on Monday as Costello and O'Rourke are going on a holiday on Tuesday the 16th. The room is in a bit of a mess but it will do for the meeting.'

C: 'The Tidy Towns Committee want to know if we would put on a bit of street theatre during the last week of August.'

S: 'It's a bad time to get people together. Anyway, the committee can discuss it and decide what to do. By the way, the rooms are in a terrible mess; they need to be cleaned up.'

C: 'Well, it might be possible to get a few volunteers, but if people were considerate it wouldn't need to be done at all.'

S: 'Oh, Louise and Ann are going to Australia for a year. We probably should have a bit of a do for them.'

C: 'Put it on the agenda and see what people think.'

S: 'I don't think there is anything else except the usual items.'

Based on the above conversation, write the notice and agenda for the next meeting of the Golden Dramatic Society.

Now hold the meeting

This exercise can be carried out by groups of six. You are now members of the
Golden Dramatic Society and you have the agenda for the meeting from the previous
exercise. Each person plays the role of one of the committee members based on
the details below.

Chairperson: M. O'Neill

Secretary: S. McSweeney

Treasurer: J. Lonergan

Committee members: M. Costello
J. O'Rourke
P. Murphy

Chairperson: M. O'Neill

Open meeting.

Ask if any apologies.

Ask secretary to read minutes of last meeting.

Ask if you can sign them.

Ask if any matters arising.

Deal with objections to holding meetings on a Monday instead of Tuesday.

*Speak strongly to members about the mess of the rooms and ask for volunteers to
clean it up.*

Guide discussion on Tidy Towns request for street theatre.

Suggest party for Louise and Ann in local pub. Ask for further suggestions.

Ask if there is any other business.

Close the meeting.

Secretary: S. McSweeney

Apologies for absence received from J. Branagan.

Letter from Naas Drama Club thanking us for our participation in their festival.

Matters arising – booked hotel for One Act Drama Festival in December.

The cleaning up of the rooms always left to the secretary. People have very little consideration. A group should be in charge of keeping rooms clean and tidy.

Street theatre very difficult at this time of year with so many on holidays.

'Do' for Louise and Ann would need to be very soon as they're leaving on Friday. Will check with pub about a room for private party. It will be difficult to notify all members.

Treasurer: J. Lonergan

Propose signing of minutes.

Some people missing too many meetings. Should they be on committee at all?

Will Tidy Towns Committee pay us for putting on street theatre? They have plenty of money and they should pay us something.

Funds are low. We should charge for party for Louise and Ann. €5 each wouldn't kill anybody. No 'do' for self when going to US three years ago.

Committee member: M. Costello

Second signing of minutes.

Personally cleaned up rooms several times. Fed up doing it. No point of cleaning them; all will be in a mess again.

No problem putting on a bit of street theatre. Leixlip did it last year. A bit of mime and dance is all you need.

Of course there should be a party for Louise and Ann – great members. Charging is ridiculous.

Committee member: J. O'Rourke

Tidying up should not be left to secretary. Member of committee should be in charge of rooms.

Why so low in money? Where is all the money we made last year?

Party for Louise and Ann should be paid for out of funds. They deserve it.

Has idea for street theatre. Would like chance to pursue it. Idea still at the gestation stage. Would committee allow him to try to pull something together?

Committee member: P. Murphy

Nothing wrong with rooms. It's the nature of theatre premises to be messy.

Street theatre is not our work. Theatre should be in a theatre. Waste of talent and energy. It is not art. Would certainly not prostitute her own talents on such nonsense.

Parties now at the drop of a hat. In the old days remembers only one party and that to a member of very long standing and very exceptional talent. Did these girls ever act in a real play? Have they just played in what is now called 'pub theatre'? What have they contributed?

REVIEW

1. What is the difference between a notice and an agenda?
2. What is meant by 'clear days'? How are clear days calculated?
3. If you cannot contact someone who is entitled to attend a meeting, what should you, as secretary, do?
4. What is the advantage of sending out an agenda to members before a meeting?
5. Why are the minutes of a meeting read at the following meeting?
6. How and by whom is the agenda drawn up?
7. What is the value of having a secretary's agenda?
8. What is the value of having a chairperson's agenda?
9. What should a chairperson do if a member disagrees with the minutes of the last meeting?
10. What are standing orders?

PITFALLS

its it's

The confusion of these two words is one of the most common errors in English.

Its, without an apostrophe, denotes possession.

Examples

The dog broke *its* leg.

The government at *its* meeting yesterday made the decision.

The class decided in *its* own interest to study hard.

It's is a contraction of *it is*. The *i* of the *is* is omitted and the apostrophe is inserted instead.

Examples

It's a fine day.

It's the best I have ever seen.

It's great to be alive.

CONFUSING WORDS

already	all ready
altogether	all together
appreciable	appreciative
bazaar	bizarre
congenial	congenital

QUIZ

Here is a famous sentence attributed to an Irish politician, Sir Boyle Roche, in 1798:

'I smell a rat; I see it floating in the air, and if it is not nipped in the bud, it will cause a conflagration which will deluge the world.'

Why do you think it is famous?

SPELLINGS

The words most commonly misspelled are highlighted.

label	lantern	ledger
labelling	latitude	legacy
laboratory	laud	**liaison**
labour	laudable	**livelihood**
labourer	laugh	loose
lament	laughter	**lose**
lamentable	laundry	**losing**
landscape	lawyer	**lounge**
language	**league**	**lying**
languid	lecturer	

13

LISTENING

'He's actually a really intelligent person, he's really deep, which I like. He's really frustrated because people think that because he doesn't say a lot he doesn't have a brain.'—Victoria Adams ('Posh Spice') on her husband, David Beckham, quoted in the *Sunday Observer*, 8 August 1999.

'We have two ears and one mouth, that we may listen the more and talk the less.'—Zeno (335–263 BC).

Listening is an essential element of effective communication. However, in our culture more emphasis is placed on the oral aspect of communication. An effective communicator is usually appraised on his or her verbal skills. Listening is an under-rated skill, though it is 50 per cent of the communications process. At best, we hear but we do not listen. Carl Rogers, the humanist psychologist, said: 'Rarely do we listen with real understanding, true empathy. Yet listening, of this very special kind, is one of the most potent forces for change that I know.' Listening with understanding and without pre-judgment is essential in communications, whether it is between parent and child, teacher and student, leader and team member, or manager and staff member.

Listening is part of the perceptual process through which we interpret and make sense of the world around us. When we are sitting quietly listening, we are not passively absorbing sounds but are decoding these messages and putting meaning on them. Like the information coming through the other senses, we have to be selective in what we choose to hear, otherwise we would be bombarded with stimuli.

Although we hear many sounds, we can make sense of and remember only the sounds we attend to. The process of receiving information from the outside world, translating it and transmitting it to the brain is called sensation. The process of interpreting that information and forming ideas about it is called perception. How we make sense of what we hear is a very individual process and depends on past experience, expectations and motivation. Hearing becomes active listening, according to Rogers, when the listener echoes, restates and clarifies.

In the 1970s the Sperry Corporation in the US brought in consultants to help them to deliver a better service to their customers. The consultants found that the typical employee could remember no more than 20 per cent of what he or she had been told twenty-four hours earlier. Even when questioned about material they had just heard, they were likely to get facts mixed up. The management of Sperry decided that improving the listening skills of their customer service representatives was vital. They brought in a team of trainers to develop listening skills. The top management were so impressed with the improvement that they expanded the programme to the whole firm. Today, all Sperry employees attend training workshops to develop their listening skills and they must also attend refresher courses periodically. Now Sperry have even entered the market as a provider of listening skills workshops.

Most people have never practised listening, but it is like any other skill in that if practised, it can be improved. Thomas J. Peters and Robert H. Waterman, in their influential book on management, *In Search of Excellence* (New York: Harper & Row, 1982), identified the ability to listen as one of the keys to success.

In traditional organisations it was assumed that all expertise resided with the top management. Thus, managers issued directives and employees implemented them. In modern firms it is assumed that expertise can be found at all levels. It is not uncommon now to find that new employees have higher educational qualifications than some top managers. Active listening involves not only listening to others, but listening to ourselves. Listening to what we say and how we say it can teach us a great deal about ourselves. Being aware of the statements we make about ourselves and others is a major step towards personal growth and development, and it also makes us aware of our individual filter system, through which incoming information passes. For example, a barrier to effective listening occurs when you hear only what you want to hear or what you expect to hear. Another barrier to listening occurs when you have a negative experience with a person with whom you are communicating.

You can develop your listening skills every day in college by listening attentively to lectures. This can take effort, but in the long run it pays.

Like all skills, listening has to be worked at, and it takes energy. When you are attending a lecture, it is not necessary to take in every word, as this would lead to overload. A more effective way of taking in the message is to focus on the speaker's central ideas. Make meaningful notes of the main points, and review these later on to make sure you understand them. Sit where you can see and hear without distraction – concentrate. In your notes, summarise what the speaker said in your own words.

You cannot listen attentively for long periods. The mind will wander and try to take a rest. Your listening ability will depend on anxiety, tiredness and boredom. We can listen to a stimulating speaker for much longer than to a dull one. We listen attentively for short periods (less than half a minute), and then we process or try to make sense of what we have heard.

Certain factors will affect our listening:

- distractions
- preconceived negative ideas about the speaker
- dull voice or message, or both
- a message we find disturbing and therefore do not want to listen to.

IMPROVING LISTENING

- *Remove as many distractions as possible.* These distractions may consist of music, radio, people talking or traffic. Some distractions perhaps cannot be moved, but even the noise of traffic can be softened by closing a window.

- *Listen actively.* Be alert. When people say their name, listen to it. It is often a good idea to repeat the name to help you remember it.

- *Ask questions.* Ask questions of the speaker every now and then. If the speaker in some formal situation is not taking questions until the end, form questions quickly in your mind as you listen.

- *Watch non-verbal elements.* People communicate by voice but they also communicate by posture, gesture and facial expressions. Listen to the tone of voice used. We should listen with our eyes as well as with our ears.

- *Listen objectively.* Try not to allow your personal feelings to prevent you giving the speaker a chance. If you are not favourably disposed towards the speaker, you are then obliged to try harder to listen objectively. It is easy to listen to people we agree with. Good listeners are able to listen to those with whom they disagree.

- *Withhold judgment.* Hear the speaker out and do not make up your mind immediately. You have not heard the full story until the speaker is finished. First judgments are difficult to change, so you should not jump to them too quickly.

Essential points on listening

- Listening is a very important skill.
- Many people do not listen well.
- Effective listening requires active listening.
- It is important to ask questions.
- Listening is different from hearing.

LISTENING SKILLS ACTIVITY

(Taken from Morley et al., Principles of Organisational Behaviour, *Dublin: Gill & Macmillan, 1998, pp. 119–20.)*

Good listening skills are essential for effective communication and are often overlooked when communication is analysed. This self-assessment questionnaire examines your ability to listen effectively. Work through the following statements, marking 'Yes' or 'No' in the space next to each one. Mark each statement as truthfully as you can in the light of your behaviour in the last few gatherings or meetings you have attended.

	Yes	No
1. I frequently attempt to listen to several conversations at the same time.	—	—
2. I like people to give me the facts and then let me make my own interpretation.	—	—
3. I sometimes pretend to pay attention to people.	—	—
4. I consider myself a good judge of non-verbal communications.	—	—
5. I usually know what another person is going to say before he or she says it.	—	—
6. I usually end conversations that don't interest me by diverting my attention from the speaker.	—	—
7. I frequently nod, frown or in some other way let the speaker know how I feel about what he or she is saying.	—	—
8. I usually respond immediately when someone has finished talking.	—	—
9. I evaluate what is being said while it is being said.	—	—
10. I usually formulate a response while the other person is still talking.	—	—

11. *The speaker's 'delivery' style frequently keeps me from listening to content.*   —   —

12. *I usually ask people to clarify what they have said rather than guess at the meaning.*   —   —

13. *I make a concerted effort to understand other people's point of view.*   —   —

14. *I frequently hear what I expect to hear rather than what is said.*   —   —

15. *Most people feel that I have understood their point of view when we disagree.*   —   —

Scoring: *The correct answers according to communication theory are as follows:*

No for statements 1, 2, 3, 5, 6, 7, 8, 9, 10, 11, 14.

Yes for statements 4, 12, 13, 15.

If you missed only one or two responses, you strongly approve of your own listening habits, and you are on the right track to becoming an effective listener. If you missed three or four responses, you have uncovered some doubts about your listening effectiveness, and your knowledge of how to listen has some gaps. If you missed five or more responses, you are probably not satisfied with the way you listen, and your friends and co-workers may not feel you are a good listener either. Work on improving your active listening skills.

GROUP ACTIVITY

1. *Think of a person who you consider an effective listener. What makes them an effective listener? How do you feel when you talk to this person?*

2. *Tell one member of the class the following message. 'The end-of-term test will be given on Thursday, unless the preceding Tuesday is a holiday, in which case the test will be on the following Monday. It will take place in the Seminar Room in the Barrow Centre at 9.30 and will cover the first seven chapters of the text.'*

   Exercise: *Now have each member of the class relay the message one at a time to each other so that the others cannot hear it. The last member of the class to hear the message should write it down. Then compare this with the original version to see how much of the message was lost.*

3. *Tell one member of the class the following message. 'The new prospectus is almost ready but there is a little difficulty with the cover. The colour separations have not worked out as well as we hoped for and will have to be done again. It will have to be taken to Dublin but there will be no extra cost involved. One of the colour pictures, the one on page three, is blurred and will not be used at all. The*

prospectuses will be ready on Wednesday but the first 1,000 will have a cover that is not as good as it should be. The rest of the run will have a perfect cover. They will be delivered on Tuesday night by courier. The printers will pay the courier. The error in the map on page seven has been corrected. Posters to go with the prospectus will be ready on Thursday.'

Exercise: *Now have each member of the class relay the message one at a time to each other so that the others cannot hear it. The last member of the class to hear the message should write it down. Then compare this with the original version to see how much of the message was lost.*

REVIEW

1. Explain the importance of listening in an organisation.

2. What is active listening?

3. Explain the difference between hearing and listening.

4. Discuss the factors which affect listening.

5. How can listening be improved?

PITFALLS

The problem of the unattached or dangling participle is common, e.g. 'Having received your letter, it will be answered today.' The participle *having received* has no corresponding subject (noun or pronoun). 'Sitting within my orchard, a serpent stung me,' says the ghost of Hamlet's father to a surprised Hamlet. It would seem from this that it was the serpent, and not Hamlet's father in the flesh, who was sitting in the garden. If care is not taken to attach a participle to a noun or pronoun, we may have absurd sentences like the following: 'While writing this, the telephone rang.'

CONFUSING WORDS

contemptible	contemptuous	dessert	desert
council	counsel	disease	decease
credible	credulous	emaciated	emancipated
decent	descent	eminent	imminent
device	devise	equable	equitable

QUIZ

Can you form ten words from the word BRANDY? The new words need not contain all the letters of the word BRANDY.

SPELLINGS

The words most commonly misspelled are highlighted.

magician	margarine	mechanic
magnetise	**marriage**	**medicine**
magnetism	martial	**Mediterranean**
magnificence	martyr	melancholy
maintain	martyrdom	melodious
maintenance	marvel	merciless
majority	massacre	metropolis
management	mathematics	microphone
maniac	meagre	migrate
manoeuvre	meagrely	militarism
manufacture	measurement	millionaire

4

PART

RESEARCH

SKILLS

14

BASIC SOURCES OF INFORMATION

INTRODUCTION

As a person working in business, there are certain books and websites you will need to access on a regular basis. No one is capable of spelling all the words in the English language, so a dictionary is of vital importance. Dictionaries have fallen in use with the increased use of new technology in the office and the advent of the spellchecker facility in word processing packages.

DICTIONARY

Always have a dictionary available to you at work. Read the introduction to your dictionary and it will tell you how to use it. Even the smallest dictionary will indicate the spelling, pronunciation, meaning and grammatical function of words. It also explains abbreviations, foreign words and phrases in common use, and some will also give synonyms and antonyms. The last two items mentioned will be explained later in this chapter.

Word processing programs now usually provide a spelling check, grammar check and thesaurus. These are useful but should not be relied on completely, as the spellings are often those of American English.

ACTIVITY 1

Read the introduction to your dictionary and it will tell you, for example, how its entries are arranged, what type of pronunciation it is putting forward and the conventions it is following in spellings.

In the extract from The Concise Oxford Dictionary *(8th edition, 1990), it can be seen that the word **business** can be used in several senses. The pronunciation of the word is given, as is its part of speech. The formal meanings of the word 'business' are given as well as its use as a colloquial term.*

business /'biznis/ *n.* **1** one's regular occupation, profession, or trade. **2** a thing that is one's concern. **3 a** a task or duty. **b** a reason for coming (*what is your business?*). **4** serious work or activity (*get down to business*). **5** *derog.* **a** an affair, a matter (*sick of the whole business*). **b** a structure (*a lath-and-plaster business*). **6** a thing or series of things needing to be dealt with (*the business of the day*). **7** buying and selling; trade (*good stroke of business*). **8** a commercial house or firm. **9** *Theatr.* action on stage. **10** a difficult matter (*what a business it is!; made a great business of it*).

business card a card printed with one's name and professional details. **the business end** *colloq.* the functional part of a tool or device. **business park** an area designed to accommodate businesses and light industry. **business person** a businessman or businesswoman. **business studies** training in economics, management, etc. **has no business to** has no right to. **in business 1** trading or dealing. **2** able to begin operations. **in the business of 1** engaged in. **2** intending to (*we are not in the business of surrendering*). **like nobody's business** *colloq.* extraordinarily. **make it one's business to** undertake to. **mind one's own business** not meddle. **on business** with a definite purpose, esp. one relating to one's regular occupation. **send a person about his** or **her business** dismiss a person; send a person away. [OE *bisignis* (as BUSY, -NESS)]

ACTIVITY **2**

1. *An American president once said, 'The business of America is business.' Explain the senses in which he used the word.*

2. *Find the meaning of the following words in your dictionary.*

   dyslexia ....

   expletive ....

   banal...

   bizarre ....

   obdurate..

   obeisance..

   paean...

   purblind ....

   ingot ....

   mayhem ....

   polyglot ....

3. Find the following in your dictionary.

Monetary unit in Argentina ....

Monetary unit in Israel ....

Monetary unit in Denmark ....

First letter of Greek alphabet ....

Last letter of Greek alphabet ....

Number of millimetres in one inch ....

Number of kilometres in a mile ....

What is a peck? ....

Number of acres in one square mile ....

Number of yards in one mil ....

PRONUNCIATION

Most dictionaries will give you an indication of how words are pronounced. A dictionary can only give you an accepted pronunciation. It is very unlikely that there is any word that has only one pronunciation. English is a living language which is growing and changing, and the world itself would be a very dull place if everyone pronounced every word in exactly the same manner. Sometimes your dictionary will give more than one pronunciation.

ACTIVITY 3

1. Find out how your dictionary suggests that the following words should be pronounced and write the pronunciation in the space provided.

temporary	Thomas ....
veterinary	Thames ....
controversy	Tipperary ....
February	supple ....
Wednesday	garage ....
implement	object ....
conduit	insult ....

2. Form small groups and make a list of ten words that are pronounced in different ways in different parts of the country.

THESAURUS

As well as a dictionary, you should also have a thesaurus available to you at work. It will help you use the correct word for every occasion. If you use the same word again and again in a short document it can lead to boredom, so a thesaurus is necessary to allow you to add variety to your writing.

A thesaurus groups words which are related or which have similar meanings. An index at the back of the thesaurus guides you to the right group of words. Suppose you want to find a short or different way to describe the sort of loan that helps a person buy a house. First you look up the word *loan* in the index of the thesaurus. In the index to *Roget's Thesaurus* (London: Longmans, 1966), you will find the following:

Loan	lending 784n
	borrowing 785n

The number is not a page reference; it is the number of a particular entry in the thesaurus. The 'n' for noun after the reference indicates that in both these instances the equivalent nouns for *lending* and *borrowing* are listed. Since you are looking for a word to express the idea of a 'loan' in the context of borrowing for house purchase, you must turn to reference 785 in the thesaurus. There, you will find the following:

785. Borrowing – N. *borrowing*, request for credit, loan application; loan transaction, mortgage 803 n. *debt*; hire purchase, never-never system; pledging, pawning; loan, repayable amount, debenture 784 n. *lending*; infringement, plagiarism, copying 20 n. *imitation*.

Vb. *borrow*, touch for; mortgage, pawn, pledge, pop, hock; get credit, take on loan, take on tick; hire-purchase 792 vb. *purchase*; run into debt 803 vb. *be in debt*; promise to pay, float a loan; invite investment, accept deposits; borrow, or steal; plagiarize, infringe 20 vb. *copy*.

hire, rent, farm, lease, take on lease, take on let, charter.

The word you require is *mortgage*.

SYNONYMS

A synonym is a word that is similar in meaning to another word, e.g. cold/chilly, big/large, small/tiny.

ACTIVITY 4

Write synonyms for the words listed below in the spaces provided. The first letter of each word is given to help you.

mysterious	s	cold	i ....
profit	g	hard	s ....
harsh	c	youth	a ....
evil	m	girl	c ....
stay	r	nest	h ....
difficult	c	question	q ....
unbelievable	i	inflame	a ....
anger	i	ignite	l ....
coarse	r	liberal	f ....
desire	w	net	r ....
clear	t	change	a ....
proud	h	see	p ....
reveal	d	shout	h ....
potent	p	remedy	c ....
forbid	d	position	s ....
yearly	a	puzzling	b ....
tedium	b	terrible	a ....
fat	o	throw	f ....
disaster	c	try	a ....
wealth	a	hide	c ....
dark	d	jovial	h ....
courtesy	m	journey	t ....

ANTONYMS

Words of opposite meaning are called antonyms, e.g. good/bad, clean/dirty, big/small.

ACTIVITY 5

Write antonyms for the words below in the spaces provided. The first letter of each word is given to help you.

leave	a	abstain	i ....
wicked	g	betray	p ....
abandon	s	benefit	l ....
hate	l	defeat	v ....
stay	g	defer	e ....
cleverness	s	definite	i ....

shout	w	hardy	w ....
beautiful	u	heavy	l ....
question	a	hide	e ....
excellent	t	high	l ....
blame	p	insipid	t ....
certain	u	inspire	d ....
deep	s	intellectual	u ....
respect	d	painstaking	c ....
clear	c	principal	i ....
scatter	g	probable	u ....
abbreviate	l	reckless	c ....
abhor	e	raw	c ....
ability	i	silly	w ....
stand	s	absent	p ....

HOMONYMS

Words that sound alike but are spelled differently and have different meanings are called homonyms, e.g. hair/hare, knows/nose, alter/altar.

ACTIVITY 6

Find homonyms for the following words.

air	....	aisle	....
all	....	aloud	....
arc	....	bail	....
bard	....	beach	....
bear	....	calendar	....
elude	....	ewe	....
eye	....	sail	....
scene	....	stair	....
sum	....	sun	....

IPA *YEARBOOK & DIARY*

Very often in the course of your work you will need to know the names, addresses and secretaries of various organisations or who is the chairperson of a certain company. The Institute of Public Administration

(IPA) *Yearbook & Diary* will answer all these questions and every business should have at least one copy.

The IPA *Yearbook* is very useful for anyone working in Irish business. This yearbook is a comprehensive directory of Irish life, covering the private as well as the public sector. Its information ranges from county councils to embassies; private companies to government departments; religious orders to youth organisations; statistics on agriculture, industry and population to holidays in EU member states. It is issued yearly and is constantly updated. It may be somewhat expensive for a student, but if you go along to some company one of the managers will probably give you an old copy and this will do you for the present. Much of the information would not change from year to year. However, at work you would need an up-to-date copy.

ACTIVITY 7

Using the IPA Yearbook & Diary, find the following information.

1. The population of Munster ....
2. The population of Leinster ....
3. The percentage of the population aged between 0 and 14
    in Ireland ....
    in Belgium ....
    in Germany ....
    in the UK ....
4. The number of
    males in third-level education...
    females in third-level education ....
5. The value of dairy products in Ireland ....
6. The number of people in Ireland employed
    in public health services ....
    in agriculture ....
7. Who is the County Manager in Westmeath? ....
8. What is the address of the Censorship of Publications Board? ....
    ....
9. How many kilometres is it from
    Athlone to Cavan? ....
    Clonmel to Wexford? ....
    Dublin to Derry? ....
    Waterford to Tullamore? ....
    Ennis to Ballina? ....
    Sligo to Dublin? ....

Tralee to Cork? ....

Letterkenny to Dundalk? ....

10. What is the stamp duty for a first-time buyer on a property of €190,500?
....

11. If it is 10.00 a.m. in Ireland, what time is it in

Paris? ....

Athens? ....

Madrid? ....

Bonn? ....

New York? ....

Singapore? ....

Seoul? ....

Tokyo? ....

Calcutta? ....

12. Who is the Minister for Education and Science? ....

AN POST SERVICES

Despite the growing use of e-mail and mobile telephones, there is still a need to use the services of An Post. It may be your task at work to deal with the post, so you must be aware of the various costs charged by the post office and the variety of services available.

Full details of all services available from An Post may be obtained by contacting your local head post office or the GPO, Dublin. Full details can also be obtained by accessing www.anpost.ie.

WORDGLOSS

Another book which would be useful is *Wordgloss* by Jim O'Donnell, published by the Institute of Public Administration in 1990. It gives definitions and uses of words and terms used in common speech and which speakers rarely define. Such terms include *laissez-faire*, a draconian measure, forensic evidence, *caveat emptor* and caucus.

ACTIVITY 8

Use Wordgloss to find the meaning of the following:

balance of payments, carpet-bagger, charisma, primus inter pares, codicil, compos mentis, cornucopia, Delphic, demagogue, fiscal rectitude, lobby, maverick, parochialism, prolific, separation of powers, sinecure, white paper.

REVIEW

1. Use your dictionary to find the origin of the following words: argue, bikini, bilingual, bomb, cholesterol, courier, bank, knave, leaflet, previous.

2. Find all the possible synonyms for the following words: girl, boy, student, business, children, parent, secretary, bold, fastidious, discreet, hinder, summary, compute, teacher.

3. How many public holidays are there each year in the Republic of Ireland and how are their dates determined?

4. What services does An Post offer their businesss clients?

5. What is the difference between Swiftpost and registered post? If you were sending an important document, which would you use?

PITFALLS

less fewer

Less and *fewer* are often confused. *Less* is used to denote quantity, and *fewer* to denote number. For example:

'*Fewer* people than usual attended the seminar.'

'There was *less* snow this year than last year.'

CONFUSING WORDS

formally	formerly	elicit	illicit
infer	imply	envelop	envelope
flair	flare	bought	brought
border	boarder	cannon	canon
cash	cache	cast	caste

QUIZ

It is sometimes possible to take a line of poetry and add a second line which makes the two together amusing. For example:

'I think that I shall never see –

My contact lens fell in my tea.'

Could you add an amusing line to the following?

'When lovely women stoop to folly,

_____ .'

SPELLINGS

The words most commonly misspelled are highlighted.

narrate
narration
narrative
national
nationalism
naughty
navies
navy
necessarily
necessary

necessity
negative
neglect
negligence
negligible
negotiable
negotiate
neighbour
nephew
nervous

niece
notice
noticeable
notification
notify
nourish
novelty
nuisance
numerous
nymph

15

BASIC RESEARCH

INTRODUCTION

Undertaking research for any piece of work is a daunting task. Whether it is searching for material for an assignment for college, undertaking an investigation into the options available to a company changing its suppliers or preparing a proposal for a client, people often ask 'Where do I start?'

'Where can I find...?' This question is asked constantly at work. A good employee needs to be able to find information quickly and accurately. Good decisions are based on good information.

In undertaking research for college or completing a task allocated to you by your manager, it is important to devise a timeframe, taking careful note of the deadline the work must be submitted by. Allow enough time for last-minutes hitches, including printing problems. *Always* make a back-up copy of your work and where you found the information.

SELECTING THE TOPIC

When faced with an essay title, assignment topic or project, students often wonder where to start. It is vitally important to prepare a clear structure of what you envisage as the finished piece of work. In order to write about the material and conduct your research, you need to systematically tackle the topic. Break down the topic into areas, prepare a mind map or just brainstorm and see what ideas you come up with.

Once you have a clear vision of what areas are to be covered in your assignment, it is time to tackle the research. Faced with the prospect of looking for material on a topic which you may never have researched before, the first and final stop for many students is the internet. However, keep in mind that while it is a good starting point, it should not be your only source.

WHY RESEARCH?

Properly conducted research should produce a variety of sources. Using more than one source allows you to support or challenge the topic you are writing about. In addition, it is important to reference material to show that there is some substance to your arguments or viewpoints.

PLAGIARISM

Presenting material taken from books or the internet as your own is plagiarism and is a serious breach of copyright and academic procedures. Students are often concerned about using material they have gathered. There is no need to worry as long as you acknowledge your source and use quoted material sparingly, allowing for your own words and opinions to come through.

PLANNING THE RESEARCH

In undertaking your research, you should plan it as carefully as the final outline of the assignment. The next step is deciding on what sources to use. There are many sources available to students, yet many fail to look beyond the internet. In this chapter we are going to examine a variety of sources available.

Vast amounts of information are available online. So much information is available that we can tend to be overwhelmed with websites, books, newspapers and periodicals.

Allow plenty of time to complete your research, as there may be books in the library which are out on loan, or you may need to avail of the interlibrary loan facility. If you are depending on other people, always bear in mind that they may not be available when you want them to be.

Some types of information are more difficult to find than others, e.g. information about the future always presents a difficulty. How many babies will be born between 2005 and 2010? Nobody knows with certainty, but estimates must be made. The government must plan for crèche facilities, school buildings and local amenities.

Stages in the research project
- Devise a timeframe.
- Identify the topic and its various components.
- Break down the topic. Brainstorm and note all the issues which may be relevant to the topic.
- Identify the research techniques you wish to use.

- Identify where you may access relevant material.
- Find your source material.
- Access the material.
- Analyse the material you gather.
- Select relevant quotes you wish to include.
- Use quotes, acknowledging the source.

SOURCES OF INFORMATION

The library

The local library is generally the first source of information. The librarian will explain the types of information available and the classification system.

The Business Information Centre, Ilac Centre, Henry St, Dublin 1 is of particular interest to people being trained for business positions, as this centre caters for the needs of business and industry. The Business Information Centre is a reference service specialising in company and market information. It is operated by Dublin City Public Libraries. The centre holds books, directories, Irish government legislation, business magazines, databases, newspaper cuttings (from the late 1970s on) and has a collection of Irish company reports. Items cannot be borrowed. Photocopying and printing facilities (where applicable) are available, though note that the Copyright and Related Rights Act 2000 applies. Further information about libraries in the Dublin area can be accessed at www.dublincity.ie/living_in_the_city/libraries.

A useful tool is the Dublin City Public Libraries' Online Catalogue, which lists all items in the Dublin City Public Libraries system. The catalogue enables you to check which libraries an item is held in and see if the item is currently available to borrow, is reserved or is for reference use only.

The catalogue can be searched by author, title or keyword. It can be accessed at http://libcat.dublincity.ie/dublinc/catalogue/home-frame.form.

A list of all registered libraries, both public and private, can be obtained on the library associations' website. It can be accessed via their website at www.libraryassociation.ie.

CATALOGUES ONLINE: IRELAND AND WORLDWIDE

- Irish public library catalogues online: www.library.ie/public/index.shtml
- Ireland online catalogues: www.libdex.com/country/Ireland.html

- British Library catalogues on the web, including access to the Integrated Catalogue, the main catalogue containing records for over 12 million books, serials, printed music and maps: www.bl.uk/catalogues/listings.html
- Library of Congress Online Catalog: the Library of Congress Online Catalog contains approximately 12 million records representing books, serials, computer files, manuscripts, cartographic materials, music, sound recordings and visual materials at http://catalog.loc.gov/
- Worldwide index of library catalogues and websites: www.libdex.com/country.html

ACTIVITY I

1. What is the library classification number given to computers?

2. Who wrote the book The Past is Myself?

3. List five different facilities which your local library offers.

4. List ten periodicals taken by your local library.

5. Find two books in your local library about the Spanish Civil War. Write down the title, author, date of publication and classification of each book.

6. Name two books under the following classifications: 826, 350.8, 651.78, 823.8.

7. What classifications are used for the following subjects: communications, speech, plastics, shorthand?

8. Go to the reference section of your local library and write down the titles of two reference books.

9. What books do you have in your local library by the following authors: W. B. Yeats, Peter Drucker, Garret FitzGerald, T. S. Eliot, Charles McCarthy?

10. Write down the titles of two magazines of business interest which your local library stocks. Find out from the librarian how back issues are stored.

11. What classification would the following books receive: The Tools of Social Science, The Concise Oxford Dictionary, Writing the Executive Report, Modern Irish Poetry, English and Communications for Business Students?

12. Does your local library stock tapes, cassettes, slides and videos?

13. Who is the editor of The Sunday Tribune?

14. Does your library have a book written by Ernest Gowers?

15. Who was Taoiseach in 1973?

NEWSPAPERS

Many newspapers now have their own websites which offer a search facility of past issues. Past issues not accessible on the website may be accessed on microfilm in their offices. Newspapers and magazines often have an advantage over books in that they tend to be more up to date. However, many articles are opinion pieces and as such should be treated with caution, as they express the views of the writer.

The following are some useful newspaper websites. Some may require registration and a fee to access some services. Others are free. The following are the most popular Irish newspaper websites:

Irish Times	www.ireland.com
Independent Newspapers	www.unison.ie
Examiner	www.examiner.ie
Sunday Business Post	www.sbpost.ie
Sunday Tribune	www.tribune.ie

Local newspapers often have their own website. In addition, many are listed on the *Irish Independent* website (www.unison.ie).

When using material from newspapers, it is important to note the date of the article or news report and check whether there have been any new developments since that date. For example, your research on the private security industry on *The Irish Times* website may produce a display of reports on the reading of the first stage of the Private Security Bill; however, it is important to view all the results concerning this topic, as the Bill became law at a later date.

REFERENCE BOOKS

In addition to the books mentioned in Chapter 14, there are many other sources of information you should be aware of. A good starting point is an encyclopaedia such as the *Encyclopaedia Britannica*. This will usually give you a good introduction to the subject and refer you to other books. *Encyclopaedia Britannica* is now available on two CDs, which means that it is easy to search for any type of information you need. It is also available on the internet. The following reference material is particularly useful and will probably be available in your local library:

- *Books in Print* is published annually by Bowker and details all books in print in the US.
- *British Standards Institution Catalogue*, a CD that can be used to search for details of all British standards. Though of use to all disci-

plines, it is of particular use in the areas of construction, engineering and design.

- *Guide to Current British Journals*, David Woodworth, 4th edition, Library Association, 1986.
- *Guide to Reference Material*, A. J. Walford (ed.), Library Association (3 vols.); vol. 1, Science and Technology (1996); vol. 2, Social and Historical Sciences (1998); vol. 3, Generalities, Language, Arts and Literature (1995).
- *Whitaker's Almanack*, first published in 1899, presents information about public affairs, government, industry, finance, commerce and the arts in Britain (published annually).
- *Factfinder Irish Business*, a CD that contains five different databases: (1) the full text of *Business and Finance* and twenty-five other business and marketing journals; (2) abstracts of the business pages of the national newspapers; (3) an overview of the top 4,000 Irish companies; (4) a database on doing business in Ireland; and (5) research reports on trends in various sectors of business. This CD is updated twice yearly and is fully searchable and printable.
- *Oxford Reference Shelf*, a CD containing the equivalent of a shelf of sixteen books. It contains *The Pocket Oxford Dictionary, The Oxford Dictionary for Writers and Editors, The Oxford Guide to English Usage, The Oxford Minidictionary of Quotations, A Compact Encyclopedia, A Concise Dictionary of Business, A Concise Dictionary of Law*, etc.
- *Sources of Economic Information—Ireland* (2nd edition), Institute of Public Administration, 1999.

THE INTERNET

The internet is one of the fastest-growing methods of communication in the world. E-mail and the World Wide Web are the most familiar elements of the internet. Each source of information on the World Wide Web is referred to as a website. Web addresses usually begin with 'www'. In this chapter we are going to examine the web as a source of information and method of research. In Chapter 20, the internet and other emerging technology will be explored in more depth. At this point it is only necessary to understand the value of the internet as a source of information.

Using the search facility on the World Wide Web, you can search for any topic by typing in a word or group of words. If that topic is listed on any site on the web, then you will get a listing of the sites.

Anyone with access to the internet can post websites about topics that interest them. These sites are not always accurate. Researchers should check the age of the information provided on a website. It may have been set up recently or have been in existence for a long period of time. The website itself may also not be updated on a regular basis and may contain inaccurate information. It is important that all information is checked for authenticity, bias and can be verified.

There are many points of entry to web resources, but search tools differ. Some of the information you may find may be too broad for your needs and you may have to refine your search to find the precise details you are seeking. For example, if you type the word 'Ireland' in your search you will find over 352 million results.

Using a search tool

Most internet users are familiar with search tools such as Yahoo!, MSN, Google and Ask Jeeves. There are literally dozens of these sites to help you locate what you are looking for. It is important that you understand how they work so that you can use the right search tool and site and analyse the results it presents to you.

Websites tend to change often. Older versions may still exist when the company adopts a new name or changes their website address. These changes are not always reflected in the search engine database. Typically, websites are registered with search engines when they first go online. After that, changes are not generally reported. The result may be that a link from a search engine to a particular website is no longer valid.

All search tools are not alike. Each uses a slightly different methodology, so your results will vary. You may not always find what you are looking for on the first try.

Search engines can be divided into two categories: directories and indexes. Directories are good at identifying general information. The results of your search will be a list of websites related to your search term. For more specific information, you should use a web index, because they search all the contents of a website.

The most popular search tools on the net are:

Google	www.google.ie	www.google.com
Yahoo!	www.yahoo.co.uk	www.yahoo.com
MSN Search	www.msn.com	www.msn.co.uk
Ask Jeeves	www.ask.com	

Each search engine is slightly different from the others, but they all have frequently asked questions (FAQs) or instructions that explain how that specific site works. Taking a few minutes to read these FAQs before you start searching will save you time later on.

It is important to clearly and concisely define the topic you are seeking information on. If you are seeking information on engineering, then it may be more relevant to decide whether it is civil or mechanical engineering that you wish to obtain information on as opposed to the general term 'engineering'. If you use broad or general terms, your search will return thousands of possible sites. Try to use terms that are more specific to your topic.

For example, if you type in 'Ireland' on the Yahoo! website, you will find over 352 million websites. Many of them are irrelevant and may refer to books referring to Ireland which are for sale on Amazon.com. You may also have sites for people whose last name is Ireland. If you want your search engine to search for an exact phrase, put quotation marks around the phrase, e.g. 'Mullingar'.

In the case of 'Mullingar' and 'Ireland' we combined terms, using Boolean operators. Boolean operators are words that allow you to combine search terms in most search engines:

- *AND*: AND tells the search engine to find both terms on the same site. For instance, entering 'Cavan and education' would instruct the search engine to find web pages that contain both words.

- *OR*: OR instructs the search engine to find one term or the other. Entering 'Cavan or education' would cause the search engine to look for web pages that contain either word but not necessarily both words. Using OR results in the search engine returning thousands of sites. OR is most useful when the same term may appear in two different ways. For instance, you could use 'the Gaelic Athletic Association or GAA' to find web pages about the Gaelic Athletic Association.

- *NOT*: NOT tells the search engine to find pages that contain the first word but not the second. This limitation is helpful when you know your search term is likely to appear with another term that does not interest you.

YEARBOOKS AND DIRECTORIES

- *Administration Yearbook & Diary*, see Chapter 14.
- *CIF Directory and Diary:* directory of the construction industry.
- *Student Yearbook and Careers Directory.*

Several other yearbooks and directories are published, and the Business Information Centre in the Ilac Centre will have them in stock.

JOURNALS/PERIODICALS

- *Accounting Ireland* (bimonthly): journal of the Institute of Chartered Accountants.
- *Books Ireland* (monthly, except January, July and August): provides news on books and libraries.
- *Checkout Magazine* (monthly): information on the food trade in Ireland.
- *Engineers Journal* (monthly): official journal of the Institution of Engineers of Ireland.
- *Industrial Relations News* (weekly): provides coverage of industrial relations issues.
- *Inside Business* (bimonthly): magazine of Chambers of Commerce of Ireland.
- *Iris Oifigiúil* (twice-weekly): gives details of Acts passed and official orders being enforced.
- *Irish Banking Review* (quarterly): review of economic trends.
- *Statistical Bulletin* (quarterly): contains information collected by the Central Statistics Office.
- *Trade Statistics* (monthly): up-to-date statistics on trade.
- *Consumer Choice* (monthly): consumer magazine.

ORGANISATIONS

Organisations such as government departments, local authorities, semi-state bodies, companies, trade and other professional organisations are usually very helpful in providing information. You should contact them in good time by writing to the information officer or other relevant person.

Government departments

Government departments are valuable sources of information. Address your query to the minister or to the secretary of the appropriate department. If information is urgently required, a local TD may be able to speed up the matter.

Embassies

Embassies and cultural institutions are good sources of information. Most of them have websites.

European Union

The European Union maintains offices in each of its member states and these are a valuable source of information. The European Commission has an office in Dublin, as does the European Parliament. Direct your enquiries to the head of information.

Local administration

Sources of information under this heading include:

- *Local authorities*: urban councils, county councils, corporations, town commissioners.
- *Vocational education committees*: there are thirty-three such committees and they provide and manage community colleges and vocational schools.
- *'Leader' Groups*: the function of 'Leader' is to make funding available to rural groups to implement a business plan.
- *County enterprise boards*: they foster economic development in the various counties.
- *Central and regional fisheries boards*: there are seven regional fisheries boards.
- *Harbour authorities*: these are responsible for the operation and maintenance of their harbours.

State-sponsored bodies

State-sponsored bodies can be divided into five categories according to the nature of their work:

- commercial, e.g. ESB
- developmental, e.g. Fáilte Ireland
- health, e.g. Comhairle na nOspidéal
- cultural, e.g. RTÉ
- regulatory/advisory, e.g. National Economic and Social Council.

Financial institutions

Financial institutions in Ireland can be divided into the following:

- Central Bank
- Associated banks, e.g. AIB, Bank of Ireland
- non-Associated banks
- hire purchase finance institutions
- building societies
- insurance companies
- venture capital institutions
- credit card companies
- stockbrokers
- European Union financial institutions

- International Financial Services Centre.

Major companies and co-operatives

Most companies, both public and private, will be willing to help you with research. Address your letter to the personnel officer or the public relations officer. Information on companies may be obtained from the Companies Office in Dublin Castle.

Trade, professional and other organisations

The following are just some of the organisations which would provide business-related information:

- *Chambers of commerce*: most towns have a chamber of commerce which provides useful local business information.
- *Trade unions*: these are always a good source of information on employees' attitudes, levels of employment, wages and working conditions. For information of a broader nature, contact the Irish Congress of Trade Unions.
- *Irish Business and Employers' Confederation (IBEC)*: represents industry in all matters.
- *Institute of Public Administration*: provides training, education and research as well as publishing books and periodicals dealing with Irish government.
- *Irish Management Institute*: provides a comprehensive programme of management development and training. It holds conferences, seminars and publishes books. It is a very useful source of information on Irish business.
- *Credit unions*: an excellent source of information on people's spending habits.
- *Irish Farmers' Association*: will supply information on agriculture.
- *Irish Creamery Milk Suppliers' Association*: will also supply information on agriculture.
- *Irish Countrywomen's Association*: particularly valuable for local information. Records have been well preserved by this organisation and would be very useful in researching women's attitudes during various times in the twentieth century.

Social, cultural and political organisations

May be divided into the following:

- health organisations, e.g. Asthma Society, Coeliac Society

- Irish language associations, e.g. Comhaltas Ceoltóirí Éireann, Cumann na bhFiann
- political parties, e.g. Fianna Fáil, Fine Gael, Labour, Progressive Democrats, Green Party
- youth organisations, e.g. National Federation of Youth Clubs, Foróige
- other social, cultural and political interest groups, e.g. ACRA (Central Body for Residents' Associations), Consumers' Association of Ireland, GAA, IRFU, FAI, Royal Dublin Society (RDS), Royal Irish Academy.

INTERVIEWS

When the object of research is to gauge attitudes or to collect opinions, then interviewing knowledgeable and interested persons is an appropriate procedure. Information gathered in this way, however, must be cautiously sifted.

It should always be remembered that people have a tendency to tell an interviewer what they think the interviewer wants to hear. However, interviews have the following advantages over questionnaires:

- People often enjoy being interviewed, while filling in a questionnaire is considered a chore.
- If a response needs to be clarified, it can be done immediately.
- A person's behaviour or attitude can be observed during an interview, and this can often convey useful information.

However, in an interview a person needs to be aware of factors which may distort the information:

- the tendency to find what one wishes to find
- intrusion of interviewer, who may interpret the information given on the basis of personal experience
- tendency of interviewed person to modify her ideas and behaviour to meet the known expectations of the interviewer.

This type of interview demands careful planning. The following steps should be taken:

- write to person concerned requesting an interview
- give full details of purpose, format and approximate duration of interview
- give outline of areas to be covered
- request permission to tape the interview if necessary

When conducting an interview you must have some means of recording responses if you are not using a tape recorder. The usual method is to have a form where the responses can be recorded easily.

FIG. I — SAMPLE INTERVIEW FORM

Name of interviewee: _____ Position: _____

Place of interview: _____ Date: _____

Time begun: _____ Ended: _____

Number of people employed: _____ Men _____Women   Total: _____

Comments:_____

_____

_____

Number of employees who left in 2004: ___ Men _____ Women Total: _____

Comments:_____

_____

_____

_____

Reasons for leaving: _____ Retirement _____ Going to other jobs

_____ Not happy _____Dismissed _____ Other

Comments:_____

_____

_____

_____

Reasons for dismissal: _____ Sub-standard work _____ Poor attendance

_____Dispute _____ Other

Comments:_____

_____

_____

QUESTIONNAIRES

Where information of a statistical nature is required, a questionnaire will be useful. The advantages of using a questionnaire for gathering information are:

- it is capable of reaching a large audience
- the same questions are asked of each person
- questions are asked in the same order
- answers are easy to tabulate.

The disadvantages are:

- person may misunderstand the question
- person may not return questionnaire at all
- person may return an incomplete questionnaire.

Points to remember

- The objectives of the questionnaire should be absolutely clear.
- A pilot survey of a number of respondents should be undertaken.
- Talk the questionnaire through with a potential or typical respondent.

Parts of a formal questionnaire

There are normally four main parts in a formal questionnaire. Each part contains specific information.

1. Identification of survey

This section should include the survey title and, where appropriate, the name of the company and the identity of the interviewer.

2. Identification of the respondent

The rank and status of the respondent; it does not necessarily mean the name of the respondent.

3. Control questions

Control questions are designed to determine whether or not the respondent is giving consistent answers. The most common devices are (a) asking questions twice in different parts of the questionnaire and (b) inserting bogus options in the questionnaire that would deceive an unknowledgeable respondent.

4. The survey questions

This is the main part of the questionnaire. Consideration here must be given to the length of the questionnaire and to the necessity for instructions.

Types of questions

There are four types of questions that can be asked on a questionnaire.

1. Dichotomous questions

These are the simplest of the questions to ask, as they are designed to be answered in only one of two possible ways.

    Do you smoke? Yes ☐   No ☐

These questions are easy to ask, answer and analyse.

2. Multi-choice questions

Respondents are able to choose from a range of possible answers. Often an option you have never considered emerges, so it is a good idea to include 'Other (please specify)' as one of the options.

    You bought your trailer from

a manufacturer	
a merchant	
an importer	
a second-hand centre	

       other (please name) ....

3. Open-ended questions

These questions, also known as free-answer or free-response questions, call for a wide variety of responses. The respondent structures the reply as he or she wants.

    Why do you use diesel instead of petrol? _____

_____

You should avoid these questions whenever possible, as they are difficult both to record and to analyse. However, they are very useful when assessing attitudes and opinions.

4. Scaling questions

There are two main types of scaling questions: Likert scales and semantic-differential.

(a) Likert scales

In this type of question a respondent is asked to what extent he or she agrees or disagrees with a particular statement.

The price of houses will rise in the next six months.

1 Strongly disagree	2 Disagree	3 Uncertain	4 Agree	5 Strongly agree

(b) Semantic-differential

This type of question is used to test the respondent's attitude to specific issues or products. The respondent is presented with a list of the attributes to be measured; they are then asked to judge each attribute on a scale of descriptive phrases.

The following are some adjectives that could be used to describe politicians:

good	❑	❑	❑	❑	❑	bad
peaceful	❑	❑	❑	❑	❑	violent
original	❑	❑	❑	❑	❑	unoriginal
exciting	❑	❑	❑	❑	❑	boring

Points to remember about questionnaires

- Questionnaires should be developed carefully and tested before large-scale use.
- Decisions must be made on the following:
  (a) the form of the questions
  (b) the wording of the questions
  (c) the ordering of the questions.

The lying game

(Observer, *1 August 1999*)

The market research was unequivocal: the Leeds Royal Armouries Museum would be a stunning success. Fifteen million lived in the great cities of Yorkshire and Lancashire, and analysis of their tastes showed that one million would visit the collection each year. To date in 1999, less than 200,000 have paid to enter a museum which is now near to closure. It is a sad, but common story.

The supposed science of market research is facing a crisis of mass mendacity. Average punters do not want to show themselves up as plebs. They tell canvassers they'd love to tour a museum and suppress the small voice that says they will catch the latest *Star Wars* instead. The pollsters have also been undone by liars. They cannot gauge Tory support because some Tories are ashamed to admit their prejudices while others are so greedy they refuse to spend time giving researchers answers for nothing and thus pass by unrecorded.

Deplorable though fibbing is, this growth of deceit has an advantage. Perhaps our leaders will now develop original ideas rather than second-guessing an increasingly treacherous public.

FIG. 2 – SAMPLE QUESTIONNAIRE

CAREERS SURVEY OF AWARD RECIPIENTS, 2006

INSTITUTE OF TECHNOLOGY, CARLOW
KILKENNY ROAD
CARLOW
TEL: 059-9170400

Careers Survey

Dear Graduate,

We are conducting a survey of our former students. We hope you will complete the enclosed questionnaire, as we expect that the result will be of great benefit to us in evaluating and planning our courses. The results will also be of great interest to you and we plan to send you a resumé of our major findings. This will enable you to compare your career with those with whom you studied here.

We are contacting all students who completed the course for which they registered and we hope that the response rate will be very high. If you have any queries about the survey, you may contact us at the college and we will be delighted to help you.

A stamped addressed envelope is enclosed and we would urge you to complete the questionnaire today and return it to us immediately.

Many thanks for your help.

Yours sincerely,

Juliann Coogan, Brenda Murphy, Michelle McGroarty

**SECTION 1: GENERAL INFORMATION –
TO BE COMPLETED BY ALL RESPONDENTS**

1. Surname

2. First name

3. Permanent home aaddress

   Line 1

   Line 2

OFFICE USE ONLY

Code No.

Location code

4. Age in years

5. Sex (enter code
   in box)

   Female = 1   Male = 2

Line 3 ☐☐☐☐☐☐☐☐☐☐☐☐☐

Line 4 ☐☐☐☐☐☐☐☐☐☐☐☐☐

6. Award obtained in 2005 ....   Please write relevant code on line

1 = FETAC Level 6 Award   2 = HETAC Level 7 Award

3 = HETAC Level 8 Award

Please write the exact title of your award

....

....

7. Present situation ....

Please read the categories listed below and then write relevant code on line.

1 = Full-time employment, i.e. you have already commenced or are due to commence full-time employment either in a temporary or permanent capacity.

2 = Part-time employment, i.e. you are working less than normal hours.

3 = Work experience scheme, i.e. you are engaged on a work experience scheme organised by FÁS or any other statutory body.

4 = Further studies, i.e. you are primarily engaged in further studies.

5 = Seeking employment, i.e. you are unemployed, and are not engaged in any form of work experience scheme or further studies, and you are actively seeking employment.

6 = Other, i.e. you are not engaged in or seeking employment for reasons such as ill health, travel, domestic circumstances, etc.

SECTION 2: TO BE COMPLETED BY RESPONDENTS WHO ARE OR WHO HAVE BEEN IN EMPLOYMENT SINCE RECEIVING AWARD

1. Please write the exact title of your job ....

Please specify the primary duties and responsibilities of this position ....

2. Was the qualification you obtained a requirement for appointment to your present position?

Please enter relevant code in box.

1 = Yes   2 = No   ☐

3. Was the course you took relevant to the job which you are now doing?

Please enter relevant code in box.

1 = Very relevant   2 = Relevant   3 = Unsure

4 = Largely irrelevant 5 = Irrelevant   ☐

4. To be completed only by those in full-time employment.

Present salary (per annum)   Please enter relevant code in box.   ☐

1 = Up to €12,999   2 = €13,000 – €14,999   3 = €15,000 – €16,999

4 = €17,000 – €18,999   5 = €19,000 – €20,999   6 = €21,000 – €22,999

7 = €23,000 – €24,999   8 = €25,000 – €26,999   9 = €27,000 +

5. Name of company or person   ☐☐☐☐☐☐☐☐☐☐☐☐☐☐☐
   with whom you are employed.   ☐☐☐☐☐☐☐☐☐☐☐☐☐
   If self-employed state
   'self-employed'.

   Address of employer   ☐☐☐☐☐☐☐☐☐☐☐☐☐☐

                                 Office use   ☐☐

SECTION 3: ANY OTHER COMMENTS?

....

....

....

....

....

....

ACTIVITY 2

1. How would you find out how many chambers of commerce there are in Ireland?

2. Where would you discover how many publishers there are in Ireland?

3. What periodical would be useful if you were thinking of changing your car?

4. Which government department would you contact to find out when new Gardaí will be recruited?

5. You wish to complain about pollution of your local river. To whom would you complain?

6. Give the name and address of the organisation you would write to to find out how many workers in Ireland are members of trade unions.

7. Find out how many books mentioned in this chapter are in your local library.

8. Draw up a form for recording an interview you are going to have with the secretary of your local chamber of commerce. You are going to ask about membership, fees, level of participation, attendance at meetings and projects being undertaken at the moment.

9. You are going to do a report on how students choose their careers. Explain the method of procedure you would use.

10. You are doing a report on emigration. You are confining it to the final-year class in your own college. Your emphasis is to find out the reasons for emigration and whether or not the potential emigrants intend to return to Ireland. Draw up the questionnaire you would use.

11. A public library produced the following statistics at the end of the year:

Books borrowed by the public	50,000	100.0%
Books borrowed by members aged 5–13	12,500	25.0%
Books borrowed by members aged 14–18	15,000	30.0%
Books borrowed by members aged 19–35	6,250	12.5%
Books borrowed by members aged 36–50	4,000	8.0%
Books borrowed by members aged 51–65	7,250	14.5%
Books borrowed by members aged 66+	5,000	10.0%

Write an interpretation of the figures.

12. The same library also produced the following figures. Of the total number of books borrowed:

15% were children's books

45% were fiction

20% were history

10% were literature (poems, plays, etc.)

5% were politics

5% were others.

Write an interpretation of these figures.

USING AND ACKNOWLEDGING SOURCES

Once you have located the information you wish to use, it is important to acknowledge the source of the material. There are good practical reasons for this, as it clearly states that this part of the work is not your own. It also demonstrates to the reader the body of knowledge you have based your work on, and it enables other researchers to trace your sources and lead them on to further information.

In order to accurately acknowledge your sources, it is important in the process of your research to make careful notes of where you obtained the information. If it was on a website, then this would include the full address of the website, including the page you accessed. You should also note the date that you accessed that site, as information on a website can change on a regular basis. There are various ways of using and acknowledging sources:

- *Citing* means formally recognising the resources you obtained information from within your text.
- *Bibliography* is the list of sources you have used.
- *Referencing* is the detailed description of the item you obtained your information from.

There are two stages to acknowledging the sources of any information or ideas you use. The first is in-text citation: this is where you acknowledge the use of a source in the body of the text. It is your way of letting the reader know that you have just taken an idea or perspective from a source, used the writer's ideas in your own words, or indeed quoted directly. At this stage in the text you give the reader an abbreviated version of the reference.

The second stage is where you give the source of the information in full. In other words, you give the reader the full reference so that she can look the source up for herself if she wishes. This may be done in a list at the end of the work in the Bibliography or References sections.

IN-TEXT CITATION

Once you have decided to use a source in your text, there are three different ways you can introduce the material: quotation, paraphrase or summary. The difficulty many inexperienced researchers face is which method they should adopt.

When to use quotations

When you take words directly from a source without changing anything, *you must use quotation marks*. It is very easy to overuse this method and end up with a report or assignment full of direct quotations. Choose select phrases and extracts to reinforce the point you wish to make. The main exception to this is where you are analysing a primary source. Primary sources are first-hand accounts, interviews, research, surveys, experiments, etc. A student of literature who is commenting on a poem, novel or play would have to quote extensively from this primary source. A student of marketing who is asked to evaluate or comment on a specific piece of research, report or set of results would have to do likewise. Qualitative research, for example, is a primary source, and if using this you would quote extensively from interviews.

However, many of the texts you cite will be secondary sources, which draw together information and research from a variety of primary sources. An encyclopaedia is a secondary source, for example. Many of your textbooks will be secondary sources. Where you are using secondary sources, the use of direct quotations need not be as extensive.

Handling the in-text citation

When quoting directly from another author, you must give the author, year and page and ensure that the full reference is given in the reference or bibliography.

Quotations should normally be enclosed in single inverted commas in the text. Use double inverted commas only for quotes within a quote.

It is common practice that quotations over about forty words in length or four lines of text should not be enclosed in inverted commas but should be *block indented* from the left and typed in single line spacing. For example:

> Gouldsbury (2004: 130–1) notes:
>> Students can often take three attempts to complete their CAO form. The complexity and selection of courses forces them to order their choices prior to an indication of their results. College Admisssions report an increase in telephone enquiries during the last two weeks in January.

> Gouldsbury (2004: 130–1) notes that 'students…order their choices prior to an indication of their results.'

When to use paraphrase

Instead of using direct quotations excessively, you may decide to paraphrase a writer's words, i.e. restating the author's idea or line of argument in your own words. The ideas are not enclosed in quotation marks but must still be acknowledged. This is achieved by including the author's name and the year of publication after the material. For example:

Leaving Certificate students change their CAO selections at least three times prior to the publication of their results (Gouldsbury 2004: 130–1).

Gouldsbury (2004: 130–1) claims that the range of courses on offer prompts students to revisit their initial choices.

The Harvard system, or author-date system, as it is also known, is the most widely used method of acknowledging quotations, both direct and indirect. It consists of a citation in the text that points forward to a list of references. Readers may then refer to a list of references, ordered alphabetically at the end of the work, for the source of the quotation.

Regardless of which system you use, it is important to be consistent.

THE BIBLIOGRAPHY

The bibliography should contain a full reference of every work *directly referred to in the text* and anything you read as background but have not used in the body of your text. It should be in alphabetical order by surname of the author, followed by the first name or initials as given in the work cited.

Books

Surname, Initials, *Title of Publication in Italics*, Edition, Place: Publisher Year of publication.

Kotler, P., *Marketing Planning Management: Analysis Planning and Control*, 8th ed., New York: Prentice Hall 1994.

Referencing a book with multiple authors:

Blattberg, R. C., Glazer, R. and Little, J. D. C., *The Marketing Information Revolution*, Boston, MA: Harvard Business School Press 1994.

Periodicals

In the case of journal articles, the place of publication and the publisher are not included since this information is usually well known. However, the volume number, issue number (if used) and the inclusive page numbers for the article are given.

Author, Initials, 'Name of Article', *Name of Journal in Italics*, Volume number/Issue number (Year of publication), Start of article page number.

Levitt, T., 'Marketing Success through Differentiation of Anything', *Harvard Business Review*, January–February (1980), 322–40.

Department of Labour, *Case Studies in Employee Participation,* Dublin: Stationery Office 1989.

Irish Congress of Trade Unions (ICTU), *New Forms of Work Organisation,* Dublin: ICTU 1993.

If you have a number of government publications, it might be better to place them under a separate heading. For example:

(a)   Government Publications

(all published by the Government Publications Office, Dublin).

(b)   Books and Articles

(all other books and articles would be referenced as normal under this heading.)

Newspaper or magazine articles are treated similarly to periodicals except that it is normal to precede the page numbers with the abbreviation p. or pp. as appropriate.

CD-ROMs

Citing information from computer databases varies. For example, if you have been using a CD-ROM to obtain journal references, you only need to cite the journal as your source of information, not the CD-ROM.

Citing internet sources

Material obtained from the internet may change, so it is important that you keep a copy of material accessed. There are a number of approaches to citing work from the internet. The following style fits with the Harvard style. It is important that *enough information* is included in order for the reader to locate the citation in the future. You should always cite the *date the document was last updated* if this is apparent, or the *date when you accessed it* if not. In internet addresses, punctuation is important and the stops and commas in a bibliographic citation may confuse the reader; hence the common convention of using < and > to indicate the start and end of a URL.

The following information should be included:

- Author/editor.
- Title: underlined, emboldened or in italics (be consistent throughout the bibliography).
- [Internet].
- Edition.
- Place of publication: Publisher (if ascertainable) Year of publication.

- Available from: <URL>. Note general points about URLs.
- [Accessed date].

Holland, M., *Harvard System* [Internet], Poole: Bournemouth University 1996. Available from: <http://www.bournemouth.ac.uk/service-depts/lis/LIS_Pub/harvardsys.html> [Accessed 22 August 1997].

INTERPRETING INFORMATION

Interpreting information is a delicately balanced affair. Nobody is totally free from bias; acknowledgment of this fact is a necessary preliminary to objective interpretation. A useful corrective to personal bias is to ask a friend with different political, economic and ideological views to interpret the facts and then to compare the interpretations.

A good example of differences in interpretation appears in a review titled 'How Much Intolerance Exists in the Republic?' in *The Irish Times* of 6 August 1977. In the article, Dr Conor Cruise O'Brien is writing a review of *Prejudice and Tolerance in Ireland* by Fr Mícheál Mac Gréil. The response to questions on the Irish language are tabulated as follows:

Desired situation

(1) Principal language of use (as English is now)	8%
(2) Bilingualism with Irish as the principal language	10%
(3) Bilingualism with English as principal language	33%
(4) Preservation of spoken Irish only in Gaeltacht and/or preserved for its cultural value as in music and art	34%
(5) Irish language should be discarded and forgotten	15%

Fr Mac Gréil brackets the first three responses and comments: 'Situations Nos. 1–3 imply a revival of the Irish language (the choice of 51%) in order that it become a spoken language throughout the country.' But Dr O'Brien comments that 'the 33% who make up the ingeniously amassed 51% said nothing about the "revival of Irish"'. Bilingualism, Dr O'Brien points out, does not necessarily mean revival of Irish; it may mean a few Irish phrases on certain occasions.

The second example appears in response to the question 'Would you say that the religious beliefs in which you were brought up influenced your growth or development as a person?' The responses are tabulated as follows:

Perceived influence of religious beliefs in which respondent was reared:

Degree of Influence	Actual %	Cumulative %
(1) Essential help	55.3	
(2) Important but not essential	13.7	81.1 (positive)
(3) Helped somewhat	12.1	
(4) Neither help nor hindrance	15.2	15.2 (neutral)
(5) Hindered somewhat	2.6	
(6) Serious hindrance	0.7	3.7 (negative)
(7) Grave hindrance	0.4	

Fr Mac Gréil says 'the perception of religious beliefs as being essential or important aids to personal development by over 80% of the sample speaks for itself'. But Dr O'Brien does not agree with that interpretation. He says an equally legitimate interpretation is the following:

- religion essential 55.3%
- religion not essential 44.7%

These differences in interpretation in dealing with the same figures show how two people with different outlooks can view figures differently.

ACTIVITY 3

1. Access the Stock Exchange site on the World Wide Web, and find out the value of Ryanair shares for today.

2. Search the web to find out how many cars can be bought for between €20,000 and €30,000.

3. Search the web to find out how much you would have to pay each month for three years if you borrow €20,000 to buy a car at current interest rates.

4. Search the web to find the sites of each of the government departments. Which department has the best site? Give reasons for your answer.

5. Find out from your librarian how the interlibrary loan scheme works.

6. Access the website of the government, and find out how many embassies Ireland has.

7. Find the website of the European Union, and find the name of Ireland's representative on the European Court of Auditors.

8. Send a message to the Department of Foreign Affairs to discover what an

Irish citizen should do if he or she is in difficulty in a country where Ireland does not have an embassy.

9. *You are going on holidays to Italy. Access the website of the Italian embassy and find what sort of information it has that would be useful to you.*

REVIEW

1. Find out if your local newspaper has back copies of each of its issues. Is there an index to help you find topics quickly?
2. What facilities and services does your local library have for children?
3. What help can your local library give you if you want to study German?
4. What are some of the advantages of carrying out interviews rather than using questionnaires when doing research?
5. What is a leading question?
6. Why do people interpret information differently?
7. What measures can you take to guard against prejudice and bias when interpreting information?

PITFALLS

hung   hanged

Should we say 'The man was *hanged* this morning' or 'The man was *hung* this morning'?

'*Hanged*' means killed by hanging, so 'The man was *hanged* this morning' is correct. '*Hung*' is used in a general sense, e.g. 'He *hung* up his hat.'

CONFUSING WORDS

cell	sell	discreet	discrete
dear	deer	doe	dough
dents	dense	draft	draught
descent	dissent	dew	due
die	dye	dire	dyer

QUIZ

A rebus uses pictures, numbers and letters of the alphabet to make words and sentences. What is the meaning of the following rebus?

	have to		paid
I		because	
	work		I am

SPELLINGS

The words most commonly misspelled are highlighted.

oases	occupy	opposite
oasis	**occur**	opposition
obedience	**occurred**	oppression
obituary	**occurrence**	optimism
obligation	oculist	optimist
oblige	offensive	orchard
obscure	official	orchestra
obstacle	**omission**	ordeal
obstinate	omit	ordinary
obtuse	**omitted**	organisation
obviously	omitting	organise
occasion	onion	original
occasional	**onus**	ornament
occasionally	opaque	orphan
occasioned	**opinion**	ostrich
occupation	opponent	outrage
occupied	opportunity	oyster

16

READING CRITICALLY

SUMMARY

'The good die happily; the bad unhappily. That is the story of Western Literature.' This is Oscar Wilde's summary of Western literature.

An old king who was at death's door asked to be told the history of man. His minister for education told him: 'They were born, they lived and they died.'

A summary requires you to state the main message in a passage or speech in fewer words than the original. It means that you must understand the passage, be able to extract the main points and reproduce these in your own words.

Summarising is an essential skill for business and office administration students. The practical value of the summary is that it saves time and labour for someone else. A good summary must be accurate, concise and presented in readable form.

In business, summarising is a practical skill. You may have to summarise correspondence, minutes of meetings, reports, fax messages, telephone messages and statistics.

If instructions for the summary in examination questions state that it is not to be more than 110 words, then marks will be deducted for exceeding that number. On the other hand, if it is to be approximately 110 words, it is permissible to write a summary between 100 and 120 words.

Avoid faulty proportioning, i.e. two-thirds of your summary dealing with one-third of the original passage. Do not use direct questions, figurative language or illustrations which appear in the original if you can avoid it. If the original is in direct speech, the summary will have to be in reported speech.

Converting direct speech into reported speech

- *Omit quotation marks.* For example:

  Direct: Oscar Wilde said, 'To love oneself is the beginning of a lifelong romance.'

  Indirect: Oscar Wilde said that to love oneself was the beginning of a lifelong romance.

- *Verb tense changes.* For example:

  Direct: He said, 'I will be late.'

  Indirect: He said that he would be late.

Direct	Indirect
'I am interested.'	He said he was interested.
'I will go.'	He said he would go.
'I can do it.'	He said he could do it.

- *Changes in pronouns.* The first person (I/we) usually changes to the third person. For example:

  Direct: The judge said to the accused, 'I cannot hear you.'

  Indirect: The judge said to the accused that he could not hear him.

- *Changes in time and place.* Events and places become more distant in indirect speech. For example:

  Direct: He said, 'I was here yesterday.'

  Indirect: He said that he had been there the previous day.

Direct	Indirect
here	there
this place	that place
now	then
these	those
tomorrow	the next day
last year	the year before

- *Commands and questions.* Commands and questions must be rephrased. For example:

  Direct: The teacher said, 'Stop talking.'

  Indirect: The teacher told them to stop talking.

  Direct: 'Why are you crying?' the woman asked the little girl.

  Indirect: The woman asked the little girl why she was crying.

- All indirect speech is introduced by the word *that*. For example:

  Direct: He said, 'I will go.'

  Indirect: He said that he would go.

FIG. I − HOW TO WRITE A SUMMARY

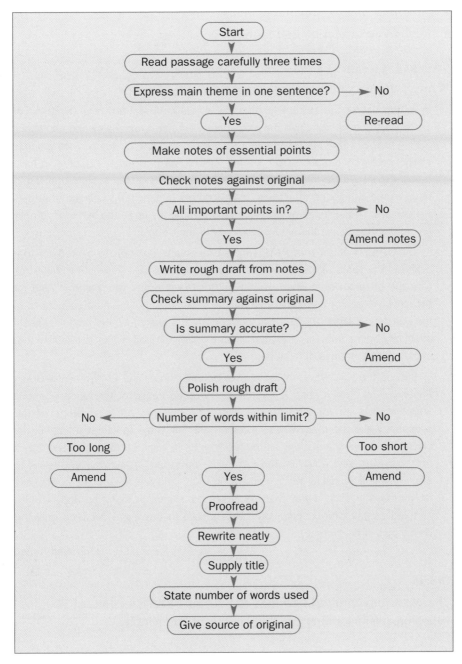

Hints on writing summaries

- Omit examples.
- Omit definitions.
- Omit additions.
- Omit lists of more than three items.
- Rephrase material in brief form.

Sample summary

Write a summary of the following passage in 125 words:

In hitting out at the current income tax regulations recently, the Congress of Trade Unions have identified the most *potent* creator of inequality and bad social feeling that is within the Government's power to control. Income tax has progressively spread its *tentacles* over the last decade as prosperity and inflation have brought more people into taxable brackets; but it is an unfair system that totally omits some categories of citizens, leaves others largely free to decide what they will declare, and includes others – the salary earners – up to the hilt, with virtually no means of reducing the amount they pay to the State.

There is no doubt that PAYE was an ingenious solution to a problem that existed forty years ago when it was introduced. Many young people without ties took the emigrant boat when the tax bill for the previous year came in, and for those who were not so mobile, the annual assessment came as a cold shock to the domestic budget. PAYE has helped the State's cash flow, too, and provides a direct and immediate link between income increases and higher tax liability that makes sense in times of inflation.

But, as the ICTU have argued in their submission on the Government's Green Paper on full employment, it has created a deep sense of grievance – *among workers who are locked into the system* – towards other sections of the community like the many whose incomes are not subjected to anything like as close or continuing a scrutiny as the luckless PAYE victim. It means heavier taxes for those who pay, which in turn increases the sense of injustice that leads to evasion where possible. Many workers on PAYE who are able to do '*nixers*' ask for payment in such a way that tax is not paid, and, in doing so, they feel as justified as the professional man who is paid in cash and declares only the visible part of his income.

(*The Irish Times*)

Theme

The government should change the current PAYE system of taxation, which creates inequality and bad feeling among people.

Notes on essential points

1. ICTU has pointed out the greatest creator of inequality – income tax.

2. It is an unfair system.

3. PAYE was a good solution to a problem which existed forty years ago.

4. PAYE has helped the state's cash flow.

5. Income tax has created a sense of grievance among PAYE workers because others are not subject to the same scrutiny.

6. It means heavier taxes for those who pay.

7. PAYE workers doing nixers feel justified in not paying tax on them.

Rough draft

As the Congress of Trade Unions has pointed out, the most potent creator of inequality and bad social feeling which the government can control is the income tax regulations. The income tax system is unfair because some people are free to decide how much income they will declare, while the salary earner is included up to the hilt. It was a clever solution to a problem which existed forty years ago, when young people with no ties emigrated when the tax bill arrived. Though PAYE increases the state's cash flow, it has created a sense of grievance because others are not subject to the same close scrutiny as PAYE people. This means heavier taxes for those who pay, it increases their sense of injustice and encourages tax evasion. Those on PAYE who can do nixers seek payment in such a way that tax is not paid and feel justified in doing this. (152 words)

Final draft

Title: Change the PAYE System

As the Congress of Trade Unions has pointed out, the most potent creator of inequality under the government's control is the income tax regulations. It is an unfair system, though it was a clever solution to a problem which existed forty years ago, when young people with no ties emigrated when the tax bill arrived. Though PAYE increases the state's cash flow, it has created a sense of grievance because others are not subject to the same close scrutiny as PAYE people. This encourages tax evasion. Those on PAYE who can do nixers seek payment in such a way that it is not subject to tax and feel as justified in doing this as the profes-sional who keeps part of his income secret. (123 words)

1. Here is a series of comments about the economy. Read them carefully, and sum up the point of view of each one in a short sentence.

    (a) We are now almost at the stage of full employment. Only just over 5 per cent of those available for work are unemployed at the moment. We are in a situation in which there are shortages of workers in certain areas.

    (b) The economy has been growing strongly over the past few years. Is it growing at too high a rate? Do we need to slow down the rate of growth? Perhaps we are too competitive. One of the problems is that wage increases have been very low. Perhaps wages need to rise significantly to slow down the growth rate and make us less competitive.

2. Select an article from The Sunday Business Post and draft a suitable summary of the article.

3. Read the passage below (from The Irish Independent, 9 October 1999), give it a title and summarise it in not more than 125 words.

I am very far from being an 'early adopter' (someone who quickly accepts innovations) when it comes to gadgets. My husband is a complete Luddite and hates all modern technology. He won't have a washing machine in the house. Call it his little eccentricity. Like Mao Tse-Tung (who tried to abolish private kitchens), Dick believes that washing clothes should be a collective, rather than a domestic, activity and the private washing machine only a capitalist plot to encourage every household to possess its own.

So we go to the laundrette. Ideally, he would prefer that the womenfolk did it by hand in the river, as may still be seen in parts of Africa. Such collectivist laundering is the natural order of things.

When I first acquired a word processor, he said that Tolstoy didn't need a word processor, and neither did Dickens. So why should we? I didn't argue, because it is flattering to be asked to compare yourself to Tolstoy and Dickens. And in any case, I partly agree that it is what is in your head that counts, not what kind of fancy technology that surrounds you. But there is one technological innovation which I really do embrace with enthusiasm, and that is the e-mail. It is surely one of the greatest aids to communication since the time of Caxton, or Rowland Hill, the inventor of the modern postal system.

The e-mail is a builder of new friendships, and a renewer of old ones. Old friends from whom you are separated by dint of time and space suddenly re-enter your life because of the facility of e-mail. It knits together families across the continents, and transmits useful and enjoyable particles of knowledge through its magic screen. It has revived the very grand old custom of letter writing, which had almost disappeared.

I don't care all that much for the telephone. It is all right as a business tool, but it's a time-waster and you have no memory or recollection of what has been said on the phone. Because modern-day lovers use the telephone rather than committing their thoughts to paper, biographers are beginning to despair that there would be mo more love-letters, no more passionate and indiscrete notes, no more rivetting footnotes of rivetting gossip to be uncovered in the future. They need fret no more. The e-mail will bring it all back. For an e-mail once written, or once received, can be stored ad infinitum, transferred to a disk, or even printed out on paper.

I love the e-mail, which I have really grown comfortable with over the past year and now I want everyone to have one. I think elderly people, especially, should have their own e-mail systems, so they can go back to writing those long and interesting letters that old folk always used to write. There are a growing number of oldies who use the internet – known as 'Silver Surfers' – but you don't even have to have recourse to the internet to use e-mail. I am not yet a habitual internet user. One thing at a time. And I'm not keen on all the drivel that is on the net. But my e-mail basket is like receiving four postal deliveries a day (as was the case, incidentally, with the postal service in Ireland in the 1930s).

I am not at all clever with technology (I needed nearly 70 lessons to learn how to drive a car), and with the e-mail, too, I needed a tutor. The tutor came and taught me how to compose, send and receive e-mail, at a cost of £55 an hour, which I consider to be money very well spent. It took me about four lessons to understand it, which means that the averagely intelligent person would probably pick it up in two.

There is, of course, the snag of unwanted mail. That is a great vexation. I get a great deal of pornography offered to me, which I consider maddening. 'Teen', by the way, has now replaced the word 'adult', to signal porn. Where once small adverts might describe their filthy offerings as 'adult material', the e-mail version is 'teen-mail'. You can block off the porn offers, but I have to get my tutor to show me how. This whole question has completely reversed the debate over censorship. Far from anyone censoring the pornographers, nowadays, the porn merchants are invading our space.

This experience has encouraged me to believe that there is a powerful symbolic argument for controls of offensive material: even if it is accessible, why should it be endorsed?

Since I live a nomadic life between Ireland and England, it's brilliant that the e-mail system will go everywhere with me, all contained within a little laptop. You do have to change the widget that goes into the telephone outlet between different countries (the British widget is different from the Irish one), but it's only a matter of carrying around two different flexes. Then you plug it in anywhere, open up, and start on your e-mail.

There are debates about the best inventions of the 20th century – the paper clip, the television, the jet engine, the computer, the contraceptive Pill. Surely the e-mail is one of the top candidates. Not just because it is such a marvellous form of communication, but because it is promoting such a traditional genre of communication. You read about the Bloomsbury group of writers who would send each other letters two and three times a day, thus creating a fabulous archive of observations, experiences and thoughts. You hear about the great days of the telegram, a written message you could keep forever. Well, the great days are back. Most innovations destroy what went before; but the e-mail has restored something we had very nearly lost – the personal letter, instantly delivered, forever kept.

4. Summarise the article below (from the internet version of the Examiner, 31 July 1999) in not more than 100 words.

Business users get latest data on one-stop internet site

by Des O'Sullivan

A one-stop internet site which offers information on companies, industries, markets, judgments, stocks and shares and news is being availed of by more and more Irish business users.

Businessgold, a subsidiary of the publicly quoted IFG Group, is the only service which offers direct internet access to the Companies Offices in Ireland and the UK. It includes on-line access to information from Dun and Bradstreet, Financial Times Information, ENKI Information Systems, CFI (Company Formations International), Interface (Irish company reports), Irish Trade Protection Association (Judgments) Ireland, RM (instant information on all registered UK companies), updated business news and stocks and shares. Sales consultant Lisa Buckley of IFG Technology and Development at 82 South Mall, Cork, says there is across-the-board interest in the service from banks, stockbrokers and financial management services to professional and service organisations and small and medium-sized enterprises.

The news service on Businessgold provides news feeds from 12,000 publications worldwide and international services such as Associated Press, AFX and Comtex. Data can be personalised to the user so that *an alert flashes on screen when any news update is recorded. The service starts from just ten pounds a month. Much of the information provided is free, while some information is charged on a usage basis.*

IFG has invested around £1 million in building and developing this service. It brings together some of the top business information services in an easily accessible internet service, which eliminates costly subscription fees and hugely speeds up access to information in, for example, the Companies Office, where searching may be conducted against a company name or number and there is viewing of all scanned documents filed. You pay as you view. Dun and Bradstreet UK, Irish and European Reports has the world's largest and most-up-to date business information database. There is concise information in the company report, which includes a maximum credit recommendation, a summary of the company's resources and the latest three years' key financial comparisons and facts on the company's principals. The report at the centre of the product range includes key detrimental indicators.

COMPREHENSION

A summary tests your ability to gain an overall understanding of a passage, while comprehension questions give you the opportunity to show a deeper understanding of the passage. People working in secretarial and business positions constantly have information before them which must be understood and assessed quickly. Practice in comprehension will develop this skill.

Tips for comprehension
- Read the passage through three times.
- Read the questions on the passage carefully.
- Refer each question back to the passage as you frame your answers.
- Write the answers accurately and concisely.
- Check answers.

Types of comprehension questions
Comprehension questions may:
- test your understanding of particular words and phrases
- test your understanding of facts in the passage
- seek explanation in detail of an important point in the passage
- ask you to read between the lines to understand the tone

- allow you to comment on the style in which it is written
- allow you to give your own opinion on some major element in the passage.

Sample comprehension questions

We will use for comprehension the passage from *The Irish Times* which we used for our sample summary (see page 222).

- Sample comprehension question (1)

  The first comprehension question on the passage asks you to explain the words in italics:

  (a) *potent:* powerful

  (b) *tentacles:* long, slender appendages

  (c) *workers who are locked into the system:* employees who are caught in the tax net and have no means of escape

  (d) *nixers:* odd jobs apart from one's main occupation, sometimes carried out with some secrecy.

- Sample comprehension question (2)

  The next type of question tests your understanding of facts in the passage:

  What is PAYE?

  PAYE stands for 'Pay As You Earn'. It is a system whereby the amount of income tax to be paid by an individual is deducted from his wage or salary in weekly or monthly contributions.

  What is a Green Paper?

  It is a document produced by the government to begin and/or encourage discussion on a particular topic. It generally sets out the various viewpoints on an issue.

- Sample comprehension question (3)

  This next type of question asks for explanation in detail of some important point:

  According to the writer, what are the advantages and disadvantages of PAYE?

  Advantages

  (a) It helps the state's cash flow.

  (b) It ensures tax is paid by would-be evaders.

(c) It ensures that as a person's income increases, so does his tax liability.

Disadvantages

(a) Workers in the system have virtually no means of reducing the amount they pay.

(b) It creates a sense of grievance among those on PAYE against those whose incomes are not scrutinised so carefully.

(c) It encourages tax evasion.

- Sample comprehension question (4)

  This type of question asks you to read between the lines to understand the tone of the passage:

  Do you think the writer of the passage is earning a salary on which he pays PAYE?

  Yes, because the passage has an aggrieved tone. The writer uses terms such as 'the most potent creator of inequality and bad social feeling' and also the word 'tentacles' in the passage. He feels discriminated against because he says non-PAYE people are not subjected to the same careful scrutiny.

- Sample comprehension question (5)

  This question allows you to comment on the style of the passage:

  Comment on the use of the phrase 'the luckless PAYE victim'.

  The use of the two negative terms 'luckless' and 'victim' clearly shows where the writer's sympathies lie. It shows his very strong feelings as they are highly emotional terms. The person on PAYE has a job and is not really 'luckless' or a 'victim' at all. It is an example of the writer using emotional language to get the reader on his side.

- Sample comprehension question (6)

  The next type of question allows you to give your personal opinion:

  Do you agree or disagree that there are inequalities in the tax system?

  The point of view you present here is not important so long as you can produce evidence for it. A reiteration of the points in the passage is not what is expected. The question offers a chance to present your own view of the matter.

1. Read the following extract from a booklet entitled Extending Your House, published by the Consumers' Association, and answer the questions which follow it.

    Most gas appliances must be separated from any combustible material in the structure of the building, either by a non-combustible material or by an air space.

    The flue requirement of gas appliances often depends on the size of the room. Some appliances do not connect directly to a flue: a gas cooker does not, nor a water heater below a certain size – for instance, a sink water heater. You can install a gas water heating appliance without connecting it to a flue only if the room is large enough and has a specified amount of permanent ventilation. In a bathroom a gas water heater should be of the room-sealed type with a balance flue.

    (a) A householder fixes a gas water heater directly onto a brick wall. Is this permitted? Give reasons for your answer.

    (b) A householder proposes to install a gas cooker in a very tiny kitchen which lacks ventilation. Is this permitted? Give your reasons.

    (c) A householder fixes a sink water heater over the hand basin in his bathroom. There is no flue. Discuss how one should interpret the regulations on this point; is there any ambiguity?

    (d) A householder shows the foregoing regulations to a builder, who says he has not read them before. What evidence do you notice which might indicate that a builder is, or is not, likely to have seen this extract?

    (London Chamber of Commerce Private Secretary's Certificate)

2. Read the following article (from The Irish Times, 30 July 1999) and answer the questions that follow.

Keep safe: don't accept e-mail sweeties from strangers

Niall McKay

Electronic music blares out of the four corners of the conference hall, a laser light show is in progress, massive video screens flash images at the crowd. Then the show begins. No, it's not the Eurovision: it's the launch of a new hacker software at the Def Con hackers' conference in Las Vegas this month.

The conference is perhaps the most unusual gathering in the computer industry calendar. Here nearly four thousand hackers, crackers (malicious hackers), script kiddies (novices) and FBI, National Security Agency and Department of Defence meet to discuss the ethics, morality and practicalities of hacking.

This year the conference was dominated by one of the hacking culture's supergroups, the Cult of the Dead Cow, which released Back Orifice 2000 (a dig at Microsoft's Back Office) – a back-door program that enables hackers to gain complete access to a victim's computer. The program runs on Windows 95, 98, and NT.

The software is sometimes called a 'Trojan horse' program, because hackers need to dupe users into installing it on their machine, usually by sending it as an e-mail attachment.

Trojan horse programs are a real threat to computer systems, because they do not exploit a defect in the operating system: instead they exploit what the Cult of the Dead Cow calls a design flaw in most operating systems that enables installation software to have complete access to all aspects of the computer.

In the case of Back Orifice, this enables the hacker to steal information from the computer's hard disk, or even delete the entire contents of the computer.

The problem has become more widespread because many computer users attach 'executables' or small programs to e-mail messages. Often these little programs are jokes that show funny cartoons or dancing bears. However, users should not run these programs, because they may have Back Orifice embedded in them.

In fact, since the Cult of the Dead Cow launched the first version of the software last year, 500,000 copies have been distributed on the internet. One Australian computer security group reported last November that 1,400 Australian internet accounts have been compromised by Back Orifice.

The solution, according to Microsoft, is not to accept e-mail sweeties from strangers; to update virus software programs; and never to install any software that does not come from a recognised source. 'Back Orifice's worst attribute is that it attacks the users, not the technology,' says Mr Jason Garms, lead product manager for Windows NT security.

The Cult of the Dead Cow disagrees. Its solution is to redesign the operating system so that software does not have complete access to all aspects of the computer system, or to design a utility that tells the user exactly what the software is doing to their computer. 'Microsoft is not the cause of the problem, but they are the largest operating system in the world,' said Dil Dog, the author of Back Orifice. 'That is why we targeted their operating systems.'

The cause of the problem, according to Dil Dog, is that the computer industry is still in its infancy and has not yet learned how to create secure systems. Certainly, Dil Dog has a point. In an age when computer failure can knock billions off a company's share price (which happened to the auction website eBay recently), securing computers is of paramount importance.

Meanwhile, during the launch of Back Orifice, several participants played Def Con's oldest game, the Spot the Fed (FBI man) contest. The game goes something like this: a member of the crowd points at someone they suspect is with the FBI and shouts 'Fed.' The accused then has to go on stage and say what they do for a living. If the accused works as a law enforcement officer, the spotter is awarded an 'I spotted the fed' T-shirt.

While the Cult of the Dead Cow members call themselves hackers and go by imaginative nicknames such as Oxblood and Grandmaster Ratte, they do not break into corporate computer systems. Rather, they attack their own computers to find flaws in programs. Once found, they will then release programs to exploit those flaws, giving malicious hackers the tools to attack systems.

Why? Because the members see themselves as New Age computer security evangelists. 'We see companies like Microsoft as a threat to personal security,' says Sir Dystic, co-author of Back Orifice. 'And the only way to get them to own up is to write programs that exploit security weaknesses so that they are forced to address the problem.'

Still, it's all a matter of spin really. While the Cult of the Dead Cow will never make money from Back Orifice, it has become the most famous hacker group in the world.

(a)   Sum up the main point of the passage in one sentence.

(b)   Why is the program sometimes called a 'Trojan horse'?

(c)   What is a Trojan horse, and what is the origin of the term?

(d)   What does the writer mean by the phrase 'don't accept e-mail sweeties from strangers'?

(e)   Write one paragraph for and one paragraph against computer hackers.

REVIEW

1. Why are summarising skills useful for working in business?
2. What is the difference between direct speech and reported speech?

3. Turn the following into reported speech:

   (a) In his address the chairman said, 'This has been a successful year for our company, but we hope that in future things will be even better.'

   (b) 'We will meet here week,' he said.

   (c) He declared, 'I ask you, can this go on?'

4. How do you render the following in reported speech?

   now   today   last week   tomorrow

   here   mine   next week   ourselves

   us   may   can   last year

5. What is meant by 'reading between the lines' of a passage?

6. How do you gauge the tone of a passage?

7. Find two reviews of the same book and compare them.

8. Find two different pictures of the same event and compare them.

PITFALLS

two-first two-last

It is impossible to have more than one first or last of anything, and expressions such as 'the two-first', 'the three-last' should be avoided.

CONFUSING WORDS

waist	waste	deduce	deduct
write	right	negligent	negligible
riot	rite	official	officious
popular	populous	impressive	impressionable
insolvent	insoluble	ostensible	ostentatious

QUIZ

The figurative expression 'to call a spade a spade' is sometimes modified to 'call a spade a shovel'. What do you think is the difference between the two phrases?

SPELLINGS

The words most commonly misspelled are highlighted.

paganism	peaceable	physique
pageant	peasant	picnicking
pamphlet	peculiar	piety
pantomime	penance	plague
parachute	**penicillin**	**planning**
paraffin	peninsula	**pleasant**
parallel	penniless	pleasurable
paralleled	perceive	pneumatic
parallelogram	perennial	pneumonia
paralyse	perilous	poisonous
paralysis	**permanent**	porcelain
paraphrase	**permissible**	portrait
parchment	**perseverance**	**possess**
pardonable	persistence	**possesses**
parliament	persuasion	postpone
particular	pessimist	**potential**
particularly	pheasant	precaution
pastime	philosophy	precede
patience	**physical**	**preceding**

PART 5

NON-VERBAL

SKILLS

17

INTERACTIVE SKILLS

VISITORS

In most firms the telephonist/receptionist is the first person in the organisation to meet visitors. Tact and diplomacy in such a position are vital. He or she must be skilful in dealing with people and be able to deal with awkward situations. He or she should have a thorough knowledge of the organisation's activities and know the jobs carried out by its various employees.

The person receiving visitors needs to know about all the appointments made and know which people are available each day and who will be away from the premises. Some firms keep a reception register in which details of all visitors are entered. The receptionist should have a diary with a page for each day. This will allow plenty of space for entering appointments, taking brief notes from visitors and entering reminders of various tasks to be done.

Courtesy at all times

Every visitor should be treated with courtesy and kindness. Never appear so busy that the caller feels like a nuisance. If the person has an appointment, inform your boss before showing him in; if there is a delay, apologise for it and ask him to take a seat. It is not necessary to engage in conversation all the time. Once you have invited the visitor to sit down, you can continue with your work. If the visitor does not have an appointment, make discreet enquiries to find out whether your boss wishes to see him. If your boss does not wish to see him, there are three courses of action open to you:

- find out if someone else in the firm can help him
- get your boss to telephone him later
- try to help him yourself.

You have the option of making an appointment for some future date, but your boss may not wish to see this particular caller. You can deal with this situation by asking if he would like to leave a written message which you will pass on.

If a visitor has to be kept waiting, provide him with a magazine, newspaper or your firm's prospectus or newsletter. No one should be kept waiting too long.

It is not possible to give specific guidelines on how to deal with every situation. Sometimes you will just have to use your common sense and discretion. Some situations could be handled in several different ways and it may be difficult to know which is best. Situations arise which there are no easy answers to. You just have to 'think on your feet' and deal with it as sensibly as you can. If your boss is going to a meeting and tells you she is not to be disturbed, that is not to be taken literally. If information comes through that a member of her family has been injured, then of course you inform her.

Your boss may sometimes put you in impossible situations in dealing with customers. There may be certain situations you cannot handle, and it is unfair of your boss to put you into such a situation. You should discuss such matters with him or her and suggest some better method of dealing with the situation.

COMPLAINTS

You cannot avoid complaints. Even with the best will in the world things will sometimes go wrong. There will always be dissatisfied customers. If an organisation is big it is difficult to ensure that everyone is dealt with fairly.

Receiving the complaint

Never be rude if the person making the complaint is abusive. Find out specific details of the complaint. The matter cannot be rectified unless you get to the bottom of the problem. By doing this you also show interest and concern. If you cannot deal with the complaint yourself, refer it to someone who can.

- Do not accept blame immediately if the position is unclear.
- Do not give the customer hope if he is obviously wrong.
- Tell him the procedure for dealing with complaints.
- Do not argue.
- Express regret at any inconvenience the person complaining may have experienced.

Sources of reference in reception area

- *Accommodation references*: the person working in reception should have information on accommodation available and places of interest in the area. Contact your local tourist office or the local chamber of commerce.

- *Timetables*: these are necessary for checking the times of buses, trains, aeroplanes and ferries. Contact Bus Éireann and Iarnród Éireann. You can also access timetables on the internet.

- *Road maps*: maps can be obtained from the Ordnance Survey, from the Automobile Association and from any good bookshop.

- *Internal telephone directory.*

- *Telephone directory and Golden Pages*: the telephone directory can now be found on the internet.

- *Local business and community directory*: some cities and towns have published local directories of services and facilities.

ACTIVITY I

1. *A visitor to your firm insists he has an appointment with your boss. You cannot find it in your diary. This very rarely happens, as you are careful to note all appointments. What action would you take?*

2. *Describe in detail how to deal with callers who do not have an appointment.*

3. *What information should a receptionist have on hand?*

4. *Mention three important points that should be borne in mind when dealing with visitors.*

5. *A visitor who has an appointment calls to see your boss. Your boss does not want to see him. Write down the dialogue which might take place between yourself and the visitor.*

6. *What steps would you take to shield your boss from callers she does not want to see?*

7. *Your boss has made an appointment for 9.30 a.m. The visitor arrives at 9.25 but your boss will not be able to see him for fifteen minutes. How would you deal with the visitor in the meantime?*

8. *A visitor, well known to your firm, calls to see your boss on what he says is a confidential matter. Your boss is at an important meeting with some of her staff. What action would you take?*

9. *Describe in detail the steps you would take when dealing with a visitor who has an appointment.*

10. Two visitors, neither of whom has an appointment, arrive to see your boss. Both say they are in a hurry and would like to see him first. How would you deal with the situation?

GROUP ACTIVITY

The following situations may be used to practise dealing with complaints. One person complains and the other person responds to the complaint. It may be helpful to record the situations on video and have discussions about how the complaint was made and how well the other person responded.

1. You are shopping in the supermarket. Only two out of eight checkouts are open. The queues at these are getting longer and longer. No attempt is being made to open extra checkouts. The manager is on the phone. You are in a hurry and can no longer put up with this. Approach the manager to complain.

2. Your daughter has applied to your local college to get a place on the Business Studies Certificate course. Two hundred points in the Leaving Certificate is the minimum required to gain a place. Your daughter, in fact, has 226 points, but the course director informs you that only six subjects are counted for making up the points. Your daughter sat seven subjects in her examination. If you count just six subjects your daughter has only 185 points. Complain about what you see as the unfairness of this to the course director.

3. You have hired a chainsaw from a hire equipment company. The two previous occasions you hired it, the saw broke down after an hour's work and much of your day was wasted. Complain to the manager about the standard of equipment available for hire.

4. A customer complains that your telephonist is seldom available at 9.00 a.m. and that sometimes the phone rings for long periods before being answered. Deal with the person complaining.

5. You bought some crystal glasses, but when leaving the shop the bag burst and the box in which the crystal was packed fell on the tiled part of the shop. When you check the box you find that three of the eight glasses are broken. Complain to the manager and ask for replacements.

USING THE TELEPHONE

On the telephone, courtesy and good manners are essential. The consideration shown to a caller in person is just as important when she is at the other end of a telephone. The receptionist/telephonist is the first contact many people have with an organisation and it is vital that this first impression be positive. The telephonist/receptionist should have the following available:

- telephone directories as needed
- index book for keeping a list of numbers used frequently
- notebook for recording telephone messages. Many firms have printed forms for this purpose.

Making a telephone call

- Ensure you have the correct code and number.
- If the call is non-routine, jot down the main points you must cover.
- Have any documents you need available.
- Speak clearly into the mouthpiece.
- Identify yourself by name of firm, department or your own name.
- Explain clearly and concisely your business.
- Always repeat numbers to ensure they have been correctly heard.
- Repeat important parts of the message.
- Spell out difficult names and words.
- Express thanks at the end of the call.

Receiving a telephone call

- Answer the telephone quickly, but not after the first ring. It is better to allow it to ring three times.
- Identify yourself by name of firm, department or your own name.
- Adopt a friendly tone.
- Listen carefully.
- Ensure you know the caller's name and address or telephone number so that you can reply.
- If you can't find the person sought or the information requested quickly, promise to return the call as soon as possible.
- If you must put the caller through to an extension, do not just flip a switch and leave the caller not knowing what is happening. Say 'I'm putting you through now to Ms Scully.'
- If the person being sought is not available, suggest a time when he will be back.
- Express thanks for calling at the end of the conversation.

Taking messages
Many firms have special printed forms for messages.

FIG. 1 – FORM FOR TAKING TELEPHONE MESSAGE

For: _____	Date: _____
From: _____ Number: _____	Time: _____
Urgent_____	
Message: _____	
_____	
_____	
_____	
_____	
_____	
Taken by: _____	

In taking telephone messages, the following points should be noted:

• date and time of call
• caller's name, firm and telephone extension
• name of person for whom call was intended
• precise details of message.

Read these points back to the caller to ensure you have them correct. The message should be placed where the person it concerns will find it. It is prudent to check later that the person has, in fact, seen it.

Spelling words on the telephone
When it seems likely that some words may be confused, it is a good idea to use the alphabetical code. It goes as follows:

A for Alfred	J for Jack	S for Samuel
B for Benjamin	K for King	T for Tommy
C for Charles	L for Lucy	U for Uncle
D for David	M for Mary	V for Victor
E for Edward	N for Nellie	W for William
F for Frederick	O for Oliver	X for X-ray
G for George	P for Peter	Y for Yellow
H for Harry	Q for Queen	Z for Zebra
I for Isaac	R for Robert	

1. What do you think the caller is saying in the following exchange?

> Telephonist: 'Grange Products Limited.'
>
> Caller:..
>
> T: 'Putting you through.'
>
> Assistant: 'Retail Department.'
>
> C: ....
>
> A: 'Yes, we have plenty of that in stock. It is sold in either five-metre or one-metre lengths.'
>
> C: ....
>
> A: 'Well, the five-metre lengths work out cheaper; €14.50 per length or €130 for the ten lengths.'
>
> C: ....
>
> A: 'Yes, we can deliver them to your home on Wednesday. So that's ten lengths. What is your name and address please?'
>
> C: ....
>
> A: 'Padraic Scully, Tirshannon, Gorey, Co. Wexford. Is that correct?'
>
> C: ....
>
> A: 'Thank you very much and goodbye.'

2. What criticisms would you make of the person receiving this call?

> Bus Company: 'Hello.'
>
> Caller: 'Is that the bus company?'
>
> BC: 'Yeah.'
>
> C: 'Could you tell me what time the bus goes to Dublin on Wednesday?'
>
> BC: 'On Wednesday! Wednesday! Let me see now! Monday, Tuesday, Wednesday! Here we are now! What time did you want to go?'
>
> C: 'Well, what times do the buses go?'
>
> BC: 'There's one at ten to nine and there's another at three o'clock.'
>
> C: 'What times do these get into Dublin?'
>
> BC: 'Ah, it takes about an hour and three-quarters, all going well.'
>
> C: 'What is the return fare please?'
>
> BC: 'God, I don't know. They're always changing it. The fare is not on this leaflet I have here; I think the new one will be out next week.'
>
> C: 'Does the bus stop in Naas?'
>
> BC: 'Oh God, I haven't a clue; but I'd say so, more than likely.'
>
> C: 'Ok, thank you.'
>
> BC: 'You could always ring Dublin now and they'd know the exact fare and whether she stops in Naas and all that sort of thing.'

C: 'Ok, thank you.'

BC: 'Right.'

3. How should a receptionist deal with the following call?

Receptionist: 'Good morning, Athassel Products.'

Caller: 'Hello! I wanted to make a . . .'

R: 'Sorry, just hold on a sec please.'

(Half a minute later)

R: 'Now, we're right. You were saying.'

C: 'I wanted to make a complaint about . . .'

R: 'Oh, we don't deal with complaints here at all. You'll have to ring 062-71124. They deal with complaints – Mr Foran.'

C: 'Can you transfer me to him?'

R: 'No, I'm afraid not.'

REVIEW

1. When dealing with people, why are first impressions very important?
2. Why is the telephonist/receptionist so important in an organisation?
3. How should you deal with a visitor who is abusive?
4. If your boss says she is not to be disturbed for the next two hours, how should you interpret that message?
5. Firms and organisations should welcome complaints. Why?
6. How would you deal with a customer whose complaint is unjustified?
7. List the common mistakes people make when answering the telephone.
8. List the common mistakes people make when making a telephone call.
9. A person has telephoned your organisation and complains that your boss never seems to be available. She has telephoned six times in the past two weeks and she was always told he was not available. How would you deal with this complaint?

PITFALLS

sewage sewerage

These two words are often confused. *Sewage* means the matter conveyed in pipes to, for example, a septic tank. *Sewerage* is the conduit or channel or pipe system to carry the sewage to the septic tank.

CONFUSING WORDS

recent	resent	human	humane
dependent	dependant	uninterested	disinterested
horde	hoard	beside	besides
waive	wave	ascent	assent
plaintiff	plaintive	popular	populous

QUIZ

What is a limerick? Write one.

SPELLINGS

The words most commonly misspelled are highlighted.

quadruple	quantify	questionnaire
quagmire	quantitative	queue
quaint	quantity	quicken
quake	quarrel	**quiet**
qualification	quarry	quit
qualify	quarter	quite
qualifying	quarterly	quorate
qualitative	quay	quorum
quality	queasy	quota
quandary	querulous	quotation
quantifiable	query	quote

18

MEDIA ANALYSIS

INTRODUCTION

In 1998 Chief Justice Judge Ronan Keane, commenting on the Irish media in the case of Judge Murphy vs *The Irish Times*, stated that 'the media are the eyes and ears of the public, and the ordinary citizen is almost entirely dependent on them for his knowledge.'

Media owners, editors and journalists should be subjected to the same codes of public standards as those that govern politics and business if the integrity of the media is to be protected, according to Prof. Onora O'Neill of Newnham College, Cambridge: 'Today the media are among the most powerful and least accountable players in public affairs. Yet we continue to exempt the press, in particular newspapers, from many of the sorts of accountability required of other organisations and individuals.' She believes that false and unreliable reporting now poses a major threat to democracy because it marginalises large sections of the public.

The Archbishop of Dublin, Dr Diarmuid Martin, speaking to a conference on 'Ethics and Values in a Digital Age' in 2004, stated that transparency of media ownership is a matter of public interest and requires specific legislative norms. What do you think? Does the media have such power in Irish society? Is it right that they do? Are there any dangers involved in placing so much responsibility on the media?

WHY STUDY THE MEDIA?

There are basically five reasons why you should study the media.

1. *Your interest*: you may be personally interested in radio, TV, newspapers and magazines. You may want to know more about these.

2. *Media power*: many people believe that the media have great power and influence. Most people believe they have some power. They are the main source of ideas for many people and they help shape our opinions and attitudes. They may shape how we think and act.

3. *Economic power*: the media employ thousands of people directly and many others indirectly. The income and expenditure of the media are vast. Then there is the question of advertising and how much money is spent on it. The media need advertising to survive.

4. *Audience*: the media have a huge audience. Some media such as radio and TV come right into our kitchens and bedrooms. Few households do not have at least one radio and one TV.

5. *Information and entertainment*: people want entertainment and they want information. They get most of these from the media. Most people no longer have just RTÉ 1 and Network 2. The idea of preventing outside influences is no longer practical. We can tune into TV stations in Britain, France, Germany and the US. The world has become a 'global village'. Some surveys show that nearly 90 per cent of people get their news from TV and that for the most part, they believe it. The media – TV, radio, books, newspapers and magazines – provide most people's entertainment. So if the media are the main providers of information and entertainment, it makes sense to study them. We should look at what they provide and why.

MEDIA OWNERSHIP

The Irish newspaper market is dominated by the Independent News and Media Plc. It publishes *Irish Independent*, *Sunday Independent*, *Evening Herald*, *Sunday World*, *The Star* and *Daily Star Sunday*. The Independent group also holds a 29 per cent stake in *The Sunday Tribune*. It is Ireland's leading media company, publishing five national newspapers and twelve regional newspapers. All Independent news and media publications can be accessed on the www.unison.ie website.

The Independent News and Media group publishes over 176 newspaper and magazine titles worldwide, including *The Independent* and *The Independent on Sunday* in the UK. It also owns the Belfast Telegraph group, the largest newspaper publisher in Northern Ireland.

Thomas Crosbie Holdings, a private company based in Cork, publishes *The Irish Examiner*, *The Evening Echo*, *The Sunday Business Post*, *The Irish Post* and ten local newspapers. It also has interests in local radio and owns www.recruitireland.com.

The remaining Irish-owned national newspaper, *The Irish Times*, is published by The Irish Times Trust, a private company. It also owns the www.ireland.com website.

In the past decade there has been a decline in the sales of individual newspapers and an increase in the number of newspapers available in the Irish market. Irish editions of UK tabloids have a firm foothold in the Irish market. The main market leaders are *The Irish Daily Mirror* and *The Irish Sun*. Both print Irish editions. In addition, British-published newspapers, including *The Guardian*, *The Financial Times* and *The Independent*, are available to Irish readers.

Claims about the number of readers contrast with no apparent growth in circulation. In recent years the Sunday newspaper market has seen a growth in the number of titles. It now has fifteen competing newspapers.

Local or regional newspapers and weekly publications such as the *Farmers Journal* feature strongly in the purchasing habits of the Irish population. In many cases family-owned local or county newspapers have been purchased by Irish and UK media groups.

ACTIVITY I

1. *How many people in your class read a national daily newspaper?*

2. *What were the readership figures for* The Irish Times *in 1999?*

3. *What was the circulation of* The Sunday Business Post *in 1999?*

Readership of national newspapers, 2002–3

Universe (000s)	3192
Sample	7118
Any Irish newspaper	2935 (92%)
Morning titles	
Irish Independent	607 (19.0%)
The Irish Times	347 (10.9%)
Irish Examiner	207 (6.5%)
Irish Daily Star	456 (14.3%)
Irish Daily Mirror	239 (7.5%)
Irish Sun	296 (9.3%)
Any daily	**1891 (59.2%)**
Any morning	**1720 (53.9%)**

Sunday titles	
Sunday Independent	1093 (34.2%)
Sunday Tribune	219 (6.9%)
Sunday World	841 (26.4%)
Sunday Business Post	168 (5.3%)
Ireland on Sunday	481 (15.1%)
Sunday Times	315 (9.9%)
Irish News of the World	531 (16.6%)
Irish Sunday Mirror	198 (6.2%)
Irish People	151 (4.7%)
Any Sunday	**2501 (78.3%)**
Irish Farmers Journal	273 (8.5%)

Based on readership by any adult (aged 15+).

Source: JNRS July 2003–June 2004; conducted by Lansdowne Market Research

ACTIVITY 2

1. Do a survey of your class to ascertain how many hours are spent each week on TV, radio, books, magazines and newspapers. Find out which medium is the most popular and on which days of the week students spend the most time on each medium.

2. Find out which programmes are the most popular with your classmates on radio and TV. Is there a difference in the programmes watched by men and women?

3. List the newspapers, in the order of popularity, which the students in your class read.

4. How many radios and TVs do your classmates have in their homes?

5. What TV channels are the most popular among your fellow students? Is there a difference in the channels watched by men and women?

6. Which newspapers do the families of your classmates buy every week? Do they buy a local newspaper? Do they buy two newspapers on Sunday?

7. What percentage of your classmates' families buy a British newspaper?

MEDIA STUDIES

In Chapter 1, models of communication were introduced illustrating the communications process. Central to this process is the concept of shared meaning. This shared meaning takes place through interaction with others. Communications, therefore, is the study of interactions within societies. Human communication takes place through the use of signs and symbols (words, images, gestures). These signs and symbols represent things or ideas within a particular culture and are shared by the members of that culture through language. The study of the meaning of signs and symbols is called semiology.

Values and beliefs are another important feature of culture that are transferred by the communications process. These are what inform our behaviour in everyday life. These values and beliefs are learned through the socialisation process, which is the way the individual learns to live in society. The agents of socialisation are the family, peers, schools and the mass media. In any culture, therefore, the media both reflect and shape the central values and beliefs of the society. The media are a significant social and cultural institution in any modern society. This is why it is such an important area of study for sociologists. The sophistication of a culture is also reflected in its mass media.

What are the media?

- Newspapers.
- Radio and television.
- Cinema.
- Popular music.
- Advertising.
- Electronic media, including the internet

What these media have in common is:

- the ability to reach large audiences
- the employment of technology
- communication where there is little interaction between the source and the receiver
- communication that involves mediation.

Mediation is a process of selecting and shaping that creates a range of meaning. In other words, a representation of facts is presented.

Consequently, each of the above media can alter our perception of an event in a specific way.

ACTIVITY **3**

From the time you woke up this morning, list the encounters you have had with the media. Compare your list with others in the group.

You are probably surprised to discover how central the media are to your everyday life. What may be more surprising is the extent to which these encounters took place in your own home.

Media texts

The term used to refer to a particular newspaper article, film, television programme or advertisement is 'text'. While the text carries a message, it is not as intimate or as immediate as the message in the interpersonal communication, as there is a delay between its formulation, its circulation and its reception.

The text is made up of two sets of signs or codes:

- technical signs, which include the framing, lighting, sound
- cultural signs, which include dress, setting, narrative.

A text, therefore, is a collection of signs whose meaning can be decoded.

Just as the message in interpersonal communications needs to be encoded and decoded, the text in the media is interpreted in order to give it meaning, and people bring different understandings to texts. This is linked to a person's experience, motivation and expectations and can vary from culture to culture. Consequently, a text is open to a number of interpretations.

Narrative

In media studies, the process of producing a story is called the narrative. It is made up of:

- the theme: what the story is about
- the plot: what happens
- the discourse: how the story is told.

All texts tell stories, and different media use different techniques to produce this story.

In films and television, shots are produced in a certain way to facilitate the telling of the story. However, much of the story can be left to the imagination.

Sport is an important part of Irish life. Many sports enthusiasts who attend events return home and watch the highlights on television and then read the newspaper report the next morning.

ACTIVITY 4

Working in groups, each member takes a photograph from a newspaper and composes a story relating to the photograph. What do you think is happening in the picture? What happened before the picture was taken? What do you think happened after the picture was taken?

Genre

Take a sporting event of your choice, e.g. golf championship, hurling championship, soccer or camogie all-Ireland final. How is the story told by:

- the television broadcast
- the newspaper report
- your own story (narrative) if you were present?

What are the similarities and differences in the way the narrative in each case is presented? Is there a difference of emphasis? If so, what is it, and how is it done?

Write down how you expect the television broadcast to represent the game, and write down what you would expect to be included in the newspaper coverage. Do you think the narratives are produced for different audiences? This difference is called the genre.

ACTIVITY 5

What are the differences between a television serial such as Fair City *and the film* Titanic*?*

People are not passive when engaging with the media and can decode the message (text) in different ways. As in all human behaviour, why people interpret it in different ways is complex and may be influenced by factors such as age, sex, nationality and class. Other factors, such as political differences, geographical differences and religious differences, can influence how an individual interprets a message. In media studies this is referred to as the 'reading' (Morley). There may not be a right or a wrong way to interpret the message, and, as we said, many factors influence our interpretation of the message. However, the producers of the message usually have a 'preferred reading'. So when we look at a photograph in a newspaper we need to ask, 'How are we expected to read this?'

How is the subject portrayed? Are they portrayed in a positive or negative way? How is this done?

ACTIVITY 6

Look at the picture below and answer the questions that follow.

Photograph: © *New York Times*/Rex Features

1. *Should this picture have been published? Support your answer.*
2. *What do you think the general message of this photograph is?*
3. *Do you find any part of this photograph unacceptable?*
4. *What emotions does this photograph arouse?*

Read the article and answer the questions that follow.

Spinning a web of mass deceit

The Irish Times

23 July 2003

As a piece of media manipulation, the success of Alistair Campbell, Tony Blair's media guru, in switching attention from the falsehoods that underpinned the foreseeable killing of thousands of people in Iraq, is quite spectacular, writes **Vincent Browne**.

For now, at least, media focus here and in Britain is riveted not on whether lies were told to ordain mass slaughter, but on whether the BBC contributed by exaggeration to the death of a single person.

It isn't yet established conclusively that either Tony Blair or George Bush lied to justify war on Iraq. But the evidence is mounting that on the issues of weapons of mass destruction, including nuclear weapons, and on links with al-Qaeda, they made claims at the United Nations, the US Congress and the House of Commons that people around them knew to be untrue. And it was on those very same bogus claims that they sought UN, Congressional, Parliamentary and world support for the bombardment of a country that already had been devastated by war and economic sanctions.

Both Blair and Bush cited evidence that the regime of Saddam Hussein had sought to purchase uranium oxide from Niger as part of the build-up of a nuclear arms programme. It now emerges that this 'evidence' came from an Italian journalist, Elisabetta Burba, a foreign correspondent for an Italian news magazine, Panorama. She visited Niger in the autumn of 2002 and was given a bundle of documents that purported to show that the Iraqis had tried to purchase uranium oxide there some time previously.

On returning to Rome, she told her editor that the story seemed 'fake' to her, so the magazine ignored their own 'discovery'. However, she handed the documents over to the US embassy in Rome. Quite quickly, the CIA determined the documents were unreliable but, apparently, the British 'intelligence' services did not so advise Tony Blair, even though, according to recent reports in the US media, the CIA informed their British counterparts of their belief that the documents were bogus.

In spite of this, George Bush made reference to this 'evidence' in his State of the Union address in January. The British had cited the Niger documents in one of its now infamous dossiers. When these same documents were handed over to the International Atomic Energy

Agency (IAEA) in Vienna, four months after the US had first received them, IAEA officials were able to discover within a few days that they were false. They did so, according to the Washington Post *last Friday*, by 'using the Google Internet search engine, books on Niger and interviews with Iraqi and Nigerian officials'.

Now Tony Blair insists the 'evidence' of this attempted uranium purchase was 'confirmed' by other intelligence information the British had received. This corroborative information was not passed on to the Americans and, according to former British intelligence agents, if this is true it was a unique restraint on the part of the British services in over half a century. In other words, it is not remotely believable.

Another 'trump card' both Blair and Bush played in the lead-up to the attack on Iraq was linking the regime of Saddam Hussein with al-Qaeda. Repeatedly, George Bush, Donald Rumsfeld, Paul Wolfowitz and even Colin Powell cited 'evidence' of such links, claiming the prospect of Saddam arming al-Qaeda with weapons of mass destruction was real and imminent. Rumsfeld said it was 'bullet-proof' evidence.

Yet the CIA had repeatedly discounted this prospect and, in the *New York Times* on Sunday, two former members of the National Security Council stated that while on the NSC from 1994 to 1999, they 'closely examined nearly a decade's worth of intelligence and we became convinced, like many of our colleagues in the intelligence community, that the religious radicals of al-Qaeda and the secularists of Baathist Iraq simply did not trust one another or share sufficiently compelling interests to work together'.

In the last few days, it has also emerged that the war on Iraq was long under way before America acknowledged on March 20th last (the day the war on Iraq started formally) what it was up to. According to a report also in last Sunday's *New York Times*, from mid-2002 into the first few months of 2003 the Americans dropped 606 bombs on Iraqi installations. This was done under the cover of purported Iraqi violations of the no-fly zone in southern Iraq. However, in the course of this covert bombardment, key Iraqi command centres, radar and other important military assets were attacked – this was at the same time that the US and Britain were seeking UN support for the war they had already covertly started.

In that report by Michael Gordon, the *New York Times* defence expert, it was also reported that commanders had to obtain the approval of Rumsfeld where any planned airstrike was thought likely to result in the deaths of more than 30 civilians. More than 50 such strikes were proposed and all were approved.

But, for now at least, the BBC is the target and, in America, the issue is whether countries which opposed the war can now be induced to pick up the pieces.

© *The Irish Times*

1. *What caught your attention?*

2. *Do you accept that the article is true?*

3. *Do you disagree with parts of it?*

4. *Do you find any part of it unacceptable?*

5. *Summarise the article.*

6. *What is the dominant view of the writer of the article?*

7. *Compare your summary with others in the group.*

The power of the media lies in their role in promoting the dominant political, economic and cultural values and beliefs of a society. This power manifests itself in deciding what is the news. The media can set the agenda by presenting certain information, while avoiding other topics.

Representation

We have seen that the communication process involves meaning that is shared through language. 'Representation' is the term used to describe the active use of language.

Television is often referred to as a 'window on the world'. This phrase suggests that we are looking at reality as though we are looking out our sitting-room window. Think back to the exercise on the sporting event; think of the differences between being present at the event and watching the event on television. What is the difference?

Because the media use a process of mediation, what is presented to us is not reality but a representation of reality. In other words, what you read in the newspaper and watch on television is constructed. News programmes on radio and television use the genre of reporting objective facts, which gives the impression of reality. However, the news does not just happen: someone decides what is newsworthy. Therefore, the news is a reflection of the news values held by editors.

As certain events are constructed and represented in a certain way by the media, this informs how we think about certain events, groups and individuals. This is why the media play such a significant role in shaping our attitudes.

Determinants of news production

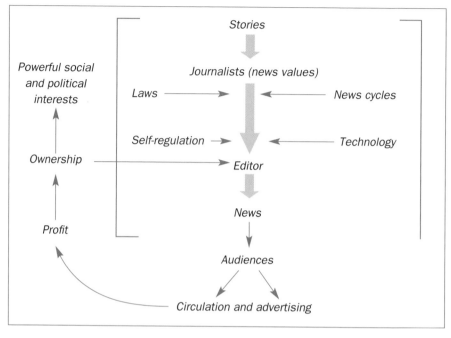

(From Brian Dutton, The Media, *London: Longman 1997.)*

ACTIVITY 8

1. *Take* The Irish Independent, The Irish Times *and* The Examiner *for one day and find out what percentage of the paper is given over to advertising.*

2. The Examiner *makes most of its sales in Munster. Is this reflected in its coverage of events?*

3. The Irish Mirror *is a tabloid newspaper. What does this mean?*

4. *Analyse the television schedules of RTE1, Network 2, TV3 and TG4 and find out how much time is devoted to sport.*

5. *Analyse the television schedules of RTÉ 1, RTÉ 2, TV3 and TG4 and find out how much time is devoted to sport.*

6. *On RTÉ Radio 1, how much time is devoted to programmes for teenagers?*

7. *RTÉ Radio 1 always interrupts its programmes for the Angelus. What does this tell us?*

8. *How much time is devoted to news on your local radio station?*

9. *What type of audience does Lyric FM have?*

FUNCTIONS OF THE MEDIA

Why does the media exist and what are they supposed to do? What are their functions for the individual and for society?

- *Entertainment functions*: the media provide entertainment for their audience. The entertainment provided may be seen as healthy and pleasurable for us or it may be viewed as a means of diverting our attention from more important issues.

- *Information functions*: the media provide necessary information about the world for their audience. It can be said that this helps us to form our view of the world, or it may be said that we are given a particular view of the world to keep us happy.

- *Cultural functions*: the media provide material which reflects and develops our culture. It could be said that they develop mass culture at the expense of subcultures.

- *Social functions*: the media provide examples of how relationships and interactions take place in our society. This helps us operate successfully as members of our society.

- *Political functions*: the media provide evidence of political events, issues and activities. This enables us to understand the operation of politics in our society and to participate in political activity. But the media may also shape our opinions and may only raise certain issues.

ACTIVITY 9

Analyse the programmes on RTÉ1, TV3, ITN, BBC2 and TG4 for one day and categorise them into the five functions above.

THE NEWS ON TV

Many more people watch 'the news' than any other programme on TV. It is broadcast several times a day and people have a strong desire to know and to see what is happening in the world. Most of us believe that it is accurate and trustworthy. This may be because we see pictures as well as hearing words. You can see what is happening and make up your own mind about it. But is the TV news neutral? Is there any distortion?

The production of TV news is very complicated. It is not like the weather that just happens. TV stations have many people who gather the news. But once the news is gathered someone must decide which items to put on and which to leave out. How do you decide what is important? If someone throws an egg at the Taoiseach, is that important enough to make the news? Visually, it might be very strong.

There are many factors which influence the decision to include some stories and not others in television news.

- The news takes up a specific number of minutes. This time has to be filled. When this time is filled nothing else will be considered unless it is of major importance. Sometimes a news bulletin is extended if a very big story 'breaks'.

- The news appears at regular times every day. Events are planned in advance so producers can decide to cover certain events. But who decides which events to cover?

- TV is a visual medium. Stories that provide good pictures are often chosen over items which do not have good visuals. A former prime minister of Britain, Mr Harold Wilson, complained that he almost had to pay people to throw eggs at him to get the cameras to cover his meetings.

- The news is also part of the night's entertainment on TV. This affects its presentation. Sometimes humorous items are tagged on at the end to entertain the audience.

ACTIVITY 10

1. Can you remember any events that resulted in the news being extended?

2. Can you recognise the elements in the news that are there for entertainment?

3. Does the way the newsreader deals with certain items determine the way you are to interpret them? For example, does she read some items in a solemn voice and some in a cheerful tone?

4. Watch the news on TV for a day and then the following day read a newspaper. Are there many items in the newspaper which did not appear on TV? Make a list of these items.

5. Did items appear on TV which did not appear in the newspaper? Make a list of these items also.

ADVERTISING

Advertising is paid-for persuasive communication. It appears between programmes on TV and radio and in magazines and newspapers. It also can appear in other places, such as shopping bags and billboards. It must be distinguished from *publicity*, which is free communication. An example would be a writer talking about her book on *The Late Late Show*.

The purpose of advertising is to create awareness of the product or service, to assure existing customers of the quality of the product, to get a bigger share of the market and to hold onto the existing share of the market against competition.

The media reflect the values and beliefs of a culture. An example of this would be in observing how men and women have been represented in advertising over the years. On the surface, an advertisement is promoting a particular product. This is what is denoted. When we analyse the message in the advertisement, we decode many of the values held in a particular culture; this is what is connoted. Media images, therefore, represent dominant ideas and values about nationality, class and sex. These representations change over time as values and beliefs change. For example, television advertisements in the 1960s represented women in the home, cleaning the house, while men were represented 'going to work' outside the home. These images reflected the roles played by men and women in society at that time. The advertisements of today reflect the changes in how men and women are now perceived.

ACTIVITY 11

1. Identify an advertisement that represents the 'working mother'.

2. Take three advertisements. How are women represented? How are men represented? Describe the social setting. Are these examples a true reflection of Irish society?

3. How are babies and children represented in advertising? Which adult is with them? What activity are they involved in? What is the social setting? Are the children passive or active?

4. How are young people represented? What products are aimed at young people? What is the social setting? Does this reflect reality?

5. How are people over sixty-five represented in television programmes? How are elderly people represented in television serials?

A culture's assumptions about people and events are reflected in the media. The media are powerful because widely held, taken-for-granted assumptions are presented as natural. The problem with this is that people outside this 'reality' are perceived as different.

Think of a minority group. When did you last see members of this group on television or in the newspapers? How were they represented? Describe the setting. How was the photograph mediated to produce the 'preferred reading'? What does this tell you about how the group is perceived in society in general?

In conclusion, media texts are social and cultural constructions. They are not natural, timeless or universal.

Analysis of an advertisement

GOLDILOCKS AND THE THREE BREAKS
A family fairytale come true.

Once upon a time, Goldilocks was looking to get away for the June Bank Holiday with all the family when she came across 3 great offers for the luxurious Jurys Hotel Cork.

A BIG BREAK
3 nights dinner, b&b, children's activities, free family passes to your choice of local attractions for 2 adults and 2 children under 12 sharing, for £381 all-in.

A MEDIUM BREAK
2 nights b&b for 2 adults and 2 children under 12 sharing for just £71.50 per adult.

A SMALL BREAK
2 adults and 2 children under 12 sharing a family room for only £69 per night. (Meals extra).

She thought about the heated pool, sauna, gym and squash court, the lively bars and superb restaurants, so she called Central Reservations on **01-667 1333**. (Of course, she could have called the hotel direct on **021-27 66 22**.) And they stayed there happily ever after.

JURYS HOTEL CORK
Western Road, Cork.
NOBODY DOES IT BETTER

Note the title 'Goldilocks and the Three Breaks', which seeks to establish the notion of a holiday as a fairytale. It begins with the usual beginning of a fairytale: 'Once upon a time'. The well-known story is carried through the advertisement with the three headings 'A Big Break', 'A Medium Break' and 'A Small Break'.

The pictures of the three little bears on the advertisement will draw the reader to it and help to break up the script and make it attractive to the eye. The extra facilities offered are mentioned by way of Goldilocks thinking about 'the heated swimming pool, sauna, gym and squash court . . .' The notion of Goldilocks contacting a modern hotel is mildly amusing. The fairytale theme is continued to the very end with the phrase 'And they stayed there happily ever after.'

The different types of script also lend variety to the advertisement. The ad has bold at the top followed by italic. A different script is used for the headings within the ad and the telephone numbers are in bold, which makes them stand out from the rest of the plain script.

ACTIVITY 13

1. Select an advertisement for a holiday break *from* The Irish Times, The Sunday World *and your local newspaper. Compare and contrast the images and words selected to advertise the holiday.*

2. Select an advertisement for three different supermarkets in a variety of newspapers. How do they get their message across? What senses do they focus on?

REVIEW

1. Find three examples of media manipulation which occurred in the past three months.
2. Find out the readership of your local newspaper and the audience for your local radio.
3. Find out how much it costs to advertise on your local radio.
4. Find three advertisements which you think do not give accurate descriptions of the product or service they are selling.
5. Give three advantages and three disadvantages of advertising.
6. What is meant by the term 'mediation'?
7. What characteristics do the mass media have in common?
8. What is meant by 'media text'?
9. What is the meaning of 'genre'?
10. What is meant by the term 'representation'?

PITFALLS

rout route

Rout can be used in the sense 'put them to *rout*', i.e. to defeat them completely. It can also be used as in to '*rout* someone out of the bed'.

Route is a course taken, e.g. 'a man's delivery *route*', or 'I took the shortest *route*'.

CONFUSING WORDS

dammed	damned	exercise	exorcise
done	deign	fair	fare
instant	instance	depravation	deprivation
dying	dyeing	intense	intents
either	ether	knave	nave

QUIZ

What famous writer can you find in this anagram?

I ask me has will a peer,

we will all make his praise.

SPELLINGS

The words most commonly misspelled are highlighted.

radical	**recommend**	relaxation
rapidity	reconcile	reliable
rarity	reconciliation	**relieve**
readability	recruit	religion
readily	rectangle	reluctance
realise	refer	relying
really	referee	remainder
reasonable	**reference**	remember
rebel	**referred**	remembrance
rebelled	referring	remit
rebuke	refugee	remittance
receipt	regiment	remitting
receive	regret	removable
recent	regrettable	renounce
recitation	regular	renunciation
recite	reign	
recognise	rejoicing	

19

VISUAL PRESENTATION

INTRODUCTION

There are several ways of presenting information. Your documents must be presented in the clearest, most effective way possible. Just writing everything, paragraph after paragraph, is not always the best means. Readers, whether they are nine or ninety years old, respond to variety and vigour in presentation.

Charts, graphs, illustrations, diagrams, photographs, posters, symbols and signs are all forms of communication that can be used to replace or enhance the written, or indeed, spoken, message. These methods of communication are called visual communication. They have several advantages over the written message. They attract attention, arouse interest, give variety and drive home the message to the reader. Pages of statistics can be uninformative and intimidating, but put them in graphs and a person can grasp overall trends immediately. Even where these methods of communication are not absolutely necessary it can be a good idea to use some of them to give variety.

Reasons for using visual presentation

- To clarify your point.
- To emphasise your point.
- To simplify your point.
- To unify your point.
- To impress your readers.

1. *Signs are generally very easy to understand. What do the following well-known signs mean?*

(a)

(b)

(c)

(d)

(e)

(f)

(g)

(h)

CLEARWAY
Mon. - Fri.
08.00-09.30
17.00 - 18.30

(i)

(j)

LUAN - AOINE
Mon. - Fri.
08.00 -18.30

Taken from Rules of the Road *(Department of the Environment)*

2. *Find ten signs, other than road signs, which would be easily understood by the public.*

3. *Draw a sign for your local library to indicate that people who steal books will be prosecuted.*

4. *Draw a sign for your school to indicate that students are to ascend the stairs on the right-hand side and descend on the left.*

5. *Find one sign, in general use, which you think would be unclear to the general public.*

TYPES OF PRESENTATION

Information can be presented visually by way of:

- tables
- charts
- graphs
- combination of the above.

The method chosen depends on the type of information, the object of the presentation and the audience.

Tables

Tables, or tabular presentation, simplify and sometimes summarise information. They facilitate comparison and contrast. Tables can be understood and interpreted by those who have a bent for mathematics. However, many people do not have the gift for drawing conclusions from tables of figures.

FIG. I — SAMPLE TABLE

Population: International Comparisons 1992			
Country	Thousands	Per sq km	Percentage under 15 years
Australia	18,289	2	21.2
Belgium	10,157	333	17.9
Canada	29,964	3	20
Denmark	5,262	122	17.6
France	58,380	106	19.3
Germany	81,877	229	15.9
Greece	10,465	79	16.6
Ireland (26 Cos.)	**3,621**	**52**	**23.9**
Italy	57,473	191	15.3
Japan	125,864	333	15.9
Luxembourg	418	161	18.5
Netherlands	15,494	380	18.4
Portugal	38,618	123	22.2
Spain	39,270	78	16.2
Sweden	8,901	20	18.8
Switzerland	7,085	172	17.6
United Kingdom	58,782	240	19.3
United States	265,557	28	21.7

(*Source*: IPA *Yearbook and Diary*, 1999.)

Design of tables

Tables should not be too large. If possible, break a large table up into a number of smaller tables. This will help the reader. If at all possible a table should not cover more than one page and should not be stretched across two facing pages. All tables should have a title. All columns should have headings. Footnotes to tables should be included by using asterisks or some other sign. If numbers are used to indicate footnotes, they may cause confusion. Unit descriptions (points, tons, acres, etc.) should be placed above the columns as part of the headings. Do not allow the table to have a cluttered appearance. Separate the headings of columns and rows with a line if necessary, but do not use lines to separate related information. Separate related information by using extra space.

Charts

There are basically two types of charts that might be useful in the presentation of a report.

- *Organisation chart*: an organisation chart shows the chain of authority in a company. It shows who has responsibility for what and the relationship each member of staff has to others in the organisation.

FIG. 2 – ORGANISATION CHART

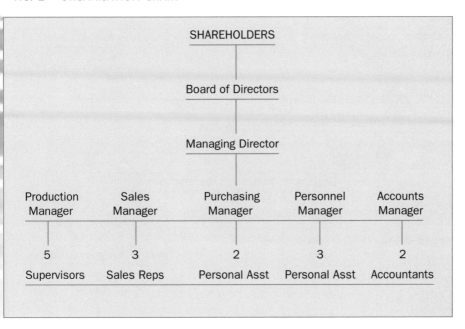

- *Flow chart*: a flow chart is a diagram showing how a job can be performed by laying out, in detail, the logical sequence of actions to be performed. It must have a single starting point and single end point.

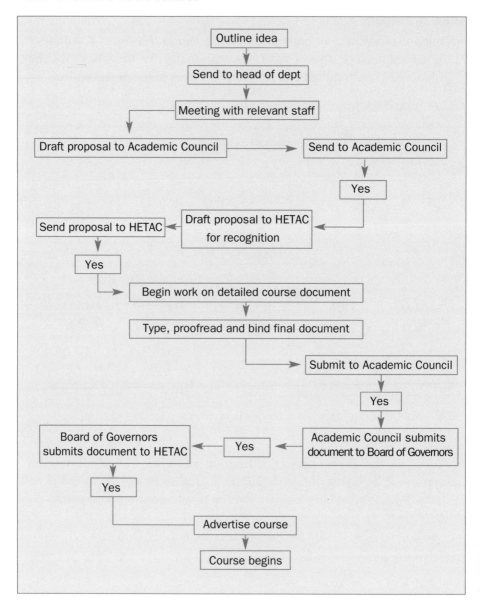

Design of charts

Charts should be given plenty of space so that they look uncluttered and clear. It may sometimes be useful to use different colours. The amateur should attempt only very simple charts. If the chart is to be in any way complicated, it makes sense to get a draughtsperson to execute it.

Graphs

- *Bar graph/chart*: these are a useful means of comparing simple magnitudes by the length of equal-width bars. They can show quantity changes over a period of time and over geographic distance. For example, if it is necessary to show the profit of a company over a ten-year period, the bar chart is appropriate as comparisons can be made.

FIG. 4 – BAR CHART

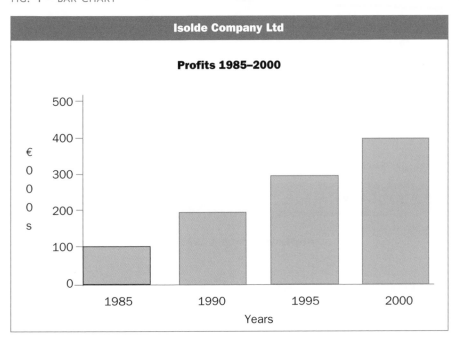

- *Grouped bar chart*: two or three variables can be compared in a single graph by the use of grouped bars. The bars are distinguished from one another by using different fill-ins in the bars.

FIG. 5 – GROUPED BAR CHART

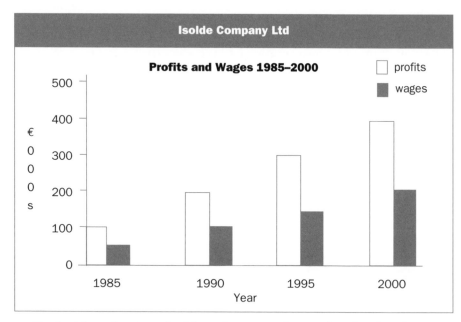

- *Stacked bar chart*: stacked bar charts may be used to display the same information as you would put on a grouped bar chart, but you wish to display it in a different way.

FIG. 6 – STACKED BAR CHART

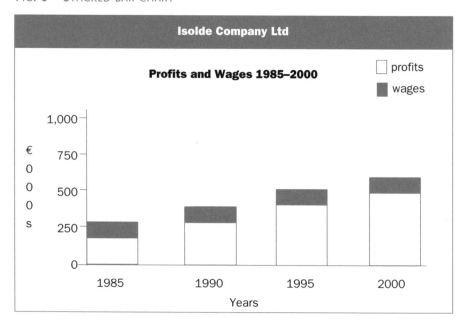

- *Horizontal bar chart*: the graphs we have shown so far are vertical graphs. But it is also possible to have horizontal graphs. Whether to design a graph vertically or horizontally is a matter of choice. It depends on which format will help clarity and look well.

FIG. 7 – HORIZONTAL BAR CHAR

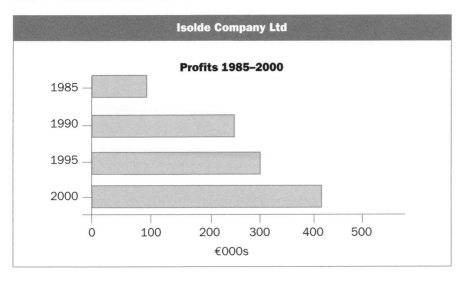

Design of graphs and charts

Computers will now draw graphs and charts in several different ways and you can choose whichever presentation best suits your purposes.

- *Histogram*: a histogram shows the frequency of occurrence of the subject being studied. For example, the speeds in shorthand for a class of forty students are shown here, first as a table and then as a histogram.

Words per minute	No. of students
60	4
70	6
80	10
90	12
100	5
110	3

FIG. 8 – HISTOGRAM

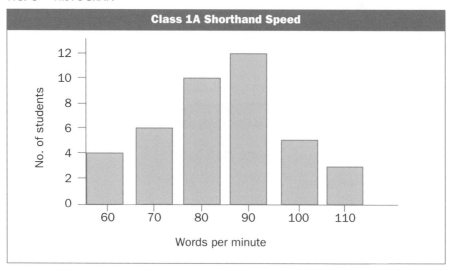

- *Pie chart*: the pie chart uses a circumference of a circle as its scale and the component parts of the chart are shown as segments of this circle. The 360 degree circle, therefore, represents 100 per cent. This type of chart is useful to show how a whole is composed. It can lose its effectiveness when too many segments are employed. Pie charts are not useful to show comparisons unless the comparisons are very obvious.

FIG. 9 – PIE CHART

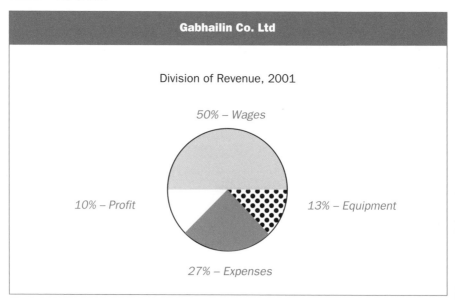

- *Line graph*: line graphs are useful for showing rising or falling trends. A line graph plots a series of quantities measured on the vertical scale against a period of time measured on the horizontal scale.

FIG. 10 – LINE GRAPH

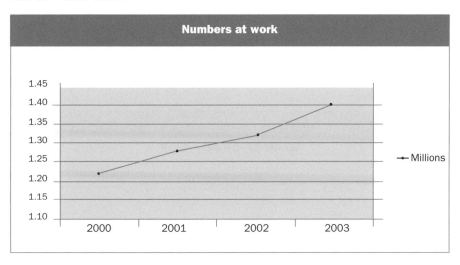

- *Z chart*: Z charts can show three types of information. Let us take the example of a shop renting videos over a period of one week. The owner may need to know the following:

(a) the number of videos borrowed each day of the week

(b) the cumulative total borrowed as the week progresses

(c) the moving weekly total. This can be found by adding the totals for the preceding seven days. For example:

	Daily total	Moving total
Monday	250	
Tuesday	300	
Wednesday	350	
Thursday	180	
Friday	400	
Saturday	400	
Sunday	450	2,330
Monday	260	2,590
Tuesday	320	2,660

No. of Videos Rented Week 24–29 July 2006

Monday	250
Tuesday	300
Wednesday	350
Thursday (half day)	180
Friday	400
Saturday	460

FIG. 11 – Z CHART

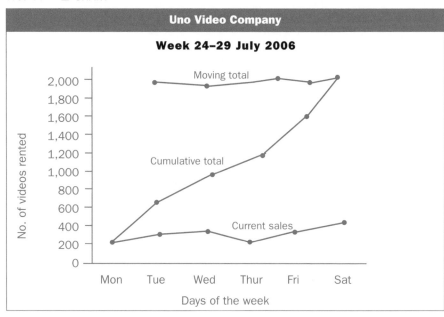

As can be seen from Fig. 11, a Z chart resembles a Z and hence its name.

- *Pictogram*: a pictogram is a picture, or series of pictures, which conveys information very simply. Pictograms add warmth and humour to what otherwise might be a cold presentation of statistics. They will not convey information in a very precise manner but will give fairly accurate trends.

FIG. 13 – PICTOGRAM

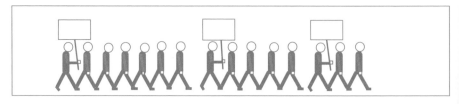

General guidelines on illustrations

- All illustrations should be numbered so that they can be referred to easily, but they should appear in the most appropriate place.
- They should make an immediate impact. They should not be included as a form of padding.
- All drawings must be to scale, and when a number of drawings refer to the same figures they should be to the same scale.
- Illustrations should have a balanced look and should be pleasing to the eye.
- Do not clutter any one illustration with too much information. If a graph or drawing has too many lines the reader may have difficulty in distinguishing what is essential to your argument.
- It should be possible to understand each illustration without reference to the text.
- All symbols used should be sufficiently explained.

ACTIVITY 2

1. Find the growth in student numbers in your college for the past ten years and present it on a suitable graph.

2. Draw a graph for the following figures:

Rathclogheen Insurance Co.
% Breakdown of Assets

	2000	2005
Mortgages	20.2	39.7
Buildings	12.5	30.6
Shares	20.6	14.3
Land	40.5	10.2
Others	6.2	5.2
	100.0	100.0

3. Find out the growth in applications for planning permission in your county over the last five years and illustrate your findings.

4. Use an organisation chart to illustrate the line of authority in your college.

5. Put the following information on a suitable graph.

Ireland: Births, Marriages and Deaths 1986–1997*

	Births	Marriages	Deaths
1986	17.4	5.2	9.5
1987	16.5	5.2	8.9

1988	15.3	5.1	8.9
1989	14.7	5.1	8.8
1990	15.1	5.0	9.1
1991	15.0	4.8	8.9
1992	14.5	4.6	8.7
1993	13.8	4.7	8.9
1994	13.4	4.5	8.6
1995	13.5	4.4	8.8
1996	13.9	4.5	8.7
1997	14.3	4.3	8.6

*Rates per 1,000 estimated population

6. Draw a graph showing how you spend your money each week.

REVIEW

1. Why use graphs in a report?
2. What is a Z chart?
3. When would you use a pie chart rather than a bar chart?
4. Should one ever use tables in a report?
5. Why might you use a horizontal bar chart rather than a vertical bar chart?
6. What is a pictogram?
7. Should one place graphs and charts in the body of a report or in the appendices? Why?
8. What is a flow chart?

PITFALLS

unique

A thing is *unique* or *not unique*. You should not say 'It is *somewhat* unique'. There are no degrees of uniqueness.

CONFUSING WORDS

fir	fur	route	root
hire	higher	their	there
its	it's	too	two
main	mane	seen	scene
not	knot	steel	steal

QUIZ

What is a metagram? It is a word that can be turned into a number of other words by changing its initial letter.

Make six different words out of *kink* by changing its initial letter.

SPELLINGS

The words most commonly misspelled are highlighted.

repetition	resolute	rheumatic
replaceable	resolution	rhubarb
reply	responsive	rhyme
reprieve	restaurant	rhythm
repulsive	restrain	ridiculous
reputation	resume	righteous
repute	resumption	righteousness
rescue	**retrieve**	riot
rescuing	retriever	riotous
resemblance	reveal	rival
resemble	revelation	rivalling
resent	revenue	rivalry
resentful	reverent	rogue
reside	reverse	roguery
residence	revival	roguish
resign	revive	rubbish
resignation	revolution	rumour

PART 6

COMMUNICATIONS

TECHNOLOGY

20

COMMUNICATIONS TECHNOLOGY

INTRODUCTION

The old traditional office with just a manual typewriter and a filing cabinet is no more. Even quite small concerns have now invested in some of the new office technology. Over the last twenty years the office has seen revolutionary changes. Firms have invested in the new technology because it is economical and efficient. It has led to major increases in productivity for office workers.

The invention of the microchip meant that computers could be much smaller and cheaper than previously. This put computers within the reach of small businesses and meant that technological advances did not just benefit large companies.

These developments have led to changes in the training and education of office staff. The traditional skills, such as the ones featured in this book, are still the most vital, but others are also necessary. The old typing and shorthand courses are gone forever. Now every employee must be able to use a range of office equipment which would have bewildered the office staff of twenty years ago.

THE INTERNET

In the 1960s, during the Cold War, it was believed that there was a need for a bombproof communications system. A concept was devised for linking computers together throughout a defined area. In the beginning only governments and a few universities were linked. The internet, as it came to be called, gradually moved from being a military tool to being a method of communication between scholars. The speed of the internet has changed the way people receive information. It combines the immediacy of broadcasting with the detailed coverage of newspapers.

The World Wide Web (often abbreviated to WWW, or simply 'the web') is a hypertext network that runs on the internet. It began in the 1980s when Dr

Tim Berners-Lee wrote a program for his own computer that allowed pages to be linked using keywords. It soon became possible to link documents on different computers, as long as they were connected to the internet. The web remained primarily text-based until 1992. In that year the first web browser was created and this made it easier to access different websites. Soon sites contained not just text but sound and pictures as well.

In most web pages, certain words or phrases appear in text of a different colour from the rest. When you click on such a word or phrase you will be transferred to the relevant page, whether it is at the same site or a different one. Sometimes there are buttons, images or portions of images that are 'clickable'. If you move the pointer over a spot on a web page and the pointer changes to a hand, this indicates that you can click and be transferred to another page.

Web pages are sometimes called 'home pages'. A group of pages belonging to one person or organisation is called a 'website'.

Internet service providers (ISPs) are companies that provide access to the internet for a fee. Typically they are telecommunications companies such as Eircom or Esat BT. People at home can 'dial up' a connection and use their home computers to contact the servers and get or send information over the internet. Internet connection speed can be divided into two categories: dial-up and broadband. The speed at which a website downloads from the internet depends on the type of connection you are using. Dial-up connections range from free to inexpensive and require the use of a phone line. Broadband connections can be either ISDN, wireless, cable, DSL, satellite or ethernet. Broadband is faster, always on and sometimes more expensive.

Browsers

Using the World Wide Web, you have access to millions of pages of information. Browsers are programs that let you look at the World Wide Web. The two most common browsers are Microsoft Internet Explorer and Netscape Navigator. The appearance of a website may vary depending on the browser you are using.

In order to move around and change between websites, you will need to use the toolbar. It is located at the top of your screen and will look something like this:

It has images and words called 'buttons'. These buttons allow you to move between web pages, print a copy of the web page, refresh or reload the web page or search for new information. The Home button will bring you to the website that you have set as your starting point. If any of the buttons are pale in colour, then that means that particular button is inactive and cannot be used.

Web addresses (URLs)

Web addresses are what you hear said on the TV and radio when they say 'Visit our home page at www dot...'. The technical name for a web address is universal resource locator (URL). Once you know a URL or website address you can type it into the 'location' or 'netsite' space, which is usually just below the toolbar. Every web page has a URL. Whatever page you are on shows its URL in that space.

Most web addresses start with **http://**. You can type web addresses in the location space and press the return key on your keyboard and the browser will find that web page for you. Alternatively, you can also click on the Go button and it will bring you to the web page. Most Irish websites end in .ie, sites in the UK tend to use .co.uk, while international sites use .com. Punctuation is very important in website addresses, as a misplaced comma or full stop can radically alter the results produced.

In most web pages, certain words or phrases appear in text of a different colour from the rest. When you click on such a word or phrase you will be transferred to the relevant page, whether it is at the same site or a different one. Sometimes there are buttons, images or portions of images that are 'clickable'. If you move the pointer over a spot on a web page and the pointer changes to a hand, this indicates that you can click and be transferred to another page.

Searching

It is impossible to estimate the number of websites and web pages available on the internet. Suffice it to say there are billions. With such a large amount of information, it is difficult to know where to start when searching for information.

Search Engines

The most common ways of looking for things or 'searching' the web are search engines. A search engine searches the web for keywords, then produces a list of websites where that word or phrase occurs. Therefore, you may get varying returns (results) for the same phrase from a number of different search engines.

Meta search engines search other search engines. Often they also search smaller, less well-known search engines and specialised sites. The most popular meta search engines are www.dogpile.com, www.mamma.com and www.metacrawler.com.

Natural language search engines accept queries in plain English. The Ask Jeeves website (www.ask.com) accepts questions without the use of quotation marks, i.e. you can input your questions directly.

Using a search engine

Websites tend to change often. Older versions may still exist when the company adopts a new name or changes their website address. These changes are not always reflected in the search engine database. The result may be that a link from a search engine to a particular website is no longer valid.

Each search engine is slightly different from others, but they all have frequently asked questions (FAQs) or instructions that explain how that specific site works. Taking a few minutes to read these FAQs before you start searching will save you time later on.

Searching the internet

All the Web	www.alltheweb.com
AltaVista	www.altavista.com
Ask Jeeves	www.ask.com
Dogpile	www.dogpile.com
Excite	www.excite.com
Go	www.go.com
Google	www.google.com
Google Toolbar	http://toolbar.google.com
HotBot	www.hotbot.com
Lycos	www.lycos.com
MSN Toolbar	www.msn.com
Web Crawler	www.webcrawler.com
Yahoo!	www.yahoo.com

Irish sites:

Browse Ireland	www.browseireland.com
Doras	www.doras.ie
Google Ireland	www.google.ie

There is a special toolbar for Internet Explorer users that puts a Google search box right into your browser. In addition, you can use it to see the 'page rank' popularity score of any page you are viewing, search within the particular site you are viewing, see a previous or 'cached' copy of any dead pages, find pages similar to the one you are viewing, block pop-ups and more.

ACTIVITY I

1. In Yahoo! (www.yahoo.co.uk), type in the name of your county and list some of the returns you get.

2. In MSN (www.msn.ie), type in the name of the county you used in question 1. Are there different sites listed?

3. How many websites on education in Ireland can you find?

4. In Ask Jeeves (www.ask.com) type in the following question: 'Where can I find an Irish embassy?'

5. Select one of the returns from your answer to question 4 and access that site.

6. Which search engine do you find the most useful and why?

7. Find a hotel in Rome near the Vatican.

8. What information can you find on Manchester United Football club?

9. Find out what services your telephone company provides to home telephone users

E-MAIL

E-mail allows messages to be sent from one computer to another over a network, usually the internet. Each user is provided with a mailbox, where messages are stored. The same message can be sent to different people, and you can get confirmation that the receiver has read your message.

E-mail is fast, and the rules for it are less formal than for normal mail, so it is easy to compose and send. There is nothing you can say in an e-mail message that you cannot say in a letter or postcard, but how many of us will dig out a card, write a note, find a stamp and then trudge to the post office just to say 'Hello'?

E-mail guidelines

- *Addresses and personal names*: always provide a personal name if your e-mail system allows it. A personal name attached to your address identifies you better than your address can on its own.

- *Subject lines*: always use a subject line in your message. It is often the only clue the recipient has to the contents when filing and searching for messages. Make the subject line meaningful, short and to the point.

- *Message length, content and format*: the e-mail message should also be short and to the point. Do not type your message in capital letters, as this is referred to as shouting. Break it up into logical paragraphs. Just because e-mail is fast does not mean that it should be slipshod.

- *Replies*: include enough of the original message to provide a context. Use some kind of visual means to distinguish between text quoted from the original message and your new text. This makes the reply much easier to follow. The greater-than sign (>) is the usual marker for quoted text.

- *Signatures*: a 'signature' is a small block of text appended to your messages that usually contains your name, address, telephone number, fax number, etc. It is possible to add a signature to your messages automatically. Some people add quotations and phrases that they feel say something about them as a person. A person from County Clare might add 'Up the Banner!' to their signature. If you are tempted to add to your signature you should keep it short, do not be offensive and avoid meaningless quotations that have no significance in other countries or cultures.

- *Courtesy*: courtesy should be observed at all times.

E-mail etiquette

Keep your messages short and to the point

It is important to remember that some people receive hundreds of e-mail messages a day. A carefully crafted short message will be appreciated and may possibly encourage a reply quicker than a long-winded ramble. Use the subject heading to indicate the content of your e-mail.

Format and font style of e-mails

Never write messages in capital letters. This is the e-mail equivalent of shouting. Do not include fancy formatting, as the recipient may not be able to read it. When composing an e-mail, the > sign in front of the text indicates that it is part of the received message. You may wish to include this when replying to the e-mail.

You've got mail

Check your messages regularly. If you plan to be out of the office for a few days, then set your e-mail to automatically send an out of office reply. This is an automatic message from your e-mail account in reply to e-mails, stating that you are out of the office.

Beware of attachments

Avoid attaching large files when sending an e-mail, as they could block up your recipient's system. Always scan files for viruses before attaching them to an e-mail or before opening them.

Read, discard or save

In business it may be necessary to keep a record of the e-mails you have sent. It is good practice to set your account to save copies of sent messages. Avoid the tendency to print out every message. Most e-mail accounts have a facility which allows you to store messages relating to a particular topic in folders.

Saluations

A business e-mail is not as formal as a business letter. Use your own judgment, though it is standard practice in the opening correspondence to start with a level of formality and then gradually move to using their first name. If you are unsure, stick to the formal salutation.

Signatures

A signature includes all relevant contact details of the sender. If the e-mail address is a business address, the sender's position in the company is also included. Details that normally form part of a letterhead can be included with the signature. E-mail accounts provide a facility for you to preset your signature, which is then automatically included when you decide to compose a message.

Return to sender

Electronic mail indicates that the message is delivered electronically, thus speed is implied. E-mail was designed for convenience. However, this may not always occur as your e-mail may have to pass through several different types of systems before it reaches its destination. Do not presume that your e-mail has reached its destination – people accidentally delete messages before reading them and e-mail systems can go down. If the e-mail address does not accept the mail, then it should bounce back to you. Too many users assume that the minute someone receives an e-mail, the person will read it. Some e-mail systems have features that try to combat this problem. These features (usually called notification) will notify you when a person has received your e-mail and may also notify you when the person has looked at the content of the message.

Address book

This is a list of e-mail addresses that you have gathered. Never send out mass mailings to everyone in your address book unless the content of the mail applies to everyone. Send the e-mail message only to those who need to receive it.

Never send sensitive information by e-mail

Like any other IT program, e-mail programs have their weaknesses. Security breaches are common. Hackers have been known to access e-mail accounts and send viruses to all the people in your address book.

In addition, it is very difficult to ascertain whether the e-mail was sent to the correct person. You may end up receiving an e-mail meant for another person or your e-mail may go astray.

Finally, some companies monitor employee e-mail accounts to avoid unauthorised usage. You should never send anything by e-mail that you would be embarrassed by or that you would not put in writing for distribution. E-mails are similar to letters in that a permanent record of them can exist.

Flames

To be flamed means that you have sent an e-mail to a person(s) that has caused that person(s) to respond in many not-so-nice words. It is basically a verbal attack in electronic form.

Think before you send

E-mail messages are instant communication. Never write or send them before rereading what you are saying. Once you have sent it there is no way of retrieving it. There is nothing easier than forwarding an e-mail, so always double check the recipient's address. It is important to check that you have not included earlier e-mails, unless you have chosen to do so.

Emotions (smilies)

E-mail nearly has the immediacy of a conversation, but it is devoid of body language. E-mail language has grown to include visual and audio clues and a method has been designed to add body language to e-mail. E-mail users use many abbreviations and other characters called smilies. Smilies convey the writer's emotions (cues). The most common example is :-). Turn your head to the left and you should see a happy face (the colon is the eyes, the dash is the nose and the parentheses is the mouth).

Smilies are typically found at the end of sentences and will usually refer back to the prior statement. Such symbols should be used sparingly. The following are the most common smilies used in e-mail language.

:-)   smiley face
;-)   wink (light sarcasm)
:-(frown (anger or displeasure)
:-e   disappointment
:-@   Scream
:-O   yell

E-mail abbreviations

Like mobile telephone language (text), e-mail has developed a language of its own and abbreviations are commonly used. Some of the more common abbreviations are listed below.

BTW	by the way
FYI	for your information
IMHO	in my humble opinion
OBO	or best offer

ACTIVITY 2

1. Find out how to add a signature automatically to your e-mail.

2. Send an e-mail message to one of your classmates, and let him or her know it is urgent.

3. Send an e-mail message and add an attachment to it.

4. Send the same e-mail message to three different people by putting their separate e-mail addresses in the address section.

5. Find out how to create folders for your e-mail.

6. Organise your e-mail in the folders you have created.

7. Find out how to forward an e-mail message you received to another person.

8. Send an e-mail message and add two attachments to it.

9. Get your friend to send you e-mail with an attachment, and then read that message and access its attachment.

10. In your e-mail program, find how to confirm that your recipient has read your message.

TELEPHONE SYSTEMS

- *Private automatic branch exchange (PABX)*: this is commonly called a switchboard. The PABX is connected to the public telephone network. It allows a number of incoming calls to be received at the same time. Most PABXs have the following facilities.

  (a) *Hold and transfer*: the call is put on hold while the receptionist dials the appropriate extension number.

  (b) *Music on hold*: music is played while the call is put on hold.

  (c) *Liquid crystal display (LCD)*: this displays the number dialled, the duration of the call, etc.

  (d) *Hands-free operation*: there is no need to lift the handset.

  (e) *Redial*: you press a special key to redial the last number.

  (f) *Speed-dialling*: the switchboard can be programmed to dial frequently used numbers by assigning a short code to each number.

  (g) Many other facilities are available, such as call forwarding, call waiting, call barring, call pick-up, etc. The manual with your switchboard will explain them.

- *Cordless telephones*: these allow a call to be transferred to the required person, even though he or she is not in the office.

- *Mobile telephones*: these are becoming more and more popular. They differ from cordless phones in that their range is not limited. However, they are more expensive to use than an ordinary telephone.

Voicemail

Voicemail enables the caller to leave a message when you are unable to take a call. It is really a replacement for the answering machine. It can be used to collect telephone messages for a number of people. Each user is given a password-protected 'voice mailbox', from which he or she can receive messages remotely using any ordinary digital phone.

Voicemail can also be used to distribute messages internally to a single person or to broadcast a single message to a group of users. A user receiving a message can send a reply directly into the sender's mailbox. Messages can be recorded while you are using the phone or connected to the internet. With voicemail you can call your mailbox from any phone to retrieve messages, and no message-recording device is required in your home. As long as you keep your personal password safe, your messages are private.

Features of voicemail

You can have a small red light attached to your telephone that flashes when you have a new voicemail message.

Arrangements can be made for people who share a phone number so that each person can have voicemail. The shared mailboxes can be set up either as chain-mailboxes or as sub-mailboxes. Chain-mailboxes allow callers to enter the five-digit private mailbox number of the person they are trying to contact. These are best for extensions shared by five or more people.

Sub-mailboxes allow callers to press 1 to leave a message for a particular person, 2 to leave a message for another person, and so on. This type of voice mailbox works best for two to four people sharing an extension. One primary voice mailbox is associated with the extension, with sub-mailboxes for each person sharing the extension.

Automated attendant

An automated attendant system allows the caller to enter the extension to which he or she wants to be connected, or will ask the caller to select the person from a list. Used together with voicemail, the system allows the caller to leave a message for the extension if it is engaged or if there is no answer. The main advantage of an auto-attendant, as opposed to manually handling the calls, is that multiple calls can be handled simultaneously. This gives the caller faster access to the person they want to contact.

Automatic call distribution (ACD)

This is the ideal solution where a high level of incoming calls needs a superior answering service. ACD ensures that the longest-waiting caller is answered first. Queue announcements give information to callers, who can be routed to priority answering after waiting for an excessive time.

Call management

A call management system can be connected to any telephone system or network of telephone systems to provide up-to-the-minute management information, statistics and charts that help ensure that the telephone system performs well. It enables you to monitor and reduce the following:

- time taken to answer calls
- time taken to transfer calls to the correct extension

- time taken to deal with calls
- number and cost of calls made by an extension or department.

Computer-telephone integration (CTI)

CTI enables you to hold your customer records in a computerised database to let the computer organise and initiate the dialling. It can also have customer details displayed on the computer before you answer the phone, and it can store and display your abandoned and unanswered calls for follow-up. CTI also allows callers to query a database. A common application would be banking by telephone.

Paging

This is much more than just a 'bleep' system. Today's pagers can display complete text messages and allow two-way conversation.

Cordless

This communication system is for people, not desks. It lets you move around your workplace yet still keep in touch with the outside world.

Telemarketing services

Eircom provides a range of services to businesses for generating sales. The main services are:

- *Freefone*: Freefone numbers begin with 1800. Calls are free to the caller: the cost is paid by the business. A business can choose its own distinctive Freefone number.
- *Call-save*: these numbers begin with 1850. Calls are charged at a special rate, regardless of length. The balance is paid by the business.
- *Lo-call*: these numbers begin with 1890. Calls are charged at the local rate from anywhere in the country, the difference being paid by the business involved.
- *Premium service*: this service allows businesses to provide information to the public twenty-four hours a day, seven days a week. Such information includes the weather forecast, sports results and flight information.

1. *Find out how many telephone companies can supply a service to your home.*

2. *List and explain four services offered by Eircom to its residential customers.*

3. *What is caller display?*

4. *What services do the various telephone companies offer to their business customers?*

5. *Prepare a short report for the managing director of your company on the various options for the provision of a comprehensive land line, internet and mobile telephone service available to the company.*

OFFICE EQUIPMENT

Fax

The fax machine transmits *copies* of documents to a receiver who has a compatible fax.

A fax is connected to the public telephone system. You simply turn on your fax and dial your receiver's machine. Her fax must also be connected to the telephone. You insert your document into your fax and it is reproduced on your receiver's machine. The cost is the same as the cost of a telephone call of the same duration.

FIG. I — SAMPLE FAX MESSAGE

01/02/06 19:20   050 99999   Joe Bloggs

Joe Bloggs
Box 485
Anywhere, 5555   **FAX**   Fax No. Int.
Victoria, Australia   Nat.
Phone: (050) 88888
Fax: (050) 99999

COMPANY: *Cavan College*

ATTENTION: *Director*   **FAX NO.** *(0503) 70400*

FROM: *Joe Bloggs*   **REF:**

DATE: *1/2/2006*   **NO. OF PAGES:** *1*

I am at present doing a study of education in various countries of the world and contacting many colleges.

It would be greatly appreciated if you could forward any information available - e.g. school magazine, students and teachers information booklet etc. outlining details of your college.

If unable to assist an address where this request could be forwarded would help.

Thanks in anticipation,

Regards from Victoria

RECEIVED FROM *Joe Bloggs*

The advantages of the fax are:

- It will transmit pictures, graphs, charts, drawings and diagrams as well as text.
- It is fast.
- Once the original document is correct, the reproduction made by the fax will be correct.
- The machines are cheap.

- A fax will give you a printout confirming that your document has been received at the other end.

However, the fax also has disadvantages:

- Lack of privacy.
- Uncertainty that the fax will reach the right person.
- Uncertainty of the quality of reproduction at the receiving end. This is particularly true of handwritten material or material that contains colour. Some colours disappear completely.
- Some companies require the original document.

New development in faxes

Computers can now act as fax machines. A modem can be installed in your computer or be attached to it. Your computer will need a special program for this.

There are advantages in having a fax capability on your computer:

- Less office space is required for equipment.
- A fax can be sent to another computer or to an ordinary fax machine.
- A fax can be filed on the computer rather than in a filing cabinet.
- There is no need to print the document before you fax it.

There are, however, some disadvantages:

- The computer must be on all the time to receive faxes.
- Information must be on your computer before you can fax it. However, if it is not on your computer you could use a scanner to read it into it. This may result in distortion.

Videoconferencing

Videoconferencing allows people to speak to one another and at the same time to see one another on television or computer screens. It allows meetings to take place between participants without the need for everyone travelling to one place.

- *Studios*: a studio is set up with equipment consisting of cameras, microphones and monitors.
- *Desktop units*: a computer can incorporate videoconferencing facilities. A small camera is placed on the monitor, and a microphone is connected to the computer. You then need a loudspeaker and videoconferencing program.

'Poshare' is a popular videoconferencing program. The advantage of this system is that you can participate in a conference without leaving your desk.

ACTIVITY 4

1. Find out what type of switchboard is available at your college.

2. Does the switchboard have the capacity to provide a print-out of all calls made and their duration?

3. Is the switchboard capable of restricting certain users to local calls? If so, on what grounds does the management decide to place restrictions on certain members of the staff?

4. What are the advantages and disadvantages of voice mail?

5. Carry out a small survey of your class to ascertain their attitudes to voice mail.

6. Find out five services that are offered on Freefone.

7. Find out five services that are offered on Lo-Call.

8. Find out five services that are offered on Call-save.

9. What are the advantages and disadvantages of having your computer used as a fax machine?

10. Find out the names of three companies that offer videoconferencing facilities.

OTHER USEFUL OFFICE EQUIPMENT

- *Personal digital assistant (PDA)*: the PDA was initially developed in the 1970s. It is now more commonly known as a Blackberry. It is essentially a wireless mini computer with a keyboard, and some models can be used as a mobile phone as well. The user can manage their e-mail account, send and receive messages. It does not require a modem. Different models have additional features.

- *Electronic diary*: this does the same job as a desk diary. Several programs are available for use on your computer. They usually display a calendar with a page for each day. The day can be divided into suitable units, e.g. hour or half-hour slots. Appointments can be entered in the diary in the usual way, and the computer will ring a bell as a reminder of an appointment. Jobs can be given priority through colour-coding. If your electronic diary is connected to other computers in a local area network (LAN), you can check when other people are available for a meeting. Generally a password is needed for this.

- *Electronic organiser*: this is a portable electronic diary that can fit in your pocket. It is helpful for use at meetings where you are away from your computer. Some models can import and export data between your office and home computer. All tend to have the following features: telephone directory, memo, calculator and clock.

REVIEW

1. Write one paragraph explaining the internet to somebody with no knowledge of it.

2. List three advantages and three disadvantages of the internet.

3. Will e-mail be the death of letter-writing? Discuss.

4. 'The main use of voice mail is to relieve the secretary of the obligation of answering the telephone.' Discuss.

5. What is the difference between a browser and a search engine?

6. What does WWW on the internet mean?

7. What is a home page on the World Wide Web?

8. Which daily Irish newspapers can be found on the internet?

PITFALLS

theist atheist agnostic

A *theist* is a person who believes in a god. An *atheist* is a person who believes there is no god. An *agnostic* is a person who asserts that it is not possible to know whether a god exists or not.

CONFUSING WORDS

seam	seem	tale	tail
seas	sees	team	teem
shear	sheer	timber	timbre
sole	soul	yews	ewes
vein	vain	wrap	rap

QUIZ

The following abbreviations are often used in e-mail for shorthand purposes. What do they stand for?

AFAIK   ASAP

AMBW   F2F

SPELLINGS

The words most commonly misspelled are highlighted.

stylish	submitted	substitute
subdue	subscribe	subtle
subduing	subscription	**subtlety**
submission	subsequent	subtraction
suburb	suitable	surround
suburban	sultry	surveying
succeed	**summary**	survival
success	superintend	survivor
successful	superiority	suspicion
successfully	**supersede**	suspicious
succession	**suppression**	sustain
successive	supremacy	syllable
successor	surgeon	sympathetic
succour	surplus	sympathy
sufficient	**surprise**	symptom
suicide	**surprising**	**synonym**
suitability	surrender	**synonymous**

CAREER

SKILLS

21

THE JOB SEARCH

INTRODUCTION

On average, we change jobs and careers three to four times in our career. In this era of lifelong learning, planning your career moves continues throughout your working life. While the days of long dole queues and emigration are just a part of history for young jobseekers today, it is more important than ever to be clear, focused and organised in job hunting and interview preparation.

Unless you are willing to take any job regardless of pay and skills required, it is vital that you spend time and effort in planning your career. Changing jobs is one of the most stressful events in a person's life, next to marriage and moving house, so it is essential that you approach the task of choosing a career and finding a job seriously and not just as a solution to meeting the monthly credit card bill.

Whatever the reason, changing jobs and careers takes effort and planning. By this stage you will have taken the initial steps by selecting a course of study. Your education and training will determine the options that are available to you to a large extent.

PLANNING YOUR CAREER

Advice

Unless you have a very clear idea of the exact career you want, it is advisable to seek some help. There are many different places and people who will help you identify the career area you should focus on. Start with friends and family – they know you best, so ask their opinion. Avail of the career advice facilities in your college or university, talk to recruitment specialists and talk to people in industries and companies that you think you may have an interest in.

Think about the things in life that you really enjoy. See if they can be fitted into a job. List all the things that you would really like to do. Identify your strengths and weaknesses and contrast these with the skills required in careers you are interested in. Identify your priorities – is it location? The pay scale? The travel opportunities? The promotional prospectives? Or is it the challenges offered by the career? For most people, selecting a career is directly related to their interests, aptitude, personality and needs.

If you are still unsure about what direction you would like to head in, use your time wisely and obtain work placements with a range of companies as a method of evaluating the industries you are interested in. Work experience is also an ideal way of getting yourself in the door of a company you would like to work in.

Finally, be true to yourself. Select the career that *you* want, not the one that someone else thinks best.

TAKING STOCK OF YOURSELF

Before taking any course of action, such as deciding to apply for a particular type of job, it is important to be aware of what you have to offer.

You have particular skills, knowledge, achievements and attitudes. Knowing what you have to offer will increase your morale and confidence and give you a greater chance of success. By taking stock of yourself you can decide whether it is time to develop some of the skills you have or to gain new skills that are more in demand at present. It is important to have a permanent record of:

- your skills

- areas that you need to develop

- the goals you set for yourself.

A written record helps the memory. You can also add to it. It helps when filling in application forms and preparing for interviews.

How to take stock of yourself

- Look at significant events in your life.

- Decide what the important themes in your life are.

- Assess your own approach to learning tasks.

- Assess your own abilities in the core skill areas.

- Assess factors that are likely to help or hinder your own learning and development.

Taking stock of yourself is a process of self-assessment and self-discovery leading to the production of a personal portfolio and a plan for future development.

Taking stock of yourself is a structured approach to:

- recognising and recording achievements

- clarifying personal and career goals

- assessing strengths and weaknesses

- identifying learning needs

- constructing personal and career-related development plans

- developing and demonstrating transferable skills

- reflecting on performance.

THE JOB SEARCH

Once you have identified your key skills and qualities and linked them with a career, then the search begins in earnest. Your job search will be a full-time job in itself. Be organised – keep a list of where you applied, keep copies of your application forms, the advertisement, etc., a contacts list, information on the company, who interviewed you and the interview results. Have a clear filing system that allows you to access all the information you may require as quickly as possible. The following form (Fig. 1) may help you in recording details about your job search. Attach a copy of the application form/CV and job interviews to the form for reference should you be called to an interview.

FIG. 1 – JOB APPLICATION DETAILS

Date application sent: _____

Reply received: Yes _____ No _____ Date _____

Interview: Yes _____ No _____ Date of interview: _____

Place: _____

Time _____

List of questions asked: _____

_____

_____

_____

Comments on interview performance: _____

Positive points: _____

Negative points: _____

Special comments: _____

Job obtained: Yes _____   No _____

WHERE TO FIND THAT JOB

The internet

The internet is fast replacing the recruitment pages of the national newspapers as a place to find a job. Among the most popular recruitment websites are www.jobfinder.ie, www.monster.ie and www.irishjobs .ie. Many recruitment agencies also have websites with listings of vacancies on their books.

FÁS (Foras Áiseanna Saothair)

FÁS is the training and employment authority in Ireland. It has a network of over seventy offices throughout the country. It provides practical advice, information and training aimed at helping the unemployed find employment and employers recruit suitable employees.

What can FÁS do for jobseekers?

- Provide you with information about training and development courses.
- Assist you in finding suitable vacancies.
- Give you information and advice about starting your own business as well as informing you about available grants.
- Give you a detailed occupational guidance and counselling service.

FÁS provides an information service and a range of schemes to assist you in identifying and pursuing job opportunities.

- An up-to-date list of job vacancies from a wide range of industrial and commercial sectors is available in all FÁS Employment Service Offices.
- Details of your skills and experience are matched with these job vacancies.
- You will be provided with assistance in selecting a career path.
- Facilities are available for you to make an appointment with a potential employer.

Newspapers

All the daily and Sunday newspapers have recruitment sections. *The Irish Independent* publishes its recruitment section on Thursday, and the recruitment feature appears on a Friday in the *The Irish Times* and *The Irish Examiner*. The Sunday newspapers also carry a recruitment listing. In addition to job advertisements, all papers carry features on the recruitment and career planning process. Local newspapers are also an excellent source for jobs available in their circulation area.

Recruitment companies

Recruitment and employment agencies are private businesses whose task is to find suitable employees for their client companies. They charge the employers a fee for their service. Recruitment consultants may also screen applicants and conduct preliminary interviews prior to the employer conducting the interview. Such agencies generally have a large number of applicants on their books. People register with such agencies and submit their CV, stating the type of job and salary range that they are seeking. The recruitment agency then tries to match the applicant with a client company, or if there is no suitable position available, they keep the CV on file until a position arises. In the larger towns and cities recruitment companies may specialise in a particular sector or have specialised units dealing with particular sectors. Some recruitment companies are contracted to fill temporary positions in client companies. Try to get as much out of your recruitment company as possible. They can provide you with CV preparation tips and interview training.

College careers service

In addition to offering advice on careers and assisting in job searches, many college and university careers services also offer a recruitment service. Avail of the facilities offered by the careers office, including mock interviews, and keep an eye on the job advertisements placed by companies with the careers office. A decision by a multi-national to locate in a particular region is often due to the presence of a college or university in the region. Companies and industries in the region often recruit directly from their local college or university. Pay attention to college notice boards, as vacancies may be displayed there before appearing in the local or national media. Occasionally, company recruiters may visit the college as part of their recruitment process. In the 1980s and 1990s, such presentations were referred to as the milk round.

Cold calling

What do you do when the company you are interested in is not recruiting? It may be worth your while contacting their personnel or human resources department to find out when they will be recruiting and what qualifications they require for positions you are interested in.

Some companies never advertise, but instead may headhunt from other companies or recruit people based on recommendations from current employees. In such cases, how do you bring yourself to their notice? Submitting a CV and requesting that it is kept on file should a vacancy arise is one approach. Be clear about what you are offering and what type of job you are looking for. Follow up the CV and letter with a call. Avoid calling at a busy time in the day, as they will be more than likely to dismiss your call immediately. If you do adopt this tactic, then the key to success is getting your CV to the right person within the company.

Friends and networking

Do not underestimate the potential of your friends and family in assisting you in your job search. At the peak of the boom in the IT sector, some companies offered rewards such as a bonus to their employees for every new employee they recruited. Those days are gone, but many short-term contracts, part-time jobs, temporary positions or maternity leave positions are filled on the recommendation of a current employee. The employer is happy to save the expense and time involved in advertising and interviewing. Let your friends and family know that you are in the market for a job or change of career.

Work placements

A majority of courses now include a work placement element. You should view such a placement as a method of getting in the door of a company you would like to work in. The benefits for both the company and the student of an internship are invaluable.

Such work placement programmes often form part of a company's recruitment policy. It allows them to assess the potential of a graduate and is a method of taking stock of potential employees.

Once you are on the inside track, you have an advantage when a vacancy is advertised. Such placements help fill the gap demanded by the 'experience required' element in recruitment advertisements.

Such programmes are also useful if you are thinking of changing careers and are finding it difficult to break into a new industry with your present qualifications. Instead of viewing a work experience placement as something to occupy you for a few weeks or a semester, see it as a means to an end in getting that job.

ANALYSIS OF A JOB ADVERT

Recruiting is an expensive business, both for the applicant and the employer. Recruitment agencies charge fees, job advertisements in national media are very expensive and the cost of going for an interview in terms of time and effort is also a consideration.

The size of the advertisement generally reflects the level of seniority of the position. Placing advertisements for jobs in national newspapers is expensive, so companies will not use unnecessary words. Therefore, the advert should be read closely to ascertain the type of person the company has in mind.

SENIOR ADMINISTRATOR
required.
Excellent dictaphone exp. and WP skills.
Financial institution.
Busy environment.

Contact Siobhan at _The Recruitment Centre_

The above advert is looking for a senior person. The use of 'senior' and 'excellent' emphasises the necessity for experience, which is not expressly mentioned. However, it is likely that they are seeking a person with some years of experience, as the advert highlights that the position is in a busy office. A financial institution may mean that the company is a bank, an insurance company, a building society or a similar type of company.

In contrast, the following advert may be of interest to a graduate of an office administration course.

OFFICE JUNIOR
Req'd Immed.
MS Word skills ess.
Varied role.
Estate Agents D.1.
01 123 4567

Notice that words are abbreviated and the cost of the advert is kept to the minimum. The essential skills in Microsoft Word and the nature of the job, 'varied role', are the only details mentioned. A contact number is given instead of an address to indicate the manner in which the company expects applicants to contact it.

The majority of advertisements will list key or essential skills required. They may also indicate other requirements which, while not essential, would be advantageous.

You should analyse all job ads, noting the key and essential skills. This will help you draw up a profile of the type of person required. If this profile matches with your skills and qualifications, then the next step is to consider whether you are interested in applying for the position.

The advertisement will also indicate the method of application. Typically it is either *CVs and covering letters to the personnel manager* or *application forms available from the human resources department*. Some companies may request that you submit an SAE (stamped, self-addressed envelope) in order to receive an application form. It is very important that you read the advertisement carefully. This is your first test – can you follow the procedures which the company has requested of job applicants?

ACTIVITY I

1. Select a job advertisement in a national newspaper and write a paragraph outlining the type of person, skills and experience the company is seeking.

2. Take stock of the skills and experiences you have to offer to an employer. List them and ask a friend to review what you have written.

3. Research the career options open to you upon completion of your current course of study. Identify any skills that you are lacking for the jobs you are interested in.

4. Working with a classmate, select a job advertisement that you think he/she is suited to.

5. Log on to www.irishjobs.ie or a similar website and register on that site to receive updates on vacancies in your area.

6. Consult the Golden Pages and find the nearest recruitment agency to your school or college. Contact them with a view to registering with them upon completion of your course of study.

RESEARCH THE JOB

Once you have found a job advertisement that you are interested in, you should find out as much as you can about the company.

- Read the documentation that accompanies the application form. Most companies have additional information available and you should request a copy. Some may provide a more detailed job description.

- Access the company's website. Request copies of annual reports or other publications. See if there are any articles published about the company in newspapers or business magazines.

- If possible, speak to someone who works there. Find out whether it is a new position or an existing position. Where has the previous occupant of the job gone? Try and speak to them. Be careful, though, as they may be on the interview board.

- Find out what the future plans are for the company and how they may impact on the position advertised.

- Look at similar positions in other companies.

- Research the industry and the future developments that may affect the growth of the company.

THE APPLICATION PROCESS

Regardless of what documentation you are required to submit as part of the recruitment process, it is essential that the application form or CV and accompanying letter contain no errors and present a professional image. Companies have been known to dump CVs without considering them if they contain errors. In this day and age with spell checks and modern technology, there is no excuse for errors. This is your first opportunity to make a good impression and progress to the next stage – the interview. There are no second chances.

THE APPLICATION FORM

If you are requested to complete an application form as part of the process of applying for a job, then you should request an electronic copy of the form by e-mail. Application forms may also be available online on the company's website. This will allow you to use a word processing package to complete the form. Otherwise you should type the hard copy of the form.

On receipt of the form, photocopy it and complete a draft version of the form, referring to the advertisement and the skills and requirements requested of applicants.

Read the instructions carefully. If it requests that the form be completed *in reverse chronological order starting with your present or most recent employment*, then follow those instructions. Other requests may include block capitals or black ink. If you have been provided with an electronic version of the form, then you can assume that it is acceptable to type rather than write. Check the preferred format of indicating dates. If completing the form by hand, write legibly.

Ensure that the information and relevant dates are accurate. Any errors in information at this stage may cost you the job at a later stage. Most forms will contain a declaration for you to sign stating that the information provided is correct and that any offer of employment arising out of the application may be withdrawn if the information provided is incorrect. This may include lying about dates of employment, exam results, job details and salary benefits. Employers are now checking application details and requesting references.

Check the draft for spelling or grammatical errors. Do not correct errors with corrective fluid – start again.

If you are completing the form online, use a standard acceptable font type and size, e.g. using Times New Roman or similar at 11 or 12 point would present a professional image. Do not cram information into a tiny space; instead, attach a separate sheet unless otherwise stated. A professional presentation is the key to a successful application.

Include all relevant information. Some companies state that applications must be submitted using the application form and that where supplementary information is provided by way of a CV, it is still necessary to complete the application form in full.

Accentuate the positive rather than the negative. Complete all sections of the form. If any section of the form is not relevant to you, then state *not applicable*.

Use the information you obtained in your research of the company and job when completing the application form. When describing your previous roles, identify verbs that would apply to the current position and see when they can be used when referring to your career to date. Words such as 'managed', 'implemented', 'extensive experience in', 'in charge of', 'established' and 'proven record in' all imply someone who is able to accept a certain level of responsibility. They might be appropriate if you are applying for a management position.

Where the application form requires the names of people willing to provide a reference, be careful to include people who will support your application.

FIG. 2 – APPLICATION FOR EMPLOYMENT

Notes for applicants – please read carefully

1. All sections must be answered. Where appropriate, please put 'not applicable'.
2. When applying for more than one post, a separate application form must be submitted in respect of each post.
3. While educational certificates and references should **not** be sent with your application, you may be required to produce evidence of qualifications during the course of the recruitment and selection process.
4. The company reserves the right to assess skills for certain posts through the use of appropriate tests.
5. It is important that complete dates be given where requested, i.e. month/year (mm/yyyy).
6. Applications must be submitted using this application form. Where supplementary information is provided by way of curriculum vitae, it is still necessary to complete the application form in full.
7. In order to comply with the closing date for the competition, application forms will be accepted by fax or e-mail. **However, it is essential to return a signed copy of the application form within seven days of the closing date.**

---

1. Title of post: Communications and Marketing Manger	**Post Reference No:**

2. Title: M*s*	**Surname:** *Lynch*	**Forename(s):** *Mary*

3. Contact address: *35 Seacrest Road, Sandymount, Dublin 4*

Permanent address *(if different)*:

4. Contact tel no: Daytime: *01 123 4567*   **Evening:** *085 123 4567*

5. Education record – third level only (in reverse chronological order)

College/institution attended	Period of study From	To	Qualification obtained, e.g. Cert., Diploma, Degree, Postgraduate qualification	Level of award, e.g. Distinction, First-class Honours, Second-class Honours, Pass etc.	Date conferred (month/ year)
Westmeath Institute of Education Second Class Honours	*2003*	*2005*	*Degree in Office Information System and Business Studies*	*Second Class Honours*	*July 2005*

Please use additional sheets if necessary.

6. Subjects of certificate/diploma examination

Final year subjects of Certificate examination

Not applicable

Final year subjects of Diploma examination

Not applicable

7. Subjects of degree examination

Final year subjects of primary degree examination

Office Administration, Legal Studies, Public Relations, Accounting

Other subjects taken as part of degree

Economics, Statistics

8. Major subject(s) of postgraduate course(s)/qualification(s)/year/title of research thesis

Not applicable

9. Details of membership of professional associations, institutions, etc.

Professional associations	Period of membership	Grade of membership
Not applicable		

10. Publications, research interests or patents

Please list publications with title, date, subject and, where appropriate, journal title. Attach additional sheet(s), if necessary.

List of publications

Not applicable

Research interests/patents

Not applicable

11. Starting with your present or most recent employment, please indicate the positions you have held. **Use additional sheet(s) if necessary**

Present or most recent employment

Dates – From: *July 2005*   To: *July 2006*   Annual salary: €25,000

Name and full address of employer:

Westmeath Business Company, Main St, Mullingar, Co Westmeath

Position held: *Business Development Executive*

Title of other positions held by you in the organisation: *Not applicable*

Nature of work

My main day-to-day duties include:

- *Mentoring start-up companies*
- *Developing business plans*
- *Preparing budget proposal and submissions for funding*
- *Advising companies in public relations strategies*

Period of notice required: *One month* Reason for leaving: *Not applicable*

Previous employment

Dates: From: *May 2004*   To: *Sept 2004*   Annual salary: €17,000

Name and full address of employer:

Halford Business Learning Ltd, 2 French St, Galway

Position held: *Junior Business Executive*

Title of other positions held by you in the organisation: *Not applicable*

Nature of work

I worked as part of the sales and marketing team. I was involved in making presentations to clients, liaising with clients as part of the after-sales services and dealing with prospective clients.

Reason for leaving: *To return to college*

12. Particular interests and abilities, including hobbies

Local history, travel, gardening and cookery

13. Please give the names and addresses of three persons, not related to you, who are willing to act as referees on your behalf. You must include your current employer or most recent employer (if not currently employed).

The company will assume permission to contact referees unless otherwise indicated.

Name	Address	Position	Do not contact*
Ms Louise Hall	*Westmeath Institute of Education, Main St, Mullingar, Co Westmeath*	*Director of Business School*	
Mr Patrick Joyce	*Halford Business Learning Ltd, 2 French St, Galway*	*Managing Director*	

** Please tick only if referee may **not** be contacted at this time.*

14. Additional information in support of your application. Use additional sheets if necessary.

15. Please state how you became aware of this position.

Sunday Independent advertisement

16. Have you previously applied for a position in this Institute?   Yes ☐   No ☑
If yes, please give details.

Year	Title of the post for which you applied	Interviewed: Yes/No

17.	If appointed, please indicate the earliest date at which you would be available to take up duty.
	One month

I, the undersigned, declare that the information provided above is true and complete.

Information which is found to be incorrect will invalidate any subsequent offer of employment.

Signature: *Mary Lynch*　　　　　　　　　　　　　 Date: *12/2006*

This application should be returned to the human resources manager.

SELECTING REFEREES

Always ask a person whose recommendation will be respected. Referees should always be asked prior to the inclusion of their name on a CV or application form. It is a matter of courtesy, as you are asking them to give up their time and alerting them to the possibility of a request from an employer. Simply including them because of their position is not justified, as they may not be in a position to give a true and accurate reference. For example, a college principal may refer a student to their class tutor or year head. Update your referees as your career progresses. If you have completed a college course, you should include the principal or class tutor, and not your school principal.

LETTER OF APPLICATION OR COVERING LETTER

You may be required to submit a covering letter with the application form. As with the application form, you should prepare a draft version. Ensure that you have the correct name and title of the person you are submitting the form to. One well-respected Irish company does not consider applications that contain incorrect job titles or names on the envelope, thus ensuring that the application never goes further than the recycle bin.

You should briefly outline where you saw the position advertised and state that you are including a completed application form/CV.

Briefly outline one or two relevant points from your CV. Emphasise the qualities, qualifications or experience you have that are particularly suited to the job. This will ensure that your application stands out from the many others received.

Conclude by thanking the employer for considering your application and stating that you are available for interview. If you are planning any holidays, ensure that you include this information in your letter, as it will allow the prospective employer the opportunity to select a suitable interview time.

If a handwritten letter is requested, then ensure your writing is legible and use a good-quality black ink pen.

Get a friend or teacher to proofread the letter prior to attaching it to the application form or CV.

FIG. 3 — COVERING LETTER

45 Friar Street
Clonmel
Co. Tipperary

22 October 2006

Personnel Manager
Ballindoney Grain Company
Dromline
Co. Tipperary

Dear Sir,

I wish to apply for the position of Secretary to the Personnel Manager with your firm, which was advertised in *The Irish Times* of 20 October 2006.

Since completing the National Certificate in Secretarial Studies this year I have been employed by Marko Engineering Company in the personnel department. I am responsible for maintaining employees' files and also write minutes of meetings between the personnel manager and the unions. A high degree of accuracy in recording discussions and complete confidentiality are very important to my position.

I studied computers during my secretarial course. I worked on Amstrad, IBM and Apple computers. I have experience of using the following programs: Ability, DBase II, Wordstar, Lotus and SuperCalc.

I am aware of the work carried out by your company. Since I have some experience of working in a personnel department, I feel that I am familiar with the duties involved in the post advertised.

I enclose details of my education, qualifications and experience. I am available for interview at your convenience.

Yours faithfully,

Claire Scully

CURRICULUM VITAE (CV)

Everyone over the age of sixteen should have a CV. It is an essential tool in the search for a part-time job or a summer job. It becomes more important when you have completed your studies and are ready to enter the world of work on a full-time basis.

The days of having a standard, one-size-fits-all CV are over. It is vital that you tailor your application, including your CV and letter of application, to suit the position on offer. Be ruthless – edit your CV, removing details which may not be of relevance to the current job you are applying for.

The style and format of a CV varies depending on what book or website you consult. An acceptable format would include personal details, education details, qualifications, employment record, achievements, interests/hobbies and references. Avoid using templates on word processing packages. The use of such templates indicates that the applicant merely filled in the boxes and gave no thought to the design and layout of the CV.

Review all jobs you have ever held, including work experience positions and summer jobs. If they are relevant to the position on offer, include them. Review the duties and responsibilities associated with each position to see if they relate to the current job on offer. Remember the information you obtained during the research of the job and company. Tailor your answers to suit the position on offer.

As your career progresses, you will remove previous jobs from your CV. If there are gaps in your CV, such as if you dropped out of college and did not compete the course or you were unemployed for a period of time, then do not try to hide them.

At every stage in your career, you should update your CV. At college, ask your lecturers if they would act as referees for you. Replace a former school principal with a current lecturer. Always have a balance between an academic reference and an employer.

As you gain additional qualifications, include them in your CV. Omit Junior Certificate results once you have passed your Leaving Certificate. Include any achievements in your interests and hobbies, e.g. captaining a winning team.

A CV should be neat, tidy, well laid out and checked for errors. Keep the CV simple. Do not include fancy graphics, clip art, etc. The emphasis should be on the content, not the design. Use good-quality white or cream paper. Times New Roman font in 12 point or a similar typeface is acceptable. The use of a header or footer indicating your name lends a finished touch to the CV.

1.   *Prepare your CV.*

2.   *Select a job advertisement from your local newspaper that you think you are suitable for. Find out about the position, then draft an application letter and CV.*

3.   *Copy the application form in Fig. 2 and complete it.*

THE INTERVIEW

There is nothing to fear from an interview. It is just one of the standard methods companies employ in recruiting candidates. The fear of not knowing what to say, of the awkward question or of drying up when a question is asked all affect a candidate's ability to perform well at an interview. Preparation is the key to dealing with your fear. By preparing well, you will be confident about your ability to do the job, handle the awkward questions and deal with the unexpected.

Try to view the process from the employer's point of view. They have a position to fill. Those involved in the interview process are under as much pressure as the interviewees. If they select the wrong person, then it will reflect badly on their ability as managers.

Preparing for the interview

- Once you have submitted your application, it is time to prepare for the interview. You should not leave it until you receive notification of an interview date. Now is the time to update your knowledge about the particular industry or sector. Many companies will only provide a short period of time from the date you receive notification of the interview to the day of the interview itself.
- Update your research material.
- If you think that you may be asked to make a presentation, then start to prepare key points that you would include. Become familiar with the tools you would use to make your presentation.
- Gather all the documents that you may be required to present to the company, e.g. references and qualifications. The vast majority of companies will request these following a successful interview.
- Review your application and become totally familiar with it.
- Prepare questions based on your application form. Ask a friend or family member to assist you. Prepare standard interview questions, including questions about your future plans, your strengths and weaknesses and your reasons for applying for this job.

- Outline the key points that you wish to get across about your suitability for the job. You want to leave the interview board with a clear message that you are the person for the job and why.
- Select your clothes and accessories. Ensure that they are clean and in good condition. For men, present a clearly shaven image, while women should not overdo their make-up. Both sexes should not overpower the interview board with strong perfume or aftershave. Avoid eating garlic and other strong-smelling food the night prior to the interview.
- Establish the location of the interview and your method of transport. Make your arrangements carefully to ensure that you arrive in good time.

At the interview
- Arrive early. Take a copy of your application form or CV with you. Be aware of your surroundings and the people you meet. Be polite and pleasant, as they may be consulted about you following the interview. Women should avoid carrying handbags, etc. Leave coats, bags, etc. in the car or with the receptionist.
- If the interviewer(s) offer to shake hands, then do so, otherwise take the seat they offer you. Sit back in the seat, not on the edge.
- Pay particular attention when the interviewer introduces him or herself and the fellow members of the board. Most interviews are conducted by more than one person. Later, during the interview there may be an opportunity for you to refer back to what one member of the board said and then it is your opportunity to use their name, e.g. 'As Mr Smith mentioned earlier...'. Err on the side of formality unless they indicate otherwise.

The dreaded questions
By the time the interview arrives, you should have a fair idea of what you will be asked as a result of your research and preparation.
- Listen carefully to the questions and points made by the board. Do not pre-empt what they may ask, finish the sentence for them or interrupt.
- Avoid yes or no answers – expand on your answers.
- Answer the question asked, not the emotion in which the question is asked. Do not argue, but stick to your point of view while acknowledging that there are other points of view or opinions on the topic.
- Do not use bad language even if a member of the board does. They may be testing you or else they are untrained in proper interview techniques.

- During the interview, if you do not understand the question, seek clarification. It is better to ask for an explanation than to dig yourself into a hole. The same applies if you are asked a question you do not know the answer to. Admit that you do not know rather than showing you do not know.
- Be positive and answer the questions honestly. Admit your mistakes, as it shows maturity, and show how you have learned from them. Resist the urge to enhance your experience or qualifications.
- Remember the key points you want to get across to the board and include them when answering the questions. Illustrate your answers with examples from your career to date, e.g. 'I am a very good team player. For example, I was involved in a project in my job which involved working with people from different departments. My role was…'.
- Expect questions on information contained in your application form or CV. Instead of naming the subjects or modules you studied, tell them what was involved in the module, e.g. 'As part of my web authoring module I designed a website for a local business from start to finish, including getting a brief from the client…'.
- You should be well prepared with a list of all your achievements and be ready to explain what kind of value you could add to the company. In particular, take a look at your previous positions and show that what you achieved was in addition to what was required. Tell the board exactly why you are suited to the position and assess what added value you can bring to the company.
- The final part of answering a question in an interview is relating your experience and skills to the job on offer. Give the board details of your experience, illustrate it with examples, explain how it led you to develop your skills and then relate it to the position on offer. Show the board how you would perform if you got the job, e.g. 'As the first person customers met, I often bore the brunt of customer complaints before they were referred to the customer services department. On one occasion I had to deal with a very angry customer. I managed to defuse the situation by remaining calm, bringing the customer to a quiet area, taking details of his complaint and assuring him of a prompt answer. As a result of this and other situations, I have developed an excellent ability to handle awkward situations and remain cool. I believe that this is a key requirement for the position on offer.' While this is a simple example, you should be able to formulate your own answers based on the concept of showing how the skills and experience you have are relevant to the job on offer and how you would apply them.

- Try to convey enthusiasm. Show interest in the job and the company. Do not convey the impression that you want the job for the sake of getting a job.
- Avail of the opportunity to ask questions at the end of the interview. Avoid asking questions about information you should know about the position or the company. Never ask about the salary or working hours. These should have been made clear in the advertisement or job description. Instead, refer to issues which arose during the interview, e.g. 'I noticed you emphasised… Would this be a large part of the job?' You could also ask about the company's future plans.
- With the advent of equality legislation, there are certain questions that interview boards can no longer ask. These relate to your personal life. Questions about your martial status, your family status and other areas are no longer permitted. If a board asks such questions or comments on these areas, then they may be in breach of equality legislation. Further details on what a board may not ask can be obtained from the Equality Authority.
- At the end of the interview, thank the board for the opportunity to meet them.

After the interview

- An interview post-mortem is like an examination post-mortem. You may come out on a high and as you think back hit the ground with a hard bump. It is important to note down the questions you were asked, your responses and any other observations. These notes are a learning tool for your next interview.
- Note who was on the interview board and their areas of interest.
- Was there anything that you were asked that you were not sufficiently prepared for, and if so, how can you prepare for the next time you are asked those questions?
- Complete the evaluation section of the job application form.
- If you are not successful in obtaining the job, research the details of the applicant who did fill the position. You may identify skills that you need to develop if you apply for a similar position.

CURRICULUM VITAE

PERSONAL DETAILS

Name	Aoife Sherwin
Address	4 Main Street, Mullingar, Co. Westmeath
Date of Birth:	22 December 1970
Telephone no	086 123 4567

EDUCATION

Third-Level Education

Sept 1988 – June 1989   Westmeath Institute of Education, Mullingar, Co.Westmeath

Secondary Education

Sept 1983 – June 1988   St Ann's Community School, Mullingar, Co. Westmeath.

Primary Education

Sept 1975 – June 1983   St Mary's National School, Mullingar, Co. Westmeath

QUALIFICATIONS

Course	FETAC Award Level 5 in Office Administration
Skills achieved	Word processing, spreadsheets, bookkeeping, customer service skills

Results	**Modules**	**Result**
	Communications	Distinction
	Work Placement	Distinction
	Text Production	Distinction
	Office Administration	Merit
	Business Computing	Merit

Reception Studies	Pass
Manual Accounts	Pass
Legal Studies	Pass

Leaving Certificate Results

Subject	Grade	Level
Biology	C3	Higher
English	D1	Higher
History	D1	Higher
French	D1	Higher
Art	B3	Ordinary
Irish	B3	Ordinary
Mathematics	A3	Foundation

EMPLOYMENT RECORD

August 1995 – present **Carr Agri' Services Ltd, Main St, Ardee, Co. Louth**

Position Secretary/receptionist

Duties Manning the switchboard, faxing, photocopying, filing, typing, use of document management system (distrbution of incoming post), use of MAI package system (monthly absences), customer service duties, message taking, outgoing post.

May 1989 – July 1995 **Richardson & Co, Business Services Ltd, Dublin 2**

Position Receptionist/administrator

Duties Switchboard, small accounts,

	database, filing, typing, customer service, faxing, photocopying, taking in customer payments, message taking, use of Microsoft Word/Access/Excel, post.
August 1988 – May 1989	**Dunnes Stores, Valley Park, Dublin 22**
Position	Customer Service Operator
Duties	Exchanges, refunds, customer service, safe operator, till operator, till key holder, bureau de change, telephone.

ACHIEVEMENTS

- I have won a number of trophies and medals for camogie.
- I was awarded Student of the Year in 1988.
- I became a Youthclub Leader in my local Youthreach Centre.

REFEREES

Mr John Richardson	Ms Benadette Malone
Managing Director	Course Director
Richardson & Co	Westmeath Institute of Education
Business Services	Main Street
Crispin Place	Mullingar
Dublin	Co. Westmeath

Aoife Sherwin

Aoife Sherwin

1. *Imagine an interviewer asks you to tell him about your life up to the present. Record your answer on a tape recorder. Listen critically to the recording. Assess your own performance.*

2. *What do you consider to be your positive qualities?*

3. *What is the purpose of the interviewer's question 'Why did you apply for this job?'*

4. *Why do interviewers want to know about your hobbies?*

5. *Choose a job advertisement in a newspaper and outline how you would prepare for the interview.*

6. *What types of questions might you ask an interviewer?*

7. *How would you, as an interviewer, react to a candidate who asked only the following questions: How much do you pay? How long are the holidays?*

GROUP ACTIVITY

Each member of the class should choose a job advertisement from a newspaper and write a letter of application for it. Members of the class should interview each other as part of the preparation. An interviewer should then be chosen who will interview each student for the job for which he/she has applied. FÁS may help in this matter. If your school or college has a closed circuit television system, record the interviews. Later, play back the interviews, discuss the performances and have each student complete the evaluation part of Fig. 1.

REVIEW

1. Why should job advertisements be read carefully?

2. Visit your local FÁS office and find out how many jobs are available locally to suit your qualifications.

3. Explain to your friend who is leaving school the various sources of information on job opportunities.

4. What is the difference between an application form and a curriculum vitae?

5. What is a covering letter?

6. If called for an interview, explain the preparation you would engage in before the interview.

7. What type of questions should you, the interviewee, ask at an interview?

8. Give examples of three questions which are usually asked at interviews.

PITFALLS

amoral immoral

Amoral means 'totally unconcerned' or 'outside morals'.

Immoral means 'not conforming to' or 'opposed to a certain type of morality'.

CONFUSING WORDS

peace	piece	pealing	peeling
personal	personnel	plum	plumb
rain	rein	read	reed
relic	relict	rote	wrote
scene	seen	sealing	ceiling

QUIZ

Finish the following 'knock, knock' joke:

Knock, knock.

Who's there?

Ammonia

_____(2 words)

_____(8 words)

SPELLINGS

The words most commonly misspelled are highlighted.

umbrella
umpire
unconscious
uncouth
underrate
undoubtedly
ungrateful
unique
university
unnecessary
until
urgency
usage
usefulness
usual
usually
utensil
utterance

vacancy
vagrant
valiant
valour
valuable
vapour
vegetable
vehement
vehicle
vengeance
ventilate
verification
veteran
vicious

victorious
vigorous
villain
violence
virtuous
visibility
volcano
volcanoes
volume
vulgarity

warily
wary
wealthier
wealthy
wearily
weariness
weather
Wednesday
whether
wield
wilful
wizard
wondrous
wool
woollen
woolly
wrangle
wreckage
wrestle
wrestler
wretched
write

xenophobe
xenophobia
Xerox
X-ray
xylem
xylophone

yacht
yachtsman
yahoo
yardage
yardstick
yawn
yearn
yield
yoghurt
yogi
yoke
yolk

zany
zealot
zealous
zebra
zenith
zero
zigzag
zinc
zodiac
zombie
zoology

Bibliography

Adler, R. and Elmhorst, J., *Communicating at Work*, New York: McGraw-Hill 1996.

Bell, A. and Smith, D., *Management Communication*, New York: Wiley 1999.

Burley-Allen, M., *Listening: The Forgotten Skill*, New York: Wiley 1995.

Daunt, S., *Communications Skills*, Dublin: Gill & Macmillan 1996.

Dutton, B., *Media Studies: An Introduction*, London: Longman 1995.

Dutton, B., *The Media*, London: Longman 1997.

Evans, D., *Effective Business Administration and Communication*, London: Pitman 1992.

Gallagher, J. and Coghlan, S., *Modern Office Technology and Practice*, Dublin: Gill & Macmillan 1997.

Hall, S. (ed.), *Representation: Cultural Representation and Signifying Practices*, London: Longman 1997.

Harris, S., *Human Communication*, Oxford: NCC Blackwell 1990.

Hybels, S. and Weaver, R., *Communicating Effectively*, New York: McGraw-Hill 1995.

Institute of Public Administration, *Administration Yearbook and Diary*, Dublin: IPA 1999.

Leigh, A. and Maynard, M., *The Perfect Presentation*, London: Arrow Business Books 1993.

Little, P., *Communication in Business*, London: Pitman Publishing 1977.

Lussier, R., *Human Relations in Organizations*, Boston: Irwin McGraw-Hill 1998.

McClave, H., *Communication for Business*, Dublin: Gill & Macmillan 2004.

Mead, R., *Cross-Cultural Communication*, Chichester: John Wiley 1990.

Morley, M. *et al.*, *Principles of Organisational Behaviour*, London: Financial Times and Pitman Publishing 1998.

O'Donnell, J., *Wordgloss*, Dublin: Institute of Public Administration 1990.

Prone, T., *Get that Job*, Dublin: Poolbeg 1993.

Rawlins, C., *Business Communication*, New York: Harper Perennial 1993.